AN INTRODUCTION TO BUDDHIST* MEDITATION FOR RESULTS

PART ONE : TRANQUIL MEDITATION

PART TWO : INSIGHT MEDITATION

The highest and most perfect wisdom, through achieving omniscient enlightenment (SABBHANÑUTTAÑĀNA), leading to cessation of all suffering in life and attainment of perpetual happiness (NIBBĀNA). (Kindly refer to page 377).

Cover Photo:
Dhammacakka (the Wheel of the Buddha's Teachings), carved from the huge Tak granite, is located inside the Buddha Monthon in Nakorn Pathom Province, Thailand.

Vinai Ussivakul

An Introduction to Buddhist Meditation for Results...

Bangkok : TIPIṬAKA Study Center,

2003/2546

416 p.

1. Meditation (Buddhist)   I. Title.

294.3122

ISBN 974-90891-6-2

Printed in Thailand by

TIPPAYAWISUIT Ltd., Partnership.

240/132 Soi Sriwichai Hospital,

Jaransanithwong Rd., Bangkoknoi,

Bangkok 10700, Thailand

Tel. 0-2412-7707, 0-2412-7709, 0-24125070

Fax. 0-2412-7710

TIPIṬAKA RESEARCHER

ARCHAN VINAI USSIVAKUL
13/267 MOOBAN NANTHAWAN, SOI 12,
WONGWAEN (RING) ROAD,
PASEEJAROEN, BANGKOK 10160
THAILAND
TEL: (02) 804-1781 FAX: (02) 804-1324

THAILAND COORDINATORS

MR. MANAH AND MRS. VANNA KOVITAYA
4/2 PAHOLYOTHIN RD., SOI 15,
BANGKOK 10400, THAILAND
TEL: (02) 278-0796

U.S.A. COORDINATORS

MR. IAN AND MRS. SALLY TIMM
1505 N.E. 46TH AVENUE
PORTLAND, OREGON 97213
U.S.A.
TEL: (503) 288-9822
E-mail: istimm @ pacifier.com

Words of Thanks and Extension of Merit

With profound gratitude to my parents, who gave my sister Susan and me life and a framework for learning honorable conduct, I wish to give thanks to my mother Marion, who passed away at age 91.

In keeping with her goodwill and generous heart, funds becoming available upon her death were contributed toward the printing of the book and for its Dana distribution in the U.S.A.

The help of a dear family friend, Ms. D'Averil Ibbotson, is also gratefully and appreciatively acknowledged. She helped look over points of English usage as the preparation for printing neared completion in Bangkok.

Enough tribute could never be adequately given to Archan Wonnie Tarinchareon for her deep teachings nor to Phra Archan Boonmee Methangura, Archan Vinai Ussivakul and the Abhidhamma Foundation, with whom she acquainted my husband Ian and myself over twenty years ago.

May this precious book spread loving-kindness and wisdom in the world.

On behalf of the author and the editorial staff, may I take this opportunity to extend any meritorious wholesomeness from the printing of this book, to all living beings.

Sally Timm

APPLY THE SIMPLIFIED AND PRACTICAL METHODS OF PRACTICING TRANQUIL MEDITATION AND YOU WILL ACHIEVE...

- ❧ Deep physical rest and relaxation and improved physical health

- ❧ Complete mental rest along with the attainment of a high level of happiness

- ❧ A completely free mind

- ❧ Strengthened memory

- ❧ Increased learning power

- ❧ More effective job performance

- ❧ Initiative and creative wisdom

- ❧ A wholesome and effective outlet for coping with life's problems

- ❧ Subtle tranquility and happiness

APPLY THESE MOST UNIQUE AND EFFECTIVE METHODS OF PRACTICING INSIGHT MEDITATION AND YOU WILL...

- Cultivate the "Light of Wisdom" in dispelling the "Darkness of Ignorance" in life

- Eradicate the wrong views in life

- Eliminate the "Multipliers" of adverse feeling or suffering in life

- Get relief from mental wandering and suffering

- Achieve wholesome and highly beneficial memory power

- Be able to cope effectively with extremely harmful memory power

- Attain a mind with the most complete and highest degree of freedom

- Acquire the right techniques of living through direct and full awareness and realization, leading to the attainment of "Perpetual Happiness" (Nibbāna)

AN INTRODUCTION TO BUDDHIST MEDITATION FOR RESULTS

PART ONE
TRANQUIL MEDITATION

CONTENTS

PART TWO
INSIGHT MEDITATION

CONTENTS

XVIII

CHAPTER 18
INSIGHT MEDITATION–COPING
WITH PHYSICAL PAIN **303**

FOREWORD

In the world of today, people are living under stress and strain as a result of craving, hunger, overambition, fear, anxiety and lack of safety. A lot of people are facing malnutrition or food shortages: in addition, there are many who are homeless and wander aimlessly. Crime rates, narcotic trafficking and drug addiction cases are also on the increase. There are also many instances of serious conflicts leading to the destruction of numerous lives and properties. What are the reasons behind all these?

Although December 8, 2001 was the 100th anniversary of the Nobel Peace Prize, there have been more wars than peace in the past 100 years. The question is how to counter effectively these patterns of violence. The example of Mahatma Gandhi's peaceful alternative offers a poignant reminder that we can do better than repeating past wars and terrorism. This book explains a way each of us can improve our own loving-kindness and promote peace between all people in the world community.

The more technological progress in terms of material wealth is made, the more mental development in terms of spiritual wealth is required; otherwise people can easily become the victims of their own material achievements. This is evident in such a case as environmental pollution which adversely affects physical and mental health, leading to increased suffering as well as the shortening of life.

Problems such as overpopulation are increasing. Birth control, which is an effective means of coping with this problem, has nevertheless been misapplied in certain cases, resulting in a lowered standard of morality and a decline in spiritual values. This can be seen in the indiscriminate use of contraceptive pills or other birth control devices among our youth. As a result of such reckless behavior, the mind often becomes adversely affected, leading to increased unwholesome acts. HIV/AIDS is no longer just a public health problem, but a global human and social development problem that needs a rigorous strategy for prevention and cure.

An educational system which does not place enough emphasis on moral and spiritual values is one that encourages greediness and rivalry among individuals. At the same time, any system which brings about freedom without responsibility, discipline, and limitations has an adverse effect on self-control and judgment. This leads to exploitation of others in various forms such as resorting to corrupt practices, engaging in the narcotics trade and the promotion worldwide of commercial sexual exploitation of children, conducting a booming arms business for destructive purposes and seeking domination over others economically, politically or militarily. If these adverse conditions extensively prevail, they can bring about seizures of power and serious conflicts and problems on community, national or international levels. This can be seen in various trouble spots in many parts of the world. Under such circumstances, how can peacefulness and happiness be attained in this world?

We recognize that the world's population is moving from an Agriculture-based Society to an Industrialized Society and now to an Information Technology Society. We understand that **Information Technology (IT) is a vital part of the new globalization trend and has certainly changed human beings** especially in self-development and interpersonal relationships. If people in today's society use IT in a wrong way, such as for cybersex and child pornography, it will be a tool to create misbehavior leading to more crises in social, spiritual and in the spheres of knowledge and wisdom values. This is a most provocative disaster for each nation in the world community. An enterprising society must search for the ways reflecting pros and cons, to cope effectively with the dichotomies of the changing world; that is, destructive progress versus creative sustainability in the era of globalization.

First of all, it should be realized that **it is now time for us to promote urgently the spiritual values,** which have been fast deteriorating due to increasing emphasis being placed on material wealth. Dire consequences are likely in the near future if nuclear weapons and missiles continue to be produced in large quantities with higher destructive power. Being well aware of this great danger, should we not exert every effort to enhance spiritual wealth for the happiness and the wholesome progress of mankind?

People often overlook the importance of developing their minds; they place too much emphasis on their physical comforts without realizing how much the mind affects the body.

Modern science has recognized that the mind can produce a kind of energy like that of electricity with the capability of controlling and stimulating the brain to perform its functions relating to thinking, remembering and feeling and to physical activities. The brain serves as a medium for the mind as opposed to performing these activities directly.

In addition, it has been proven that through effective meditation the mind is able to alleviate or overcome physical suffering. Hippocrates, the Greek physician who is considered the father of medicine, said that it is the natural energy within ourself that can cure various illnesses effectively.

According to the well-known Dr. Charles Mayo, worry and anxiety will affect blood circulation, the heart, various glands and the whole nervous system. This means that mental stress is an important cause of various illnesses such as peptic ulcer, high blood pressure, asthmatic attack, diabetes, heart disease and arthritis.

Many cases of illnesses with unknown and undetectable causes originate in the mind.

If we realize the effect of the mind on the body, we are better able to control wisely the mind and prevent it from producing adverse effects; instead, the mind will produce good and wholesome effects. In other words, the mind should be effectively controlled in a way similar to the control of fire, for use in a constructive manner.

The wonders of the mind are not something beyond belief, yet few people are aware of the mind's great potential. Meditation is the first important step in the development of mental power. Tranquil Meditation will make the mind peaceful, stable and secure. It is an effective way of accumulating and utilizing mental energy with mindful awareness. On the other hand, Insight Meditation will ultimately bring about the eradication of all suffering in life, leading to the attainment of "Perpetual Happiness" (Nibbāna), through the accumulation and development of the highest level of wisdom. Tranquil Meditation and Insight Meditation are therefore both helpful in our daily living and contribute to success in life for every human being.

Regular meditation practice, which is a mental exercise, must be practiced daily in the same way as physical exercise. Both should go together to balance one's life and build a strong body and a healthy mind. In this way, one will be able to develop wisdom and mindfulness in one's daily life and relieve or get rid of the feelings and thoughts which give rise to suffering, anxiety and fear.

It has been accepted medically that meditation practice is very beneficial to human life in terms of promoting sound mental health. It is currently being used for the prevention and treatment of mental illness.

In reality, the nature of the mind and mental practice and development in the form of Tranquil Meditation and Insight Meditation which are the essence and basis of Buddhist Advanced Science (Abhidhamma), was introduced over 2,500 years ago. It is a great pity that a lot of people have not made effective use of these ancient discoveries because they lack understanding regarding the real nature of the mind and mental energy.

It is now time for all those who have not tried to seek knowledge within themselves to turn toward the study and practice of Buddhist Science in order to gain real insight into their own mind and life. This in turn will bring about subtle tranquility and happiness which everyone is seeking and will increase mental powers amazingly. These effects can be achieved by the meditator only through his/her own efforts. As the Buddha said, we must work out our own salvation with diligence.

Vanna Kovitaya, M.D., M.P.H.,
Psychiatrist
Thailand
2003/2546

PART ONE

TRANQUIL MEDITATION

I. INTRODUCTION

"A well-developed mind brings happiness."

Everyone is in pursuit of real happiness in life. Many try to find happiness through sensual enjoyment by such ways as listening to their favorite music, eating delicious food, bodily contact with pleasurable objects, or seeing pleasant sights. But they have found out to their disappointment that such sensual pleasures cannot actually relieve their suffering in life. This is because their minds could still be full of anxiety, frustration and restlessness even while experiencing sensual pleasures. This is often evident in countries abundant in material wealth. The more people blindly seek sensual pleasures, the more sorrow and disappointment they experience. Instead of making wholesome gains in life, they end up with a great loss. Some have to confront miseries with no relief, resulting in total collapse, such as in serious mental disorders or suicide.

Seeking happiness through sensual enjoyment could eventually lead to more suffering. The ignorance of the Right Path leading toward the attainment of real happiness causes one to be caught in a trap of misery without hope of being set free.

Therefore, it is the aim of this book to give guidance concerning the wholesome path leading to the further enhancement of a high level of happiness. Obtaining the subtle happiness and tranquility found through the Right Path is not beyond one's reach provided that one adheres to the procedures described in this book. This subtle happiness cannot be in any way obtained through material wealth, but it can be acquired by means of mental development through Tranquil Meditation.

The meditation methods are modified for easy and practical applications and designed for all those who wish to make wholesome progress in life. This means that the meditations can be practiced by people from all walks of life, such as teachers, students, factory workers, householders, business executives, farmers, government officials, military personnel, politicians, salespersons and the elderly and retired, for their personal benefit. This book was written with wholesome intentions primarily for the interest and benefits of the readers.

PART ONE of this book is divided into two major sections. The first section is concerned with the background and theory of Tranquil Meditation covering such subjects as the meaning, types, benefits, mental factors and mental obstacles of Tranquil Meditation, whereas the second section deals with procedures and applications of Tranquil Meditation giving detailed instructions and explanations for practicing Mettā (Loving-Kindness) Meditation,

Ānāpā (Breathing) Meditation and Odāta Kasiṇa
(White Object) Meditation.

> Oneself is refuge of oneself
> What else indeed could refuge be ?
> By the good training of oneself
> One gains a refuge hard to gain
> The Sayings of the Buddha
> Thomas Byrom

> Though one should live a hundred years
> in mind unconcentrated,
> yet better is life for a single day
> wise and meditative.
>> Though one should live a hundred years
>> lazy, of little effort,
>> yet better is life for a single day
>> making a steady effort.
>> The Sayings of the Buddha

II. BACKGROUND AND THEORY

CHAPTER 1
WHAT IS TRANQUIL MEDITATION

Tranquil Meditation is concerned with the concentration of one's mind on a suitable meditation object for a reasonable length of time so as not to cause the mind to wander or to roam about. This will bring about subtle peacefulness and pleasantness or happiness, which is far superior to that which can be experienced from watching movies, or seeking other worldly sensual pleasures.

It should be noted that Tranquil Meditation for subtle happiness in life requires that the mind concentrates on a suitable object. If our mind focuses on something improper, the right concentration will not arise; on the contrary, our mind will become more restless: **for example,** when the mind of a young man concentrates on a picture of a lovely and attractive lady. Under this adverse condition, it is rather difficult to practice effective Tranquil Meditation because of the wandering mind. Therefore, it is very important to select a suitable meditation object. In the Buddha's Teachings, 40 different types of proper meditation objects are provided and three of these are covered in this book, to enhance concentration power.

With reference to Tranquil Meditation, an object here refers to that which is perceived by one's meditative mind, such as, breathing or a white object. The verbal or mental expression of good intention for all living beings to be happy is also considered to be a suitable meditation object.

For one's mind to be able to concentrate on a meditation object, the mind must remain in a one-pointedness condition (Ekaggatā Cetasika)

In effective Tranquil Meditation practice, it is not enough just to concentrate on a suitable object for a moment. Instead, the concentration must last for a reasonable period of time until one attains certain degree of tranquility. During the practice, the meditator must have one meditation object only and he must not try to analyze that meditation object. Merely focusing mentally on the object is all that is required. Apart from this, Tranquil Meditation must be practiced with the right understanding.

In short, one should realize that the concentration of one's mind on a suitable meditation object for a long period of time will enhance one's mental power to relieve physical and mental suffering in life and at the same time, attain subtle tranquility and happiness, the taste of which excels all conventional tastes.

CHAPTER 2
TYPES OF CONCENTRATION

Concentration can pave the way either to high level and subtle tranquility and happiness or to unbearable suffering depending on whether its purpose is rightly or wrongly chosen. The former will bring about happiness and tranquility whereas the latter will result in misery. For this reason, concentration can be classified into two types according to its purpose:

1. **Concentration with wrong purpose (Micchāsamādhi)**
2. **Concentration with right purpose (Sammāsamādhi)**

1. **Concentration with wrong purpose (Micchā-samādhi)** refers to the concentration of mind on an object with deliberate ill or evil intentions of harming or destroying others or increasing one's own defile-ments (Kilesa). This is evident in the case of using psychic power in such ways as to exercise one's will power in a manner to defame others, or to cast a wicked charm or spell on another to cause blind attraction to oneself.

2. **Concentration with right purpose (Sammā-samādhi)** pertains to the concentration on a suitable

object regularly with the aims of attaining wholesome happiness and peacefulness and of overcoming the defilements (Kilesa) of mind which are the root cause of misery in life. The practice of Sammāsamādhi develops the wholesomeness of the mind.

This concentration can be classified into three categories according to its strength:

a. **Khaṇika-samādhi**
b. **Upacāra-samādhi**
c. **Appanā-samādhi**

a. **Khaṇika-samādhi** denotes concentration on the meditation object on a moment-to-moment basis. In the initial stage of meditation practice, this kind of momentary concentration is dominant and delight (Pīti) and happy feeling (Sukha) may not arise. As one keeps on accumulating the power of Khaṇika-samādhi until he becomes more accustomed to the meditation object and in addition can easily direct his concentration toward it, tranquility and serenity of mind followed by delight or happy feelings will result.

As this concentration becomes further intensified, this will in turn cause the strengthening of the meditation object to the extent of creating tranquility in the concentrated mind without having to depend on senses such as seeing. This meditation object is then termed as Uggaha-nimitta (acquired image). **For example,** at the initial stage of practicing meditation by means of concentrating on a white object, it is necessary that one must open the eyes and then close the eyes trying to visualize the white object. At this point, the white object is not yet Uggaha-nimitta. As one repeats the process of opening and closing the eyes while concentrating on the white object, one begins to see the object clearly even with the eyes closed. This white object which further strengthens the concentration power is called Uggaha-nimitta.

b. Upacāra-samādhi refers to a higher concentration which is powerful enough to arrest defilements (Kilesa). With this concentration, which arises only after having effectively developed Khaṇika-samādhi and Uggaha-nimitta, the concentrated mind becomes increasingly and firmly secured to the object which will then become entirely clear and more subtle. This meditation object is called Patibhāga-nimitta.

c. Appanā-samādhi is the highest level of concentration which can overcome the defilements. The mind remains steadfast to the object to the point of being able to concentrate on the meditation object continuously for all day long, whereas it is not possible in the other two cases namely Upacāra-samādhi and Khaṇika-samādhi.

CHAPTER 3
GENERAL BENEFITS GAINED FROM TRANQUIL MEDITATION PRACTICE

A well-developed mind brings about happiness in life. This mental development leading to high level and subtle happiness can be effectively achieved by practicing Tranquil Meditation (Samatha Kammaṭṭhāna).

It has been confirmed through scientific studies and verifications that there are numerous benefits to be gained from Tranquil Meditation practice. The practice is useful in:

- **promoting physical and mental relaxation and health, good for oneself and good for others**
- **overcoming stress and strain in life**
- **developing a mind with complete freedom**
- **lowering blood pressure**
- **increasing self-confidence**
- **enhancing good personality**
- **improving memory**
- **increasing learning power**
- **improving job performance**
- **making effective use of time**
- **enhancing creativity**
- **contributing to giving up habits of drinking, smoking and drug abuse**

- lessening worries and anxieties
- enriching one's life with subtle happiness and tranquility
- acquiring initiative and creative wisdom highly beneficial to one's life
- relieving physical and mental suffering and ridding the mind and body of certain illnesses
- providing a wholesome and effective outlet for coping with life's problems and attaining a high level of invaluable tranquility and happiness

Eight essential benefits from practicing Tranquil Meditation are further explained as follows:

1. Deep Physical Rest and Relaxation and Promotion of Physical Health

The meditation methods described in this book have been simplified for easy and effective practice which naturally brings about physical rest and relaxation as well as reduced tension. When the concentrated mind arises during the meditation practice, the body consumes significantly less energy. The consumption of oxygen in the body will be below the normal requirement by about 18% on the average. This reduced oxygen consumption reflects a much deeper relaxation compared to the condition in which there is no concentrated mind. Ordinarily, the untrained mind wanders a lot, allowing the thoughts to go from subject to subject. This wandering of the mind results in an excessive, unnecessary consumption of energy.

Apart from this, the meditation, if effectively practiced, will help to promote physical health as well as relieve or rid the body of certain physical illnesses, particularly those with psychosomatic features such as indigestion, ulcers, asthma and allergy. In addition, certain bad habits such as smoking and drug abuse can be overcome.

2. Complete Mental Rest along with the Attainment of Mindful Happiness

As the concentrated mind arises during the meditation practice, the mind will become most relaxed as never before experienced. Such mental relaxation is tantamount not to sleepiness but to the mind being set at rest. In this way, the mind will not become inert, depressed or excited. Instead, the mind will be full of awareness and alertness along with wholesome and subtle delight and happy feeling. In addition, one will become increasingly mindful, devoid of any obsession or dreamy condition.

It should be noted that these wholesome delights and happy feelings which arise during meditation practice could last for a long period of time and could be intensified through their accumulations. Furthermore, they differ from the unwholesome sensual pleasures derived through the five senses from such activities as watching movies, listening to music, smelling perfume, tasting a delicious food and bodily contact. These sensual pleasures do not last as long as the wholesome delight and happy feeling from meditation. As a matter of fact, if the same sensual pleasure is repeated too often, a tedious feeling will result. **For example:**

a. After one has filled up his stomach with fried chicken, he can no longer enjoy sensual pleasure from eating more. In fact, if he does not stop eating at this point, he will feel discomfort and experience indigestion, which bring about suffering.

b. When one has to take the same kind of food at every meal over a period of time, one will likely soon become bored and lose his taste.

It can be readily seen that these sensual pleasures as such have their own limit and could not last long. Worse than that, this type of sensual pleasure is firmly linked with craving like a fetter. As long as one experiences a desirable object according to one's craving, the sensual pleasure follows. He will become as pleased as a fish returning to water. On the other

hand, if he fails to obtain what is strongly desirable
to him, he will feel restless or miserable just like
a fish wriggling on hot sand. For this reason, the
sensual pleasure accompanied by craving can be
misleading and can eventually lead to suffering. **For
example,** the unwholesome sensual pleasures derived
through drinking alcohol can lead to suffering and
death.

Conversely, the delight and happy feelings origi-
nating from meditation are wholesome and full of
awareness and these can be further intensified so as
to relieve or overcome mental suffering automatically.

3. A Mind with Complete Freedom

During the meditation practice, the mind which
is full of awareness will experience a complete freedom
from such defilement (Kilesa) as craving. The mind
will not be under the domination of one's craving.

Such complete mental freedom cannot be found
in methods other than meditation, such as hypnotism.
Even though the hypnotized subject may experience
happy feeling as a result of hypnotism, such feeling
reflects a lack of mental freedom as its arising is
dependent on the will of the hypnotist. In other
words, the hypnotized person is substantially under
the power of the hypnotist.

In the case of self-hypnosis where one does
not come under the power of others, one can only
experience a certain degree of mental freedom. At
least self-hypnosis puts one under his own command

to attain the expected results but those results are restricted in comparison with Tranquil Meditation.

There is another case in which the mind is trained by means of methods other than meditation, and that is Yoga exercises. More mental freedom is enjoyed when compared to self-hypnosis because the expected result is directly obtained through disciplined self-practice.

But meditation practice strengthens the wholesomeness of mind in addition to bringing about tranquility, delight and happy feelings. Also, the mind will not become a victim of one's own craving and at the same time will be free from its tyranny and adverse effects.

It should be observed that wholesomeness of mind, full of delight and happy feelings, will be fully developed through Tranquil Meditation practice and not through other methods. In this way, the meditator can truly and freely enjoy this subtle happiness and tranquility as never before experienced.

4. Attainment of Increased Memory Power

Memory refers to ability to recall to mind facts previously learned or past experiences. It plays an essential role in our daily activities, such as studying, working, thinking and speaking, and enhances the chances of attaining effective results in whatever we do.

Memory is ordinarily caused by:

   a. The mind perceiving the same object several times. In other words, repetition will bring about its memory. **For example,** if one reads a book over and over again, one's memory will be intensified.

   b. The interest or the impression one has about that object. For example, if one is interested in the story, one will be able to remember better; if one is impressed by witty remarks, one is likely to remember what was said.

   c. Understanding techniques of thinking and remembering.

   d. Practicing Tranquil Meditation. The practice gives rise to the concentration of the mind on a suitable object. This will increase mental power so as to prevent one's mind from wandering or becoming restless. With concentration, one will be able to perceive the object more effectively through all senses and this in turn will have a strong and favorable effect on his recall ability. In other words, this makes it easier to remember and harder to forget.

In fact, both Western and Eastern scientists have verified from their research that meditation contributes to effective memory.

In short, of all the four causes above, meditation practice stands out as the most significant in enhancing the intensity of memory.

5. Betterment of Learning Power

Tranquil Meditation practice not only improves one's memory, but also increases the effectiveness of understanding, both of which are essential in the betterment of learning power. This is applicable to

all learning through listening, reading, thinking or writing for the simple reason that concentration power developed through meditation gives rise to the tranquility of mind which serves as an important basis in enhancing effective learning.

In the years 1970-1971, Professor Doctor Rojana Suwanasudhi and his colleagues at the Faculty of Medicine, Siriraj Hospital, Mahidol University in Bangkok conducted a research among medical students concerning the effects of meditation practice on their study. Altogether there were 32 students of both sexes with ages ranging from 19 to 23 years old. They were required to practice meditation daily during the weekdays covering a period of 20 weeks. An evaluation concerning their learning and thinking was then made. Even though the meditation was practiced under certain unfavorable conditions such as, meditating right after lunch or in a noisy room, or not having enough time to practice at home, the results were encouraging. It was found that 62% of the students were more attentive to their studies; 31% were more keen to learn and 65% felt that the meditation practice was beneficial in acquiring knowledge.

Evidently, Tranquil Meditation practice is helpful in improving the effectiveness of learning.

6. Improvement of Job Performance Effectiveness

It is generally accepted that those whose minds are wandering and restless find it difficult to perform their work effectively. Tranquil Meditation practice not only can pacify the mind but also is helpful toward enhancing the effectiveness of job performance as follows:

In our daily activities, it is not possible for us to work all the time without taking a rest. This is especially true in the case where one has to work vigorously or under stress and strain. But when one overexerts himself physically and mentally to the extent of being unable to sleep, not only will his body be weakened but his mind will also be impaired due to the lack of mental training and discipline. As a result, his job performance will be adversely affected. This reflects an uncontrollable state of mind. In many cases, such problems in turn encourage other problems, such as insomnia and emotional instability. To overcome this problem is not difficult. All it requires is to spend just fifteen to twenty minutes practicing meditation daily. Such practice can eventually relieve or get rid of these undesirable conditions. This is simply because the meditation not only trains and disciplines the mind, but also brings about physical and mental relaxation, subtle tranquility and happiness. At bedtime, the power of concentration developed through regular meditation practice will facilitate a sound sleep, free from mental wandering and restlessness. This undisturbed sleep means a complete rest, which in turn will refresh the body and mind so as to be able to start working effectively on the following day.

During work, one who works continuously and vigorously without taking an adequate rest, will become tense physically and mentally so as to hamper the effectiveness of his job performance. As a result, he may suffer from headaches or may get bored or discouraged. To cope effectively with this adverse condition requires complete bodily and mental rest through mediation practice for 15-20 minutes. This process should be repeated whenever the situation calls for it.

Many personalities from various professions such as Hollywood stars like Clint Eastwood and the British singers, The Beatles, have successfully made use of Tranquil Meditation in enhancing the effectiveness of their job performances. Apart from this, a number of large organizations, including General Motors, Westinghouse, I.B.M., Kodak, Xerox and Monsanto, have encouraged meditation practice among their staff in order to have them become more effective in their job performance.

Consequently, meditation practice is applicable to everyone in any organization, especially those who require physical and mental relaxation coupled with tranquility and subtle happiness in addition to the improvement of job performance.

> **Meditate.**
> **Live purely.**
> **Be quiet.**
> **Do your work, with mastery.**
> The Sayings of the Buddha

7. Acquisition of Initiative and Creative Wisdom Highly Beneficial to One's Life

When the mind is wandering so as to cause our thinking to scatter into different directions, it will become inefficient. But when there is mental training through meditation to discipline the thinking, there will be exceptionally enhanced concentration power to induce new ideas and creativity in our thinking process. This is comparable to iron with its molecules being improperly organized. Such disorganization tends to adversely affect its magnetism. Only when these molecules are properly arranged, will iron have the property of a magnet. As previously mentioned, daily meditation practice will bring about good memory as well as physical comfort and mental happiness and tranquility. The mind will become more prudent and alert, in addition to remembering various events and incorporating them into new lines of thinking which will be useful in our life. In other words, meditation gives rise to creative thinking.

At the same time, meditation practice will bring about new and valuable experiences due to acquiring the taste of subtle happiness as never before experienced. The meditator will realize the reality of life in that the acquisition of subtle happiness is not acquired through material wealth but rather through regular meditation practice. In fact, this subtle happiness is far superior to that obtained from sensually pleasurable objects. Apart from this, such worthy experiences enhance a more thorough understanding of the true reality of life. They also prevent one from being blindly attached to happiness derived from sensually pleasurable objects which eventually bring misery and restlessness in life.

On the other hand, the meditator, when experiencing suffering, will not resort to self-harm or suicide but instead will be able to realize the subtle happiness through past accumulations of wholesome deeds (Kamma) and present meditation practices. This is because the meditation practice will strengthen the mind to the extent of effecting subtle tranquility and happiness. In this way, the power of Tranquil Meditation will bring about creative wisdom which is of great benefit to life.

> **A fool, though awarded a high rank,**
> **is a wise man's slave.**
> **In time of need**
> **Only the wise can handle the affairs,**
> **while the fool will lose his head**
> **in such case.**
>   The Sayings of the Buddha

8. A Wholesome and Effective Outlet for Coping with Life's Problems and the Attainment of a High Level of Invaluable Tranquility and Happiness

Of all the problems one faces in life, mental suffering stands out the most in causing certain unbearable miseries. At times it could easily lead to committing suicide as evidenced in the rising suicide rate trend. In some cases, one could possibly withstand the mental suffering without turning to self-destruction, but likely would still live a miserable life with no relief in sight. It is like being imprisoned by mental suffering without knowing how to escape from it successfully.

Life's problems manifest themselves in various ways. Some people enjoy life in the usual manner until it is marred by some unexpected event such as the loss of a loved one, resulting in shock and sorrow. Other sufferings arise as a result of encountering something or someone offensive or hateful. Apart from this, sorrow, anxiety, frustration, dissatisfaction, drug abuse, alcoholic addiction and other maladies could also contribute to suffering.

Regular meditation practice can be used to deal effectively with the above problems. In addition to bringing about subtle happiness as mentioned previously, meditation can also accumulate sufficient power to prevent or relieve the arising of suffering. This is because with meditation practice the mind will become prudent, firm and calm. The power developed through effective meditation could act as a shield to protect one from the stimulus which brings about suffering. This power is tantamount to the raising of one's mind above the ordinary level so as to stay above "the wave of suffering".

There are evidences that meditation has been used also to overcome the suffering caused by drug abuse, alcoholism and certain emotional problems.

Just as a mountain
Shakes not with the wind
So the effective meditators are not disturbed
Either by praise or blame.
        The Sayings of the Buddha

CONCLUSION

In summary, meditation not only can overcome the suffering in life, but also enhance a high level of tranquility and happiness.

In view of these numerous benefits to be gained from the meditation practice, should one become hesitant in practicing and let the golden opportunity slip by without taking advantage of securing them while they are at one's doorstep?

Subtle tranquility and happiness will not automatically come to us without our reaching out for them.

We should then improve our lives through meditation practice so as to be able to open the door leading to a high level of tranquility and happiness as never before experienced.

He is clarity.
Practicing Tranquil Meditation,
He is like a lake,
Pure and tranquil and deep.

By day the sun shines,
And the warrior in his armor shines.
By night the moon shines,
And the master shines in meditation.
But day and night
The man who is awake
Shines in the radiance of the spirit.
The Sayings of the Buddha

CHAPTER 4
FIVE MENTAL FACTORS
OF CONCENTRATION

As previously mentioned, Tranquil Meditation practice is concerned with mental concentration on a suitable meditation object for a reasonable period of time. To be able to do so requires the support of the 5 mental factors of concentration.

With an understanding of these mental factors, meditators, especially beginners, will be in a better position to know the extent of the progress of their practices.

There are five mental factors of concentration:
1. **Vitakka**
2. **Vicāra**
3. **Pīti**
4. **Sukha**
5. **Ekaggatā**

1. Vitakka

Ordinarily our minds are wandering. At one moment we perceive the object through our eyes, then we change to other senses, such as hearing, smelling, tasting, touching, feeling or thinking. Sometimes our thoughts go from subject to subject.

If we cannot effectively control our wandering minds, our minds will be significantly weakened and will easily become restless, anxious and worried. **For example,** when we want to understand what we read, but we lack the needed concentration because our minds wander elsewhere instead, we will not be able to achieve our desired purpose.

For the mind to be able to perceive the intended object effectively it has to develop the power of fixation on the same object over a period of time. In other words, one has to exert the effort of lifting the mind toward the object as contemplated. This lifting of the mind is called Vitakka. Without Vitakka to cause the mind to maintain frequent contact with the object, the concentrated mind cannot arise. For this reason, Vitakka is one of the vital mental factors of concentration.

The mind which fails to adequately fix on the object often becomes dull, unresponsive or inactive. **For example,** while attending a lecture some people at the beginning listen attentively but later their attention gradually decreases. This causes their minds to be unresponsive or inactive toward the lecturer leading to a state of sleepiness. This is mainly due to their lack of developing the power of Vitakka. As a result, Vitakka is weakened to the point of being unable to fix the mind on the lecturing.

Meditation practice can be helpful toward promoting the effectiveness of daily activities in life.

It serves to strengthen the power of Vitakka and
it is required to develop the fixation of the mind on
the meditation object. When the power of Vitakka
becomes intensified, it will be increasingly difficult
for the mind to be dull, unresponsive or inactive
toward the object. This is because as long as the
power of Vitakka prevails, the feeling of drowsiness
or dullness will be overcome.

Therefore, Vitakka is one of the mental factors
of concentration.

2. Vicāra

Vicāra implies the continued exercise of the mind
on the object. In meditation practice which requires
the mind to concentrate on a suitable object for a
long period of time, Vicāra performs the important
function of helping the mind to hold on to the object.
In the absence of Vicāra, the mind cannot possibly
retain the meditation object. It is noted that when
Vitakka lifts the mind toward the object so as to
cause the contact between the mind and the object,
Vicāra will at the same time embrace this contact
relationship. The lifting of the mind as such can be
compared to beating a drum to produce a sound;
whereas, in the case of Vicāra, it is like a reverberation
of the sound.

The relationship between Vitakka and Vicāra,
which somehow are inseparable, is described by way
of a simile; it is like a bird flapping its wings in

order to ascend into the air and its subsequent calm moving of the wings while flying in the air.

As meditators are able to concentrate on the object more effectively, the power of Vicāra will be further strengthened so as to do away with scepticism and uncertainty of mind. The mind will thus become more firm with the meditation object. In this way, Vicāra acts as a strong opponent to scepticism which is one of the mental obstacles of Tranquil Meditation.

For the above reasons, Vicāra constitutes one of the mental factors of concentration.

3. Pīti

Pīti signifies the feeling of delight and contentment in varying degrees giving rise to physical sensations which permeate the body.

Pīti can arise in both the unwholesome mind as well as the wholesome. The former reflects the case where one experiences a sensually pleasurable object according to one's desire. **For example,** taking a look at a desirable picture such as that of an attractive female can make a male feel joyful or excited. This in turn creates the unwholesome condition of restlessness, disturbance, anxiety and suffering in the process of trying to fulfill his craving.

As for the latter case, Pīti arises as a result of taking such actions as relieving the suffering of others, practicing meditation or studying and understanding the ultimate reality of life, leading eventually to the eradication of suffering. This type of wholesome Pīti will result in the attainment of a high level of tranquility and happiness in life.

In practicing meditation to achieve subtle happiness, the wholesome Pīti has to be strengthened fully. As one constantly concentrates on a suitable meditation object without the wandering of the mind, Pīti will follow.

There are five types of wholesome Pīti arising during the meditation as follows:

a. Khuddakā-pīti is a slight degree of joy which can sometimes raise the hairs or "goosebumps" on the body.

b. Khaṇikā-pīti is a momentary joy like a flash of intermittent lightning.

c. Okkantikā-pīti is a flood of joy which descends on the body and breaks like the waves of the ocean on the beach.

d. Ubbegā-pīti is a "floating" joy literally lifting the body to the extent of raising it above the ground.

e. Pharanā-pīti is a suffusing joy which pervades the whole body like a flood that overflows a small tank.

When the meditator experiences Pīti regularly, he can easily and quickly concentrate on the meditation object. This is because Pīti, which arises frequently, will further intensify itself resulting in the attainment of tranquility. As this tranquility is further strengthened, the wholesome subtle happiness will become more complete which in turn will have a more favorable effect on meditation.

It should be noted that the specific function of Pīti developed from meditation practice is to effectively eliminate dissatisfaction or anger which is one of the mental obstacles to Tranquil Meditation.

For these reasons, Pīti is one of the mental factors of concentration.

4. Sukha

Sukha in this context is a happy feeling existing in the mind. It differs from Pīti in that Pīti is characterized by delight or joy as a result of obtaining a pleasurable object. Sukha denotes relishing the

*taste of the obtained pleasurable objects. This is
comparable to a very thirsty traveller in a desert
becoming very glad upon learning that there is an
oasis nearby. He will proceed to the oasis to quench
his thirst with great happiness and contentment. Pīti
is likened to the feeling of gladness arising from
knowing about the oasis, whereas Sukha is compared
to the great happiness and contentment he feels after
having quenched his thirst.*

In general, whenever there is Sukha arising it
will always be accompanied by Pīti This means that
both of them are inseparable, although they differ
from each other.

Similar to Pīti, Sukha can arise with the wholesome mind as well as the unwholesome.

Meditation practice is an effective way to
accumulate the subtle wholesome Sukha. During the
practice, the mind will be trained to concentrate on
a suitable meditation object regularly so as to cause
the mind to become relaxed and calm. The result of
this will cause Sukha to arise and this in turn further
strengthen the concentration power on the meditation
object.

The special feature of Sukha derived from the
meditation practice is that it effectively does away
with the mental obstacle, mental wandering and
worrying.

Sukha is therefore a mental factor of concentration.

5. Ekaggatā

Ekaggatā denotes the focusing of mind on the meditation object. It literally means 'one-pointedness'. When Ekaggatā arises regularly to the extent of doing away with the wandering of mind, this Ekaggatā becomes concentration itself. As Ekaggatā is strengthened, it gathers together the mind and other mental constituents arising along with it and holds them together in order to prevent them from being either distracted or scattered.

The nature of Ekaggatā can be compared to the dome of a gabled house which binds all the other building material to itself, or to the presence of an army general during a troop inspection which causes the soldiers to be orderly and to stand at attention. In other words, Ekaggatā causes the mind to fix on one object, just like a steady lamp-flame in a windless place. It is like a firmly fixed pillar that cannot be shaken by the wind.

The development of Ekaggatā plays a vital role in directly increasing concentration power. As Ekaggatā becomes intensified, it will be able to overcome specifically the craving for sensually pleasurable objects, which is one of the five mental obstacles to Tranquil Meditation.

Therefore, Ekaggatā is one of the mental factors of concentration.

CONCLUSION

These five mental factors basically bring about the concentration of the mind.

At the initial stage of meditation practice, the concentration is not strong enough so Pīti and Sukha may not yet arise. However, one should not be discouraged and should keep in mind that at least three other mental factors of concentration, namely, Vitakka, Vicāra and Ekaggatā do arise, As one progresses in his meditation practice and achieves a certain level of traquility, Pīti and Sukha will certainly follow.

CHAPTER 5

MENTAL OBSTACLES TO TRANQUIL MEDITATION

Tranquil Meditation opens the door to a high level of tranquility and happiness, far above the ordinary sensual pleasure sought after by people in general. But some meditators are not successful in opening this wholesome door simply because they are mentally obstructed by some hindrances which have unknowingly created adverse effects on the meditation practice. If they become aware of these obstacles, their meditation practice will be significantly enhanced resulting in the attainment of subtle tranquility and happiness.

There are five types of mental obstacles (Nīvarana)
1. **Craving for Sensually Pleasurable Objects (Kāmachandanīvarana)**
2. **Dissatisfaction or Anger (Byāpādanīvarana)**
3. **Sleepiness (Thīna-middhanīvarana)**
4. **Mental Wandering and Worrying (Uddhac-ca-kukkuccanīvarana)**
5. **Scepticism (Vicikicchānīvarana)**

1. Craving for Sensually Pleasurable Objects

Generally, people tend to look for and become attached to sensually pleasurable objects, such as: good looks, a sweet voice, a pleasant odor, a delicious taste, comforts through bodily contact or delightful events as mentally perceived.

Beginners, whose concentration power is still weak, are seldom able to attain subtle happiness because their cravings for sensually pleasurable objects are more pronounced to the extent of being detrimental to the meditation practice. **For example,** when practicing Mettā (Loving-Kindness) Meditation or Ānāpā (Breathing) Meditation, one may want to eat ice cream or listen to popular music or watch an interesting T.V. series, and if not well aware of this obstacle, he will try to fulfill his desire. In this way, his craving will adversely affect the meditation by diverting his concentration away from the meditation object. This results in a wandering, restless and non-concentrated mind.

Why does the sensually pleasurable object obstruct the meditation practice of beginners? In general, the beginner has habitually and constantly satisfied his craving for sensually pleasurable objects; now when he is trying to attain a high level of wholesome happiness by means of meditation, defilement (Kilesa) in the form of craving steps in as if there were fear that he would succeed in attaining this subtle happiness at the expense of the craving. Some meditators lose out to their craving to the extent of creating in their mind the wrong views, such as, "Why should I meditate any longer? Is it not better for me to follow what my craving dictates? There is no point to continue the practice. Attaining happiness through craving is a much easier and better way out. Let's quit now." Because of the failure to understand this tricky situation, the beginner tends to give up the practice. This is a great pity: he misses out on such a golden opportunity of life. He lets the chance of opening the wholesome door leading to a high level of happiness and tranquility in life slip through his fingers. If he perseveres further in his meditation practice, subtle happiness will result, the taste of which will excel all those obtained from the craving for the sensually pleasurable object.

Therefore, it is imperative that the beginner becomes fully aware of the harmful effect of such obstacles to his meditation practice, so that when this mental obstacle occurs during meditation, he will not fall prey to this craving or be tricked into it. With such awareness, the meditation practice will be free from this mental obstacle. This is similar to the owner of a house becoming aware of an impending burglary. In this situation, the burglar will likely be scared away.

If you are filled with craving,
Your sorrows swell
Like the grass after the rain.
But if you subdue craving,
Your sorrows fall from you
Like drops of water from a lotus leaf.

---

2. Dissatisfaction or Anger

Generally, the mind tends to wander from one object to another. **For example,** the mind may switch first from seeing to hearing and then to thinking. When the mind is in such a wandering state, it is no longer peaceful. For some beginners, in the course of practicing meditation, their minds are not yet steady so they cannot concentrate on the meditation object no matter how hard they try. As a result, they become frustrated, dissatisfied or angry. If this dissatisfaction is allowed to intensify, it will become even more difficult to concentrate the mind on one meditation object thereby ruining the meditation practice.

The way to deal effectively with this obstacle is to refrain from desiring that the mind must have concentration because when this desire which itself is a type of craving is not fulfilled, frustration or dissatisfaction will result. After doing away with this unwholesome desire or craving, the meditator may still not be able to concentrate because of his wandering mind. If this happens, he should let it go and try to concentrate on the meditation object once again without a feeling of frustration or dissatisfaction on account of lacking concentration. Indeed, it should be kept in mind that every time there is an attempt to concentrate the mind on the meditation object, it is tantamount to a further accumulation of concentration power. This in turn will strengthen the foundation of meditation without resorting to the unwholesome desire.

There is another caution for overanxious beginners who unrealistically expect effective results too soon. These meditators tend to overexert themselves in practicing meditation leading to physical pain or discomfort, such as tiredness, dizziness or headaches, which in turn will give rise to mental dissatisfaction. Such dissatisfaction is detrimental to the progress of concentration on the meditation object. Therefore, one should not overdo in exercising his intentions and efforts but instead he should concentrate on the meditation object in a normal manner.

Sometimes during the meditation practice, some meditators become dissatisfied recalling or thinking of something unfavorable in the past or future. **For example,** thinking of someone who did or will do harm to us gives rise to anger. This poses an immediate obstacle to progress in the meditation practice. If such an adverse feeling persists, one must be fully aware of the dissatisfaction itself directly rather than the thing giving rise to this feeling, i.e. the person or event that caused the dissatisfaction. With the right understanding and awareness of the dissatisfaction being a serious obstacle to the development of effective meditation, one should continue the practice. One should try to ignore the disruption caused by this dissatisfied feeling by continuing the practice further. In this way, the dissatisfaction will be weakened and eventually cease to exist and at the same time, the power of meditation will be further intensified.

> **If you get angry, then may be**
> **You make your enemy suffer, may be not;**
> **Though with the hurt that anger brings**
> **You certainly are punished now.**
> **Anger is like the eating rust of weapon.**
> **Anger makes the mind restless.**
> **Happy is he who has killed anger.**
> **Sorrowless is he who has killed anger.**
> The Sayings of the Buddha

3. Sleepiness

During meditation practice, some meditators often experience sleepiness which is detrimental to effective concentration.

This obstacle results in a dull, unresponsive or inactive state of mind, which constitutes unwholesomeness.

Those who feel sleepy while practicing should be aware that this sleepiness is harmful to the progress of concentration. Such awareness can relieve the intensity of drowsiness. How soon and to what extent this obstacle can be dealt with, depends on how early one becomes aware of its arising.

At the time the mind begins to become inactive through drowsiness, the meditator through his timely awareness will be able to realize the arising of this obstacle to concentration, thereby causing this mental obstacle to immediately die out. This can be compared to an approaching danger: if we know in time, we will be able to stay clear of it.

When sleepiness occurs and the meditator does not realize it in time, the degree of this mental obstacle will intensify which may jeopardize the meditation practice. To cope with this problem, firstly, one is to make use of his awareness in assessing its strength. If the sleepiness loses its intensity, one should keep on practicing meditation. On the other hand, if the sleepiness is so predominant that the meditation practice can no longer be continued, one should take corrective actions as follows:

Strengthen your mind by means of deep breathing with strong determination that sleepiness will fall away and with realization that meditation practice creates substantial benefits. Apart from this, it should be borne in mind that meditation is the gateway to wholesome and subtle happiness releasing one from suffering. The recall of wholesome incidents or the remembrance of Buddhist Science studies is also helpful in combating sleepiness.

If sleepiness still persists in spite of all the efforts above, then one should say such a thing as, "Sleepiness is one of the mental obstacles which is detrimental to meditation practice", or rub the face, arms, legs and body. This is because sound and bodily contact along with the right intention will alert the mind.

At this stage, if one still fails to rid himself of sleepiness, he should change his posture in one or more of the following ways: get up and walk; wash his face; look at the sky or leave the room to find a brighter spot. When the meditation is practiced during nighttime, imagine that it is daytime. This will brighten up the mind so as to be free from dullness.

Should sleepiness remain even after the above actions have been taken, keep the mind awake by walking to and fro.

All of these are essential steps in effectively dealing with sleepiness.

When meditating, it is advisable to select a suitable place which is well-lighted and properly ventilated. This will help prevent this mental obstacle from arising.

When the lack of adequate rest is the cause of sleepiness, a good rest should be taken before practicing meditation.

> **Wakefulness is the way to life.**
> **The fool sleeps**
> **As if he were already dead,**
> **But the wise is awake**
> **And he lives forever.**

4. Mental Wandering and Worrying

A number of beginners who are faced with this mental obstacle are often unable to focus on the meditation object.

Mental wandering, which is the opposite of concentration, implies an unsettled or distracted state of mind. It can be compared to the disturbed state of a heap of ashes when hit with a stone, whereas worrying implies a disturbed state of mind bringing about anxiety, distress or uneasiness.

With this unwholesome mental obstacle, one may be bothered by the lack of concentration power. One may even go to the extent of unreasonably blaming oneself for failing to effect a concentrated mind. This in turn will cause one to lose self-respect and self-confidence.

When this obstacle arises, the meditator should become fully aware of its presence and take care not to become mentally attached to the incident giving rise to this adverse mental condition. He should not blame or look down upon himself to the extent of being discouraged in carrying on with the meditation practice. It should be realized that to thus blame himself in this way will have an unwholesome effect on his life. On the other hand, to attain a concentrated mind during the practice, even for a moment, is tantamount to the accumulation of subtle wholesomeness of mind which is highly beneficial in life. One should also understand that this mental obstacle is nothing unusual. If we do not try to practice meditation at all, the mental wandering and worrying will further be intensified so as to worsen one's life sooner or later. But as one practices meditation, the strength of mental wandering and worrying will be weakened. The more we let this mental obstacle take over our concentration power, the worse it becomes. But if we become fully aware of its arising and try to hold on to the meditation object to the greatest extent possible, this will result in reducing the power of this obstacle. As one continues to constantly practice meditation, the concentration power which has been accumulated will eventually be able to overcome this mental obstacle.

When mental wandering and worrying become so intense that meditation can no longer be practiced, please do not be discouraged or give up. Instead, try to comfort or inspire yourself by realizing the following:

a. there are many substantial benefits of meditation practice in life;

b. to attain a high level of subtle happiness requires perseverance, strong determination and full effort;

c. it is unrealistic to expect to achieve the desired result in a relatively short time; that would be just like trying to reap what has been sown in the same day.

When the condition of the mind improves, one should continue the meditation practice as the opportunity permits.

In coping with this mental obstacle, remember that if you fail this time, there is always tomorrow. The desired result will be inevitable.

> **With concentrated mind**
> **the meditator quells his thoughts.**
> **He ends their wandering and worrying.**
> **Seated in the cave of the heart,**
> **He finds freedom.**
>   The Sayings of the Buddha

5. Scepticism

Some beginners may face this mental obstacle causing them to become irrationally uncertain so much so that their minds cannot concentrate effectively on the meditation object.

This obstacle implies irrational uncertainty coupled with indecision and unreasonable doubt concerning the real benefits of meditation. One may not be sure whether or not meditation will bring about a high level of subtle happiness. One may also doubt whether or not meditation practice is a right path in life. He may even feel he has been misled after his meditation practice fails to produce any desired result after a long period of time.

It should be noted that reasonable doubt does not come under this category of mental obstacles. In fact, this type of doubt lends itself to meditation. Reasonable doubt leads to the knowledge of its causes which in turn could relieve the doubt. **For example,** during meditation, one may be doubtful and want to know the reason why he sometimes can concentrate on the meditation object so well as to experience a high level of happiness and why at other times he fails to do so. With this kind of doubt, one will try to find out the right answers and know that perhaps overeating, for instance, is the cause. It can be seen that this doubt is helpful toward strengthening the meditation practice by identifying its causes.

When faced with this mental obstacle, one should become aware of its presence. The sooner he is able to do so the better.

To overcome this obstacle requires thorough understanding and consideration in terms of one or more of the following:

a. The uncertainty, indecision and unreasonable doubt are baseless and often exaggerated without the support of any facts and figures. Usually it takes place even before any real attempt is made to practice meditation. It is just like before tasting delicious food, one has already drawn the conclusion that the food is no good. This is a matter of denying oneself the opportunity of a new experience. This attitude is inadvisable and is something that one should try to avoid. Do not assume unreasonable doubts but instead continue the meditation practice so as to be able to prove its real effectiveness beyond any doubt.

b. Scepticism runs contrary to numerous evidences in which meditators have attained a high level of happiness through practice in the past several centuries up to the present. Why then should one be unreasonably doubtful about the effectiveness of meditation?

c. Today the fact that meditation brings about numerous benefits in life has been scientifically proved and is generally accepted. Therefore, one should dispel any unreasonable doubt which is detrimental to the practice of meditation.

When this mental obstacle has been effectively overcome, one should proceed with the meditation practice without any further delay.

An earnest person
Who perseveres in the concentration
Will attain the highest bliss.
The Sayings of the Buddha

III. PROCEDURES AND APPLICATIONS

CHAPTER 6
METTĀ (LOVING-KINDNESS) MEDITATION

1. Introduction

In our everyday life, we are bound to experience something unpleasant or undesirable which can give rise to our anger, fear, annoyance or frustration.

Some people when experiencing even a slight dissatisfaction, may become uncontrollably agitated to the extent of inflicting serious injuries or damage upon themselves and others,

All the unwholesome occurrences of anger, fear, annoyance or frustration which cause mental and physical suffering are termed in Buddhist Science as **Dosa.**

2. Characteristics of Dosa

Dosa is one of the three basic unwholesome roots inherent in the minds of living beings. It reacts with hostility against undesirable objects and works against our wholesome mind just like an enemy from within.

For example, if one is verbally insulted and becomes mentally attached to the insult, he will become angry or displeased. If this unwholesome feeling is further intensified, it will result in a form of verbal and/or physical manifestation such as scolding or injuring in return.

The term "unwholesomeness" (Akusala) connotes immorality and unsoundness which is harmful to both body and mind, giving rise to suffering such as from a knife wound, and bringing about an unwholesome resultant mind and feelings which experience undesirable objects such as hearing words of abuse.

Dosa manifests itself through:
a. **Body**: such as physical attack or injury.
b. **Verbal Expression**: such as scolding or cursing.
c. **Mind**: such as worrying or agitation

3. Adverse Effects of Dosa (Anger, fear, annoyance or frustration.)

As a burning match stick can cause hundreds of houses to burn down completely, the "fire of Dosa" can likewise ruin one's whole life and property.

If **Dosa** occurs regularly, its intensity will be increased to the extent that the mind will be burnt up by the fire of Dosa and will eventually explode like a volcanic eruption.

A person who is susceptible to **Dosa** can be compared to a mind with a chronic ulcerated wound. Whenever he becomes displeased with something or somebody, it will be just like his wound is being disturbed and he will respond most strongly.

In short, **Dosa** adversely affects both physical and mental health. It shortens one's life and increases one's suffering thereby making it extremely difficult to live happily and successfully.

4. Overcoming Dosa

As fire can be extinguished by water, the "fire of Dosa" can likewise be overcome by the power of Mettā (loving-kindness).

The opposite of **Dosa** (anger, fear, annoyance or frustration) is Mettā, which means good intentions toward self and others for the attainment of happiness in life.

While we are experiencing loving-kindness (Mettā), **Dosa** cannot arise. Thus, in overcoming the "fire of Dosa", we cultivate Mettā (loving-kindness) in our mind to the extent of building up the power of Mettā.

When the flame of **Dosa** glows, the power of Mettā can overcome it instantly in the same way a fire extinguisher puts out a fire.

5. What is to be specifically gained from Mettā Meditation

With effective Mettā Meditation, the following will be attained in addition to the general benefits described in Chapter 3:

a. Tranquility and brightening of the mind.

b. The experience of sound sleep without disturbing dreams.

c. An increased level of tolerance essential for effectively dealing with problems in life.

d. Amicability towards others.

e. Freedom from worry.

f. An increasing willingness to help others constructively.

g. An increase in the chances for happier rebirth.

6. Procedures and Steps

a. Mettā (loving-kindness) Meditation concerns itself with the development of concentration as follows:

(1.) Mention verbally or mentally these words: "Suppe Satta, Avera, Uppaya Pachcha, Anika, Sukee Attanang, Parihah Runtu", which carry the meaning, "May all living beings refrain from being hostile and destructive. May all be free from suffering and attain happiness and safety in life." Or

(2.) Repeat verbally or silently the words **Mettā Mettā Mettā.....** (loving-kindness).... in cases where step (1.) above is inconvenient or inappropriate.

In the initial stage of implementation, it is advisable to speak out the above words in order to effectively enhance concentration. As more experience is gained through practice over a certain period of time, it will be no longer necessary to pronounce the words aloud.

b. In effective Mettā (loving-kindness) Meditation, set the mind to extend loving-kindness with deep feelings of good intentions. The extension of Mettā should first be directed to oneself and then to others in the following sequence of ten directions:

From self toward **1 the front, 2 the back, 3 the right-hand side, 4 the left-hand side, 5 the right-front, 6 the left-front, 7 the right-rear, 8 the left-rear, 9 the above and 10 the below.**

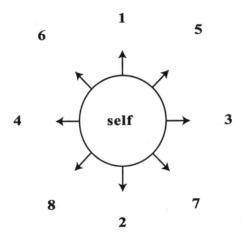

The above sequence of Mettā extension is a recommended guideline but not mandatory.

During the extension of loving-kindness (Mettā) to various directions, merely concentrate the mind without making any physical movements.

c. In practicing Mettā Meditation, sit up straight in order to concentrate better; however, this meditation may also be done in other positions such as standing, walking or lying down.

d. It is preferable to practice this meditation in a quiet surrounding especially for beginners. During the meditation, close the eyes while pronouncing the words as described in **a.**

e. In preparation for Mettā Meditation practice, good grooming and comfortable dress are also recommended simply because they induce a meditative mind.

f. Generally, Mettā Meditation can be practiced anywhere as the opportunity presents itself.

g. Do not be too hasty or too slow while repeating the words to extend loving-kindness (Mettā).

h. Mettā Meditation should be practiced regularly. To be more effective, it is advisable to meditate twice daily for at least half an hour preferably before bedtime and after getting up in the morning.

i. When **Dosa** (anger, fear, annoyance or frustration) manifests itself, mental suffering follows. In dealing with this problem, do not become obsessed with the suffering or the events leading to the suffering; such mental obsessions are not only futile but also aggravate this painful condition. Turn to Mettā Meditation instead using the method **a.** (2.) which will help relieve or eradicate the suffering.

j. When confronted with physical suffering,

such as pain or fatigue, the method mentioned in **i.** can be similarly applied. This will in turn prevent the mental suffering which is certain to follow physical pain.

k. When Mettā Meditation is effectively practiced, a subtle happiness and pleasure will be experienced and will encourage the pursuit of further practice with greater satisfaction. However, if fatigue or discomfort arises, it means that the meditation has not been properly exercised. Under such circumstances, rest, then start again.

l. During Mettā Meditation, if faced with obstacles such as the desire for pleasant objects, dissatisfaction, mental wandering, sleepiness, and scepticism, be aware that these obstacles are detrimental to meditation. This awareness will enhance the efforts which are essential to achieve further success in practicing this meditation.

m. When one derives happiness and usefulness from effective practice of Mettā Meditation, he will be likely to encourage others to follow suit. In so doing, the effectiveness of his own meditation will be further increased.

I visited all quarters with my mind
Nor found I any dearer than myself ;
Self is likewise to every other dear ;
Who loves himself will never harm another.
The Sayings of the Buddha

CHAPTER 7
ĀNĀPĀ (BREATHING) MEDITATION

1. Introduction

Breathing is a natural phenomenon, essential to all human beings. Unfortunately, the potentiality and usefulness of breathing in enriching our physical and mental health as well as our wisdom in life have not been fully realized or properly exercised,

This can be effectively rectified through the use of breathing as an important meditation object.

The practice of effective Ānāpā (Breathing) Meditation will generally lead to physical and mental relaxation in addition to various specific benefits.

2. What is to be specifically gained from Breathing Meditation

With effective Ānāpā (Breathing) Meditation, the following will be achieved in addition to the general benefits mentioned in Chapter 3:

    a. The attainment of a peaceful and happy life.
    b. An increase in the level of mindfulness in daily life.
    c. The subsidence of the defilements (Kilesa) of mind.
    d. The emergence of a firmer and stronger mind.

3. Procedures and Steps

a. Ānāpā (Breathing) Meditation should be practiced in an undisturbed and reasonably comfortable surrounding.

b. Good grooming and comfortable dress are recommended.

c. It is advisable to sit up straight with eyes closed in order to improve concentration.

d. To ensure effectiveness, one is required to commit one's mind to practicing Breathing Meditation as well as to leave behind all worries and problems to the greatest extent possible.

e. During the meditation practice, concentrate on the touching of inhaled and exhaled air on the area between the nose tip and upper lip but do not follow the inhaled and exhaled air in and out of the body; otherwise, you will be unnecessarily tired and concentration will be adversely affected.

f. When concentrating effectively, you will attain tranquility of mind with a high degree of subtle contentment and happy feelings as never before experienced. All these favorable and subtle experiences will be firmly implanted on the mind.

g. Up to this point, if effective concentration cannot be maintained due to mental wandering, do not be discouraged. Such an occurrence is very common, especially among beginners. Overcoming this problem may require that the wandering mind be occupied with a counting technique such as described below. Such occupation will greatly help the mind to wander less and to concentrate more effectively.

h. Counting Procedures

Along with the silent counting as explained below, basic concentration on the touching of inhaled and exhaled air as described under **e.** is required.

The counting procedure involves the following:

(1.) A cycle of breathing-in and breathing-out is considered as one count.

(2.) Forward Counting

    1
    1 2
    1 2 3
    1 2 3 4
    1 2 3 4 5
    1 2 3 4 5 6
    1 2 3 4 5 6 7
    1 2 3 4 5 6 7 8
    1 2 3 4 5 6 7 8 9
    1 2 3 4 5 6 7 8 9 10

Start counting "1" which corresponds to one cycle of breathing-in and breathing-out.

Repeat "1" to be followed by "2" (equal to breathing in and out twice.)

Again start with "1" and "2" and continue to "3" (equal to breathing in and out three times.)

Similarly, follow the forward counting process until reaching "10" (equal to breathing in and out ten times)

(3.) Backward Counting

10 9 8 7 6 5 4 3 2 1
  9 8 7 6 5 4 3 2 1
  8 7 6 5 4 3 2 1
  7 6 5 4 3 2 1
  6 5 4 3 2 1
  5 4 3 2 1
  4 3 2 1
  3 2 1
  2 1
  1

This is the counting in reverse of (2.) above by starting with "10" and ending with "1"

Then start with "9" and continue backward to "1"

Thus, continue the process by counting "8" until reaching "1"

Similarly, follow the reversed counting process until reaching "1"

(4.) After completing the backward counting process, restart counting forward as described under (2.) above.

(5.) During the counting process, observe whether or not you feel tired. If so, it means that the counting is too fast and should be slowed down.

(6.) In case there is a miscounting or forgetting of numbers in a line, go back to the first number of that line if remembered. Otherwise, start from the beginning.

(7.) If the counting procedure is properly exercised, the mind will begin to tranquilize and to experience a high level of contentment and happiness. Try to prolong these feelings as long as possible by maintaining the awareness that they can and will continuously arise.

(8.) When the mind reaches the state of reasonable tranquility, it is no longer necessary to continue the counting process. Nevertheless, continue the breathing procedure, i.e., concentration on the inhaled and exhaled air as described under e. until the end of meditation practice.

(9.) Breathing Meditation should be regularly practiced. To be more effective, take at least 30 minutes to meditate on a daily basis, preferably before bedtime and after getting up in the morning.

(10.) During Ānāpā (Breathing) Meditation, if such obstacles as desire for pleasant objects, dissatisfaction, mental wandering, sleepiness, and scepticism occur, realize the adverse effects of these obstacles on the meditation and further strengthen the effort to achieve concentration.

As the moon slips from behind a cloud
And shines.
So the meditator come out from behind his
ignorance
And shines
         The Sayings of the Buddha

CHAPTER 8
ODĀTA KASIṆA
(WHITE OBJECT) MEDITATION

1. Introduction

The third meditation practice involves the development of concentration through the use of eyesight as a medium while focusing on a white object. This method requires a certain aid which is easy to make. This meditation practice will eventually lead to a high level of subtle happiness and contentment in life.

2. What is to be specifically gained from Odāta Kasiṇa (White Object) Meditation

With effective White Object Meditation, the following will be realized in addition to the general benefits described in Chapter 3.

a. Brightening of the mind.
b. Alertness of the mind.
c. Elimination of drowsiness.
d. Eradication of haziness of the mind.
e. Increased powers of observation.

3. Procedures and steps

a. Preparation stage

(1.) Cut a circle with a diameter of 12 inches out of a piece of white paper or cloth.

(2.) Paste this white circle in the center of a piece of black paper or cloth which has the dimension 36x24 square inches. This will make the circle more prominent for easy focusing.

(3.) This white circle should be placed at eye level when viewed from a sitting position at a distance of 3 to 4 feet.

(4.) Before the practice, make sure that the white object (Odāta Kasiṇa) is at eye level.

(5.) It is advisable to practice in a quiet and comfortable surrounding.

(6.) Good grooming and comfortable dress are recommended simply because they encourage a meditative mind.

b. Practicing stage

(1.) Sit up straight and contemplate the value of this (Odāta Kasiṇa) meditation in overcoming suffering and simultaneously enhancing the level of serenity and happiness in life.

(2.) Focus the eyes on the white object (Odāta Kasiṇa) in an ordinary manner. If the eyes are open too wide, they will become fatigued, and if they are open too tittle, the mind will become drowsy. Both results will adversely affect the meditation.

(3.) Do not become distracted by closely examining or analyzing the meditation object. Merely focus on the white object.

(4.) Initially mention the words **"white, white, white,....."** verbally at a normal rate, while focusing on the meditation object in order to enhance concentration. After becoming used to it, merely repeat the words, **"white, white, white,....."** mentally. Even at this stage of practice, a certain degree of tranquility and happiness will be experienced.

(5.) Then alternately open and close the eyes. While closing the eyes, try to perceive the meditation object as if the eyes were open. Even in the case where there is no perception, it does not matter, as long as concentration is kept on the meditation object. The repetition of this process will further enhance the realization of all the benefits mentioned above.

(6.) To be more effective, this Kasiṇa Meditation should be practiced daily for at least half an hour as opportunity permits.

(7.) During Kasiṇa Meditation, if faced with such obstacles as the desire for pleasant objects, dissatisfaction, mental wandering, sleepiness, and scepticism, be aware of the detrimental effects of these obstacles on the meditation. This awareness will enhance the efforts which are important in attaining further success in this meditation practice.

> **By gradual practice from time to time,**
> **little by little let the meditator**
> **blow off his own blemishes**
> **just as the smith with silver**
> The Sayings of the Buddha

CONCLUSION

These meditation practices as described above, namely, Mettā (Loving-Kindness) Meditation, Ānāpā (Breathing) Meditation and Odāta Kasiṇa (White Object) Meditation, have been simplified for easy and practical application. But to achieve highly effective meditation, one is required to exercise perseverance, strong determination and wholesome intentions along with the devotion of sufficient time to practice the meditation with right understanding.

IV. CONCLUSION

If the meditator practices in accordance with the above procedures and guidelines, he/she will receive benefits ranging from the lessening of physical and mental suffering to the attainment of a high level of tranquility and happiness far above that normally experienced in life. Such subtle tranquility and happiness cannot be bought at any price. They are also much more enduring than any material wealth and cannot be destroyed by any such things as fire, flood, storm or theft, simply because they represent spiritual wealth.

This book highlights three methods of practicing Tranquil Meditation. The first method is concerned with Mettā (Loving-Kindness) Meditation which should be practiced regularly when time permits. Initially, one is often faced with mental obstacles which are detrimental to the effectiveness of meditation practice. This is a common occurrence. Try to apply the most effective methods of coping with these obstacles as mentioned in Chapter 5, "Mental Obstacles to Tranquil Meditation" along with the realization of substantial benefits to be received. One is urged to exercise further perseverance in order to successfully do away with all difficulties and at

the same time to attain a high level of tranquility
and happiness.

As for the other two methods, Ānāpā (Breathing) Meditation and Odāta Kasiṇa (White Object)
Meditation, the meditator should try practicing both
and then select the one more suitable and effective
for him/her. If both types of meditation are practiced
regularly, so much the better.

When Tranquil Meditation is effectively practiced,
the power of concentration can be utilized for the
benefits of daily living; **for example,** when becoming
angry, the meditator is able to make use of the power
of concentration to subdue his/her anger. When there
is physical pain, instead of becoming frustrated or
lamenting, the power of concentration thus developed
can contain the adverse feeling as well as relieve
the physical suffering.

Only through his/her own efforts by means of
regular practice will the meditator realize the full
benefits of Tranquil Meditation.

- The path leading toward a high level of tran-
quility and happiness is there for all of us to follow.
Why not take this path through practicing Tranquil
Meditation as described above ?

- High level happiness, the foundation of wholesome progress in life, is here before you: all that is
required is to practice Tranquil Meditation effectively.

- Some people travel a long way just to taste
delicious food while incurring a lot of expense, but

there is a taste far superior to that of any kind of food, and this taste is not far from us. In fact, this taste of Dhamma can be obtained within oneself by means of meditation practice.

PART TWO of this book is Insight Meditation (Vipassanā Kammaṭṭhāna). It involves the accumulation and development of high levels of wisdom which are most beneficial in bringing about the greatest degree of wholesome happiness and contentment in life and at the same time doing away with suffering. This is the most prudent and subtle type of meditation and cannot be found either in theory or in practice anywhere else except in the Buddha's Teachings (TIPIṬAKA). Thus, Insight Meditation is considered to be the unique characteristic of the Buddha's Teachings (TIPIṬAKA).

**By strenuous effort,
earnestness, self-discipline
and self-control,
a wise man builds himself
an island not susceptible to any flood.**
The Sayings of the Buddha

PART TWO

INSIGHT MEDITATION

DIRECT AWARENESS

SATIPAṬṬHĀNA

BODY

FEELING

DHAMMA

MIND

I. INTRODUCTION

Insight Meditation (VIPASSANĀ KAMMAṬ-ṬHĀNA) involves the accumulation and development of the highest level of wisdom among all the worldly wisdoms. It is most beneficial in bringing about the greatest degree of wholesome happiness and contentment in life and at the same time doing away with suffering. This is the most wise and subtle type of meditation and cannot be found either in theory or in practice anywhere else except in the Buddha's Teachings (TIPIṬAKA). Thus, Insight Meditation is considered to be the unique characteristic of Buddhist Advanced Science (ABHIDHAMMA).

In Insight Meditation, there is no need to exercise strong concentration power in getting rid of mental suffering as in the case of Tranquil Meditation. The latter requires the use of concentration power to subdue the mental suffering as it arises. This is because, in coping with suffering, concentration power is generated to replace the mental suffering. Tranquil Meditation is an attempt to solve the problems of life indirectly. To be effective in applying concentration power to cope with mental suffering, one is required to practice Tranquil Meditation regularly or else concentration power will diminish. It is just like playing football without regular practice thereby adversely affecting one's playing skill. When mental suffering is more pronounced than concentration power, it is generally rather difficult to get relief through Tranquil Meditation; however, with Insight Meditation, mental suffering will be eventually eradicated.

Insight Meditation subtly and wisely eliminates mental suffering by Direct Awareness of physical and mental phenomena as they really are at the present moment, without relying on thoughts and imagination. As a result, full awareness and realization of the reality of life is achieved.

For instance, when anger and/or dissatisfaction are about to arise, if those feelings are closely and directly followed, and if one becomes fully aware of their true nature, in time, one will feel neither anger nor dissatisfaction simply because they have been replaced by wisdom developed through Insight Meditation.

In Insight Meditation, the realization of the reality of life is not restricted to unwholesome arising (e.g. anger or dissatisfaction), but also extends to wholesome arising (e.g. loving-kindness). The latter serves as a further step in the development of a higher level of wholesomeness leading toward "Perpetual Happiness" (NIBBĀNA)

In spite of the above differences, Tranquil Meditation and Insight Meditation are complementary and supplementary to each other and must be used as the situation necessitates in order to more effectively attain a happier, more peaceful and successful life. Each of these meditations has its own merits. If one seeks general, wholesome happiness and contentment, development of memory, concentration power and instant relief from mental suffering, Tranquil Meditation is appropriate. However, in cases where the concentration power of Tranquil Meditation cannot be used effectively to cope with mental suffering, Insight Meditation is preferable.

II. BACKGROUND AND THEORY

CHAPTER 9

WHAT IS INSIGHT MEDITATION

Insight Meditation cultivates Insight Wisdom (Vipassanā Paññā) which fully and directly realizes the ultimate reality of life as it arises at the present moment. Its ultimate aim is to eradicate the defilements (Kilesa) of mind which give rise to suffering, leading eventually to the attainment of "Perpetual Happiness" (Nibbāna).

For a thorough and right understanding of Insight Meditation, the above definition should be further clarified on the following basis:

1. What is the unique characteristic of Insight Wisdom (Vipassanā Paññā)? How does Insight Wisdom differ from other wisdom?

2. What is really meant by a full and direct realization of Insight Wisdom (Vipassanā Paññā)?

3. What is the ultimate reality of life as realized by Insight Wisdom (Vipassanā Paññā)?

4. Why is it that Insight Wisdom (Vipassanā Paññā) must become fully and directly aware of the ultimate reality of life as it arises at the present moment?

5. What is meant by the sentence, "The ultimate aim of Insight Meditation is to completely and permanently eradicate the defilements (Kilesa) of mind which bring about suffering"?

1. The unique characteristic of Insight Wisdom (Vipassanā Paññā)

Some people are cunning and succeed in deceiving or cheating others, but are complimented as being clever or wise. In actuality, this is the wrong view simply because wisdom, in reality, is wholesome and concerned with the improvement of one's mind. On the other hand, these cunning acts stem from greediness and selfishness (Lobha), which are unwholesome (Akusala). Therefore, a person of real wisdom will not resort to any unwholesome practices.

Through studying by way of listening, reading and discussing (Sutamayapaññā), some people can distinguish between what is right and what is wrong; what is wholesome giving rise to happiness and what is unwholesome bringing about suffering. This knowledge as well as understanding about life is itself a type of wisdom, because it enables the mind to become healthy and wholesome (Kusala). Nevertheless, this is not Insight Wisdom (Vipassanā Paññā), which is on a much higher level.

Even when knowledge of reality is gained through conventional scientific methodology, this wisdom is not Insight Wisdom (Vipassanā Paññā) because it uses conventional or symbolized reality as a medium in discovering certain truths of nature. Insight Wisdom (Vipassanā Paññā), however, is not dependent upon any conventional reality as a medium in getting at the ultimate truth of nature. Instead, it directly and fully realizes the ultimate reality of nature.

In short, only Insight Wisdom (Vipassanā Paññā) can fully and directly realize the ultimate reality of nature, which is not possible in other cases, and this is its unique characteristic. Therefore, Insight Wisdom (Vipassanā Paññā) is far superior to the other types of wisdom with respect to the complete and direct realization of the ultimate reality of nature, leading eventually to the cessation of suffering in life.

2. A full and direct realization of Insight Wisdom (Vipassanā Paññā)

Insight Wisdom (Vipassanā Paññā) directly realizes the ultimate reality of nature at its present moment without relying on the use of conventional or symbolized reality as a medium. The light of Insight Wisdom (Vipassanā Paññā) extends far beyond any other lights, even the sun's. The sunlight cannot penetrate a cave while the light of Insight Wisdom (Vipassanā Paññā) can, with thoroughness and realization of ultimate reality. **For example,** Insight Wisdom (Vipassanā Paññā) fully and directly realizes the ultimate reality of light or sound without the conventional or symbolized reality used by the physicists. The scientists, through their conventional scientific methodology, still cannot directly and fully realize the ultimate reality in the same way as Insight Wisdom (Vipassanā Paññā) does. This is because they come to know about light or sound through the use of conventional or symbolized reality, as a medium. **For instance,** they depend upon facts and figures obtained from mathematical calculations, scientific instruments, comparisons, and so on. The knowledge gained in this way does not constitute the direct and complete realization of ultimate reality at the present moment. This can be illustrated by the following case: *A foreigner tries to describe the taste of an apple to his Thai friend who has never eaten it before.*

The foreigner: "An apple is not sour, not bitter, but sweet".

The Thai: "Is it sweet like a mango ?"

The foreigner: "No, it's not as sweet as that, and its sweetness is not of the same type".

The Thai: "Does it taste sweet like a grape ?"

The foreigner: "No, it tastes differently, and is less so".

The Thai: "Are there any other fruits that taste the same as an apple ?"

The foreigner: "Not exactly".

From the above conversation, will the Thai know exactly how the apple tastes ? Of course not. Does the Thai know nothing about the taste of the apple ? Certainly he has some idea about the taste of the apple through a comparison with other fruits. However, in no way will he know exactly the real taste of the apple. Still, there is a way of making the Thai know precisely about the taste of the apple without giving any explanation which is a form of conventional reality. This can be done by simply giving the apple to the Thai to eat. The Thai will then know exactly and immediately what the taste of the apple is like.

The realization of Insight Wisdom (Vipassanā Paññā) reflects the penetration of the basic core of reality, such as the knowing of light or sound directly as it really is at the present moment. This can be compared to the case of tasting the apple directly. As for conventional scientists, their knowledge of light or sound is indirectly gained, just as in the above case of explaining the taste of an apple.

The realization of Insight Wisdom (Vipassanā Paññā) and that of conventional scientific method-ology can be illustrated as follows:

REALIZATION OF OTHER TYPES OF WISDOM

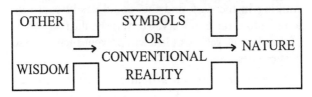

REALIZATION OF INSIGHT WISDOM
(VIPASSANĀ PAÑÑĀ)

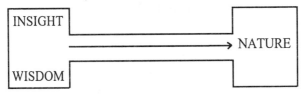

3. The ultimate reality of life as realized by Insight Wisdom (Vipassanā Paññā)

The ultimate reality of life once realized by Insight Wisdom basically serves to relieve or overcome the defilements (Kilesa) of mind which bring about suffering. This is its real benefit. This is like the following case: if we happen to meet an unscrupulous person who outwardly behaves nicely; and we are not well aware of his destructive intention, which is a form of ultimate reality, we may easily fall into his trap and suffer adverse consequences. By contrast, if we are fully aware of his ill intentions, we are not likely to become his victim. Similarly, if we do not realize the ultimate reality of life, we will be just like a person walking in the dark and this could easily cause us to fall into a trap of misery. Conversely, the realization of the ultimate reality of life will prevent such adverse occurrences.

What then is the ultimate reality of life, as realized by Insight Wisdom (Vipassanā Paññā)? This reality basically consists of Nāma and Rūpa.

Nāma means the mind and the mental constituents (Cetasika). In Insight Meditation, the following types of Nāma can be used as meditation objects: physical pain, mental suffering, mental wandering, sleepiness, (these are mental constituents), the mind accompanied or not with craving, the mind accompanied or not with anger, seeing, hearing, smelling, tasting, and bodily sensing. (these are types of mind). In fact, the above Nāma arises regularly and frequently in daily life. But generally, people are not directly aware of this ultimate reality (Nāma), leading to suffering.

Rūpa means anything other than the mind and the mental constituents, and changes due to cold or heat. In Insight Meditation, Rūpa as a meditation object consists of various types such as: a visible object, an audible object, an odorous object, a taste object, a bodily contact object, and different postures (standing, walking, sitting and lying down). In a way similar to Nāma, Rūpa arises regularly and frequently in everyday life. Nevertheless, people in general do not directly realize this ultimate reality (Rūpa), leading to suffering.

4. The reason why the realized ultimate reality of life must occur at the present moment

Insight Wisdom (Vipassanā Paññā) realizes directly the arising of Nāma and Rūpa as its meditation object at their present moment. It is not imagining or thinking about Nāma and Rūpa, but the Direct Awareness of them as they really are. This means that the arising of Nāma and Rūpa must be realized at their present moment and not in the future, nor in the past. In fact, there can never be a full and direct realization of ultimate reality with respect to Nāma and Rūpa , if one comes to know about Nāma and Rūpa before they arise, or after they have already fallen away. This is because the true characteristics of Nāma and Rūpa manifest themselves only at the time of their arising and falling away.

The full and direct realization of Nāma and Rūpa at their present moment will eventually lead to the eradication of suffering in life. Why is it so? This is because normally the defilements (Kilesa) of mind such as craving (Lobha) and ignorance (Moha) which bring about suffering in life, arise swiftly, frequently and without awareness. In order to get rid of these defilements, one must cultivate wisdom to the extent that it can arise more swiftly and more frequently, with full awareness. There can never be any other wisdoms but Insight Wisdom (Vipassanā Paññā), which can directly and fully realize Nāma and Rūpa at their present moment. Nāma and Rūpa at the time of their arising are a basis for strengthening defilements (Kilesa) as long as there is no Insight Wisdom (Vipassanā Paññā) to take their place. **For instance,** at the sight of one's favorite fried chicken (Nāma and Rūpa), one's craving (defilement) sets in automatically and as one starts eating, one's craving is further strengthened. In this case, the taste object in the fried chicken is Rūpa while the tasting sense is Nāma. If, on the contrary, at the time of arising of such Nāma and Rūpa, one has Insight Wisdom (Vipassanā Paññā), one's craving cannot come into existence. This is due to the fact that the wholesome mind and wholesome mental constituents (e.g. Insight Wisdom) and the unwhole-some (e.g. defilements) cannot arise at the same time. Similarly, the experiencing of loving-kindness (Mettā) and anger (Dosa) cannot arise together. Thus, in order to eliminate the defilements, there must be Insight Wisdom (Vipassanā Paññā) which thoroughly and directly realizes the Nāma and Rūpa as they arise at their present moment. *In short, cultivation of Insight Wisdom (Vipassanā Paññā) through Insight Meditation practice is the sole path leading to the complete destruction of all suffering in life.*

5. Ultimate aim of Insight Meditation

The ultimate aim of Insight Meditation is to put an end to the defilements of mind which give rise to suffering in life. This means that the defilements which have been destroyed can never arise again.

The Buddha compared this eradication of defilements, (Kilesa), at the time of attaining the highest level of Insight Wisdom (Vipassanā Paññā), to the complete destruction of the roots of a tree so that it will never grow again.

CHAPTER 10

HOW DOES INSIGHT MEDITATION DIFFER FROM TRANQUIL MEDITATION

Nowadays there is much confusion and misunderstanding among meditators as well as among those who study the Buddha's Teachings (TIPIṬAKA) concerning the practices of Tranquil Meditation and Insight Meditation. Many have the wrong idea that Tranquil Meditation is the same as Insight Meditation. Some even go as far as to believe mistakenly that Tranquil Meditation will automatically bring about Insight Wisdom (Vipassanā Paññā). In reality, although Tranquil Meditation practice gives rise to a certain level of wisdom, it is incomparable to Insight Wisdom, which is on a much higher level.

The basic difference between Tranquil Meditation and Insight Meditation can be simply explained as follows:

1. **Different meditation objects**
2. **Different levels of concentration**
3. **Different types of wisdom**
4. **Different effects**

1. Different meditation objects

Basically there are two types of reality. One is called "conventional reality" (Sammuti-sacca) and the other "ultimate reality" (Paramattha-sacca).

Conventional reality is reality by supposition or reality through symbols. **For example,** the red color in the traffic light signifies "stop", ♀ = female, and $ means money.

Ultimate reality is reality which exists in nature. It does not depend upon any symbolization or supposition. **For example,** an actual feeling of pain, anger or frustration, etc. (Please refer to its detailed description in Chapter 9 under **3.**).

How does an object of mind influence people ?

Ordinarily, we are experiencing an object of mind which can either be conventional reality or ultimate reality. The former is called a conventional object of mind while the latter an ultimate object of mind. These objects of mind can have an unwholesome or wholesome influence on people.

An object of mind which brings about unwholesome mind

Due to the lack of knowledge and understanding of the true nature of mind, people react to it emotionally and irrationally. Such a reaction comes from the unwholesome mind.

This object of mind adversely influences our mind in four different ways :

a. Being blindly attached to a conventional

object of mind

When being praised by others with ill or unwholesome intention, most people will respond favorably without being truly aware of the real intention. **For example,** a man called George becomes blindly attached to his friend's inducement to drink as indicated by such remarks as, "Drinking will enhance your personality and your social status. It will make a real man out of you. It reflects your good taste and increases your popularity among friends. It is good for your health and your life". As a result, he becomes an alcoholic. This is a case of experiencing an adverse consequence from being blindly attached to a desirable object of mind which is conventional reality.

b. Being blindly displeased with a conventional object of mind

When someone with good intentions tries to warn George about doing something harmful to himself, he becomes offended, instead of being appreciative and thankful. **For example,** a well-wisher says to him, "You have drunk too much already, and you had better stop at once, or else your health will be ruined". Upon hearing this, he becomes furious.

c. Being blindly attached to an ultimate object of mind

If a person who is not fully aware of a desirable object of mind, which is ultimate reality, becomes blindly dominated by this object, this could easily lead to immoral or destructive behavior. **For example,** when one is blindly attached to the feeling of happiness arising from sexual activity, which is a type of ultimate reality, regardless of its morality or adverse consequences, he could end up committing adultery or rape.

d. Being blindly displeased with an ultimate object of mind

If a person who is not well aware of an undesirable object of mind, which is ultimate reality, becomes blindly dominated by this disliked object, this could easily lead to immoral or destructive behavior. **For example,** when one experiences physical suffering such as body pain or a headache, which is a type of ultimate reality, and becomes blindly displeased with this object, this will result in more frustration and more painful feelings. For another example, on a very warm day, if one becomes emotionally displeased with this undesirable object arising from the weather, he is quite likely to get angry at the weather, thereby worsening his aversion.

From the above, it can be clearly seen that the lack of real awareness of these objects of mind not only will hinder mental development but also will increase mental defilements (Kilesa).

An object of mind which gives rise to wholesome mind

In our daily life, the arising of our wholesome mind can be caused by objects of mind which are either conventional reality or ultimate reality. An example of the former can be seen in the thought of the Red Cross, with its wholesome mission of relieving human suffering, which can give rise to a wholesome mind. That of the latter can be seen when one recalls his own past meritorious deeds in such forms as saving his friend's life from drowning or donating his savings to a charitable institution: as a result, he becomes deeply impressed with his wholesomeness. This in turn can serve as an object of mind which will bring about a wholesome mind. However, this type of wholesomeness is not a direct way of developing the mind, even though it could be helpful in its mental development.

How can an object of mind be directly used in developing the mind?

In the true sense of Buddhist Meditation practice, development of the mind is concerned with the practice of purifying one's mind by eliminating defilements (Kilesa).

However, the mind has the basic characteristic of knowing an object (Ārammaṇa) and in fact cannot arise without the object. Thus, it follows that mental development must have an object of mind.

What then is the kind of object of mind to be used in mental development? When practicing Tranquil Meditation, the object of mind used is conventional reality, while Insight Meditation practice makes use of ultimate reality as its object of mind.

Tranquil Meditation: concentrating on a suitable conventional meditation object

The development of the mind through Tranquil Meditation practice must rely only upon a conventional object of mind. An ultimate object of mind cannot be applied here simply because it has the basic characteristics of impermanence (Anicca), arising and falling away rapidly and successively, and inability to retain its original existence (Dukkha). But in practicing Tranquil Meditation, the concentration of one's mind on a suitable meditation object must be for a reasonable length of time. Since a conventional object of mind does not have the same basic characteristics as that of an ultimate object of mind, the mind is able to concentrate more effectively.

For example, when the mind focuses on such an ultimate object of mind as the mere sound of orchestral music which is made up of numerous high and low pitches and which is constantly changing, it means that the mind has to concentrate on these numerous objects rather than on one object over a period of time. This adversely affects the effectiveness of Tranquil Meditation practice.

On the other hand, when the mind focuses on a conventional object of mind such as the words "Mettā, Mettā, Mettā....." (Loving-kindness) which are not subject to change, the mind, in effect, has to concentrate on one meditation object only, as opposed to the numerous objects in the previous example, which keep on changing over a certain period of time. As a result, the power of concentration is enhanced.

In addition, Tranquil Meditation requires not only that the mind concentrates on a meditation object which is conventional reality, but also that this object must be of a suitable type. If our mind focuses on a meditation object which is improper, the right concentration will not arise. On the contrary, our mind will become more restless; **For example,** when the mind of a young man focuses on an attractive woman, or the mind of a young woman focuses on a handsome man.

Insight Meditation: directly experiencing an ultimate meditation object

In practicing Insight Meditation, the meditation object used must be ultimate reality, not conventional reality. This is simply because the development of mind through Insight Meditation is concerned with the cultivation of wisdom in order to become fully and precisely aware of the ultimate reality of life at the time of its arising.

Therefore, conventional reality, which is the reality of supposition or symbols, cannot be used as a meditation object of Insight Meditation.

2. Different levels of concentration

There are three levels of concentration according to the degree of its strength, namely: Khaṇika-samādhi, Upacāra-samādhi, and Appanā-samādhi.

Khaṇika-samādhi is a momentary concentration on an object of mind

Upacāra-samādhi refers to a higher concentration which is powerful enough to prevent only five senses i.e. seeing, hearing, smelling, tasting and touching from arising. The only sense left open is the mind door. This means that with this type of concentration, the meditator cannot be disturbed by object through five senses, namely, visible, audible, odorous, taste and bodily contact object. This level of concentration is very high and is almost up to the highest level of concentration.

Appanā-samādhi is the highest level of concentration, in which the mind remains steadfast on the meditation object to the point of being able to concentrate on it continuously all day long, or for several days.

In Tranquil Meditation, the practice begins with momentary concentration (Khaṇika-samādhi) with the eventual aim of attaining Upacāra-samādhi and Appanā-samādhi respectively.

In the case of Insight Meditation, all that is required is momentary concentration (Khaṇika-samādhi). There is no need to go beyond this level. This is due to the fact that the ultimate reality arises and falls away very rapidly, and that if there is too much concentration, the meditation object will no longer be at its **present moment** but at its past. So in practicing Insight Meditation, the meditation object must be the one which arises at the present moment and not the one in the past or the future. Again, if there is too much concentration, it is not possible for Insight Wisdom to follow the present arising of ultimate reality. This is because too strong a concentration means that the mind focuses on one object for too long a time during which ultimate reality arises and falls away many times. In other words, the present arising of ultimate reality has been overlooked or neglected so that Insight Meditation cannot be effectively practiced. This is the reason why Insight Meditation practice requires momentary concentration only.

3. Different types of wisdom

Wisdom attained through Tranquil Meditation enables the mind to concentrate upon a suitable object for a period of time in order that the mind will be **free from mental wandering or other defilements (Kilesa),** which are mental obstacles to Tranquil Meditation. With this wisdom however, the full realization of ultimate reality cannot be achieved.

The practice of Insight Meditation, on the other hand, cultivates a higher level of wisdom, which **fully realizes the ultimate reality.** It is not concerned with enhancing a firm concentration of mind on any object for a lengthy period of time.

4. Different effects

Tranquil Meditation produces subtle tranquility and happiness with the ultimate aim of subduing or

containing the defilements (Kilesa) of mind. This can be illustrated by placing a big stone over some grass. So long as the stone remains there, the grass cannot grow, but if the stone is removed, it will start growing again. In a similar way, effective Tranquil Meditation practice (like the stone) can prevent the defilements (like the grass) from arising, but if Tranquil Meditation practice is no longer effective, the defilements can arise once more. In other words, the subduing or containment of the defilements is effective only as long as the power of concentration remains. Therefore, in no way can Tranquil Meditation completely eradicate the defilements of mind.

On the other hand, Insight Meditation is concerned with the accumulation and development of the highest level of wisdom, which fully realizes the ultimate reality of life with respect to:

- **suffering (Dukkha)**
- **the basic causes of suffering (Samudaya)**
- **the cessation of suffering (Nirodha)**
- **the path leading to its cessation (Magga)**

Thus, the ultimate aim of Insight Meditation is to bring about the complete and permanent elimination of defilements of mind. The Buddha illustrated the effect of Insight Wisdom (Vipassanā Paññā) by the following:

If the roots of a tree after having been dug up, are cut into very fine pieces by a sharp knife and then thrown into a fire and burned up, this tree can never grow again. Similarly, Insight Wisdom (Vipassanā

Paññā) which has been developed to the fullest extent through Insight Meditation will completely destroy the defilements (Kilesa), just as the roots of the tree were destroyed in the preceeding example. In this way, the defilements of mind can never arise again.

In short, Tranquil Meditation and Insight Meditation produce different effects. The former merely arrests or puts a stop to the arising of defilements without eradicating their root causes, while the latter completely and permanently destroys them all.

CHAPTER 11
GENERAL BENEFITS GAINED FROM INSIGHT MEDITATION PRACTICE

1. Attainment of the "Light of Wisdom" in dispelling the "Darkness of Ignorance" in life

Insight Meditation practice is a unique, and the most effective, method of bringing about the greatest degree of mental illumination or enlightenment in life. This is simply because the practice is directly concerned with the cultivation of high level wisdom in life in order to thoroughly realize ultimate reality, while doing away with ignorance of the true reality of life (Moha) - the cause of all sufferings.

In our daily living, if we are lacking in wisdom, which is the "light of life", we are bound to fall into pitfalls of life giving rise to suffering or even death. This is like driving a car at night without headlights, which could easily lead to injury or death by accident.

Therefore, the light of wisdom is most essential with respect to guiding oneself along the right path of life while avoiding the wrong and dangerous ones.

However, of all the wisdoms, Insight Wisdom (Vipassanā Paññā) gained through Insight Meditation practice, shines the brightest, in entirely and definitely dispelling the ignorance of life which brings about suffering.

2. Elimination of wrong views in life

Nothing is more serious or disastrous than the lack of the right views in life (Sammādiṭṭhi). The absence of the right views automatically gives rise to the wrong views in life (Micchādiṭṭhi), which in turn lead the mind away from the path of real happiness. This means that one's life will be farther and farther away from the goal of happiness while getting closer and closer to misery.

In this context, the wrong views in life (Micchā-diṭṭhi) are characterized by mental attachment to the regard of the unreal as real and the real as unreal. Such an attachment is a strong driving force for unwholesome intention, which in turn causes one to act physically, verbally or mentally in an unhealthy or adverse manner. This results in suffering.

All things we experience in life through seeing, hearing, tasting, smelling, bodily contact or thinking are generated from causes and are impermanent. Unfortunately, many of us have been misled by our own wrong view that they are permanent and/or arise by themselves without any causes. When one mistakenly regards what is impermanent as permanent, one can end up with suffering. **For example,** a wife who holds the wrong view that her beloved husband or loved one will be with her permanently, will suffer immensely if he dies suddenly and unexpectedly. Others with such a wrong view even go to the extreme of refusing to believe that their loved ones have passed away, denying that it is true. In some cases, when it has dawned upon them that their loved ones actually are no longer with them, they become pervasively shocked or even psychotic. This shows that the wrong view (Micchādiṭṭhi) misleads the mind and causes it to be contradictory to the reality of life, with respect to the impermanent characteristic (Anicca) of all existence. The wrong view distorts the mind into thinking that existence is permanent as desired by one's own craving (Lobha), thereby aggravating the adverse situation.

Those who possess the wrong view that the arising of various things is without any causes and just simply happens by itself, are not in the position of giving reasons based on the reality of life. On the other hand, they often rely on wrong or illogical reasoning which contradicts the reality of life, and this could easily lead them into pitfalls, With this kind of wrong view, they will think that the outcome of their lives just simply happens and does not come from any causes. To them, a good life comes about by itself without having to stem from corresponding causes. Thus, they think they can just sit idly or live a carefree or reckless life, not needing to do anything with respect to generating the right causes for a better life. It is like letting their life drift along with a current which eventually leads to an open sea of suffering. It is here that Insight Meditation can cultivate the right view, in realizing the ultimate realities in nature as they really are at the present moment. This in turn will automatically dispel all the wrong views which bring about suffering in life.

The right views gained from practicing Insight Meditation are of the highest level when compared to the levels obtained from other means. This is simply because it is only these right views that can eradicate all suffering in life.

3. Elimination of "Multipliers" of adverse feeling or suffering in life

Generally, when people experience desirable objects such as words of praise, tasty food or pretty sights, they will feel satisfied. But when coming into contact with undesirable objects, such as rude words, bad food or ugly sights, they will feel dissatisfied. Thus, when one becomes disturbed as a result of these undesirable objects, such an adverse feeling itself is not desirable to him. This in turn leads to an unreasonable wanting to get rid of such feelings but without any success. This is like trying to extinguish a fire through mere wanting rather than taking any right action. By so doing, it is impossible for the fire to be put out. Likewise, when the fire of adverse feelings or suffering is burning within oneself, merely wanting this fire to disappear without taking any appropriate actions will have no effect. Due to this wanting being unwholesome, when the thing does not turn out the way one wants, one will become frustrated or agitated. It can readily be seen that this wanting or craving (Lobha) further intensifies the degree of adverse feeling or suffering in life. In this respect, it is therefore called a "multiplier".

When practicing Insight Meditation, one will have the opportunity of becoming directly aware of and thoroughly realizing the nature of craving as a multiplier of adverse feelings or suffering in life, and can appreciate their harmful effects. This is because when mental disturbance arises, the meditator who knows the right way of practicing Insight Meditation will not resort to the unreasonable wanting of this adverse feeling to fall away; instead, one will become directly aware of this disturbance, leading to its elimination.

4. Providing the most unique and effective method of relieving mental wandering

Many people seek sensual pleasures endlessly and blindly to the extent that they become restless and mentally attached to them. Such overindulgence leads to mental wandering and the weakening of the mind.

There are many ways of coping with this mental wandering, such as turning to something of interest. Some examples are: exercising or gardening, practicing hypnotism, and gaining general knowledge and understanding of the nature and causes of mental wandering.

Although the above-mentioned methods are useful, their effectiveness is relatively limited and short-lived. Even when Tranquil Meditation is used to deal with mental wandering, this method, because it is effective only in subduing it, does not extend to eradicating its root causes. In fact, none of the above methods lead to the direct and thorough realization of the ultimate nature of mental wandering. On the other hand, *Insight Meditation, which is the cultivation of high level wisdom in directly and thoroughly realizing its true nature, will eventually bring about the permanent and complete elimination of this mental wandering.*

Even beginners who have just started practicing Insight Meditation correctly will be able to relieve this mental wandering without any attempt to force it to fall away. They merely have to become directly aware of this mental wandering through right understanding and this will automatically cause the mental wandering to fall away or to lose its strength and then fall away without any more arising.

Therefore, Insight Meditation is the most unique and effective technique and can be highly beneficial to everyone in daily life, especially to those who live constantly under stress and strain.

5. Preventing the adverse and harmful unwholesomeness (Akusala-dhamma) which is about to occur from arising

"Unwholesomeness" refers to the mental nature

which brings about suffering in life. This nature manifests itself through adverse thoughts, feelings or other mental constituents (Akusala Citta or Cetasika) such as anger, craving, ignorance, jealousy, worry, anxiety and conceit. Those who have not yet practiced Insight Meditation are susceptible to becoming slaves of their own unwholesomeness, and are being unconsciously and automatically influenced by it. **For example,** when some people signal a bus to stop, but the bus driver simply drives past even though he notices the signal and has some empty seats, they might become angry or curse at the bus driver. This clearly shows that the unwholesomeness of Dosa or anger arises within oneself very rapidly and that it can unconsciously lead to offensive behavior. However, for those who have practiced Insight Meditation and become directly aware of the true nature of unwholesomeness, their anger will not arise even though the bus driver does not stop for them. Instead, they may experience good feelings for becoming aware and realizing that their own anger is about to arise. With such awareness and realization, there is no chance for anger to occur.

From the above, it can be seen that those who practice Insight Meditation properly will be able to prevent unwholesomeness, the enemy of the mind, from bringing about mental suffering. This is because they are well aware of that unwholesomeness when it is about to arise, thereby preventing it from occurring. On the contrary, for those who have not yet practiced

Insight Meditation, it is very easy for unwholesomeness to arise unconsciously. This is due to the lack of accumulations of Direct Awareness and the lack of realization of the ultimate reality of unwholesomeness.

Therefore, those who have a chance to practice Insight Meditation will be in the best position to lessen the causes of suffering while at the same time enhancing the causes of happiness, which in turn will lead to the path of real happiness.

6. Effective weakening or elimination of the power of the past unwholesomeness

Generally, when our mind is unwholesome, the unwholesomeness will become intensified through its accumulations. **For example,** some people feel angry whenever they come into contact with someone whom they hate, or think of someone who has harmed them. As this anger is allowed to arise more and more frequently, its power will be further strengthened.

Some people, when their minds become unwholesome in such forms as anxiety or frustration leading to much suffering, will try to relieve or get rid of this adverse mental condition by unwholesome means, such as drinking alcohol or harming others. In this way, they have not weakened the power of unwholesomeness. In fact, by so doing, they not only insure that the present problem will remain unsolved, but also create a new one.

Those with wisdom will realize that the effective way to cope with their suffering is through the use of wholesome rather than unwholesome means. These wholesome means can include giving donations for charitable activities, observing moral disciplines, appreciating the meritorious deeds of others, extending good intentions, taking meritorious actions, developing general understanding through the study of life's reality which is useful in dealing with life's problems, and practicing Tranquil Meditation and Insight Meditation.

The cultivation of wholesomeness brings about happiness as well as the power to directly overcome unwholesomeness. **For example,** when one is angry, the extension of loving-kindness towards others will relieve adverse or unwholesome feelings. However, although the power of wholesomeness gained through wholesome means other than Insight Meditation, can overcome some unwholesomeness, it cannot eradicate its root causes. Unlike other methods, Insight Meditation will ultimately lead to the complete elimination of the root causes of unwholesomeness. In fact, Insight Meditation is the most unique and effective method of overcoming unwholesomeness, ranging from weakening it to the eradication of it from one's life.

Unwholesomeness is like sediment in a jar, while general wholesomeness (with the exception of Insight Meditation) is like an agent which makes the turbid water clear. Although the water appears to be clean, this does not mean that the subtle sediment of unwholesomeness has been wiped out entirely. In reality, it still lies dormant and latent in oneself.

Insight Meditation can penetrate any unwhole-someness no matter how subtle, leading to its purifi-cation or eradication, just like the elimination of any subtle sediment which lies dormant and latent in the jar.

Thus, the practice of Insight Meditation will lead the meditator towards the weakening or the eradication of the power of unwholesomeness in the most effective manner.

7. Bringing about the wholesomeness which has not yet arisen and intensifying the power of past wholesomeness

With respect to the cultivation of wholesomeness, Insight Meditation far excels all other means. This is because only Insight Meditation, if properly practiced, leads to the attainment of the highest level of whole-someness (Ariyamagga Kusala), in which all the unwholesomeness or defilements (Kilesa) within oneself are completely and permanently destroyed. Thus, the more one progresses in his practice of Insight Meditation, the more his wholesomeness will arise or be intensified. This is due to the fact that even though the wholesomeness gained through Insight Meditation practice has fallen away, its power still remains. This means that as one practices Insight Meditation more and more, he automatically accumulates and intensifies the power of wholesome-ness. This is comparable to charging a battery in order to further increase its power.

According to the Buddha's Teachings, whole-someness is the only power upon which one's real happiness depends. For each individual, happiness or suffering is directly and respectively caused by wholesome or unwholesome deeds (Kamma). Nobody but oneself can actually and ultimately eliminate his or her own life suffering. The Buddha merely shows the way leading toward the cessation of life's suffer-ing. But in order for each individual to eliminate this suffering, he or she must himself or herself follow the path. In other words, the actual doing rests solely with each individual. Without the cultivation of wholesome-ness, no one can eventually reach the stage whereby there is no suffering in life.

However, in order to attain life's ultimate goal of eradicating all defilements (Kilesa) and sufferings, the general wholesomeness will not serve the purpose. Such a goal can be achieved only through high level wholesomeness gained from Insight Meditation practice because Insight Meditation can bring about the arising of wholesomeness that has not yet arisen as well as intensifying the power of past wholesomeness.

8. Increasing the effectiveness of wholesome and highly beneficial memory power and the ability to cope effectively with unwholesome and extremely harmful memory power

Memory refers to the ability to recall to mind past experiences or what has been previously learned. No other memories are more beneficial than the one which is helpful in eventually leading one's life toward the attainment of "Perpetual Happiness" (Nibbāna). In order to attain such highly beneficial memory power, one must cultivate the wisdom of thoroughly realizing the ultimate reality as well as *the 4 Noble Truths of life (Ariyasacca) consisting of:*

a. **Ultimate reality of suffering (Dukkha)**
b. **The causes of suffering (Samudaya)**
c. **The cessation of all suffering (Nirodha)**
d. **The Right Path leading to its cessation (Magga)**

As one begins to practice Insight Meditation regularly in becoming directly aware of ultimate reality as it really is at the present moment, he or she will develop the memory power to recall strongly the ultimate reality of life. This type of memory power is very helpful in daily living for the reason that its consistency with the ultimate reality enhances creative or constructive thinking which will automatically give rise to wholesome happiness and progress in life.

Normally, people are under the influence of their own defilements (Kilesa) of mind such as craving (Lobha), so that their memory power is not in harmony with ultimate reality and, in fact, is contradictory to this reality, giving rise to suffering in life. This can be illustrated by the following actual case of a young wife who loved her husband very dearly. She cherished the belief that she would always be with her husband

and nothing could separate them. This belief was firmly implanted in her mind, thus giving rise to her memory which contradicted the reality that life is quite delicate and death is unpredictable. In fact, life could easily come to an end. **For example,** if one breathes in without breathing out or breathes out without breathing in, such as in the case of strangulation, this can simply mean the end of life. Later, her husband died from drowning and she was in deep sorrow and great shock. On the other hand, her husband's mother had practiced Insight Meditation in becoming aware of ultimate reality with respect to every life being impermanent. Such awareness was instilled steadfastly in her mind so as to bring about her wholesome memory power which was accompanied with wisdom. After her beloved son had passed away, instead of feeling the same way as her daughter-in-law, the mother, because of her awareness, reminded herself of the ultimate reality that nothing is permanent. Thus, the mother would not experience profound mental and physical suffering, due to her wholesome memory power which is based on ultimate reality.

Apart from this, those who have been under excessive influence of their own defilements (Kilesa) of mind such as craving (Lobha), aversion (Dosa) or ignorance (Moha), cannot help thinking of various things or events such as their enemies whom they want to defeat or money which has been stolen, giving rise to mental suffering. This in turn leads to an emotional and unreasonable attempt to discard such adverse thinking. The more they try to do so, the worse off they become. Under this unhealthy condition, intensification of memory power with respect to harmful things or events will be inevitable. In this way, mental suffering will be further increased.

Some people have been so adversely affected by their unwholesome and extremely harmful memory power that frightening hallucinations occur. In some cases, they suffer from obsessive neurosis or even become psychotic.

Insight Meditation is the most unique and effective method for coping with this unwholesome and extremely harmful memory power. In practicing Insight Meditation, there is no attempt to discard by force all the unwholesome thinking under the influence of this adverse memory power. Instead, Insight Meditation leads to the Direct Awareness and realization of it as well as the elimination of its causes.

9. The attainment of a mind with the highest degree and most complete freedom

As our own craving (Lobha) is the root cause of suffering in life, to let our life come under the complete control of our own craving or be its slave is tantamount to further increasing the intensity of the suffering in our life. *The Buddha compares the craving as a fetter which binds one's life to the heap of suffering and to be able to free oneself entirely from this fetter of craving is equivalent to*

*leading one's life with the highest degree and most
complete freedom.*

Among various methods used in trying to achieve
mental freedom such as self-hypnotism, Yoga exercises,
Tranquil Meditation, and Insight Meditation, Insight
Meditation is the only effective means of attaining
the most complete mental freedom of the highest
degree.

With self-hypnotism, where one does not come
under the power of others but rather puts oneself
under one's own command to attain the expected
results, one can only experience a limited degree of
mental freedom. **For example,** when one succeeds
in getting rid of a mental attachment or craving for
alcohol through self-hypnotism, the mind will be
free from craving for drink, as one will no longer
be under the influence or command of this mental
attachment. This will allow more opportunity to engage
in constructive activities instead. However, through
effective self-hypnotism, one can attain only a certain
degree of mental freedom; other kinds of cravings will
remain intact.

As for Yoga exercises, one makes use of concentration along with physical exercise. If one does
these exercises effectively, the mind will become
wholesomely relaxed and firm while the physical health
is being enhanced. As a result, one will experience
wholesome happiness instead of unwholesome happiness and, at the same time, the desire for sensually
pleasurable objects will be somewhat relieved so as

to be free from the influence of various types of cravings instead of just one specific craving, as in the case of self-hypnotism. Thus, more mental freedom will be enjoyed when compared to self-hypnotism.

But mental freedom gained through Tranquil Meditation practice will be significantly higher than the one obtained from Yoga exercises, simply because in the effective practice of Tranquil Meditation, the concentration of one's mind is much deeper. Normally, in order to achieve a high level of concentration power, one must focus his or her mind on one suitable object only, for a reasonable length of time. If the focus is made on more than one object, the concentration power will be reduced. This power will become much worse or become completely destroyed when the mind focuses uncontrollably on numerous objects or wanders from one object to the other. Tranquil Meditation is concerned with the direct focusing of the mind upon only one suitable meditation object for a reasonable length of time, while in Yoga exercises, the concentration is fixed on more than one object. Thus, with Tranquil Meditation, as the concentration becomes intensified, it strengthens the mental power through gathering and holding together the mind and mental constituents so as to be able to overcome the craving for sensually pleasurable objects much more effectively than with Yoga exercises.

Nevertheless, at its best, Tranquil Meditation can only subdue the craving; it cannot absolutely eradicate it. This is like placing a big stone over grass, which can only temporarily prevent the latter from growing rather than completely destroying it. In addition, the type of craving being subdued by Tranquil Meditation is not the most subtle and latent. This means that craving in its most subtle form, still remains in the mind and can subconsciously exert its influence. Tranquil Meditation can lead to the attainment of a high level and subtle happiness, which can become a desirable object bringing about an unconscious mental attachment in the form of the most subtle and latent craving. It can therefore be seen that although the effective practice of Tranquil Meditation brings about a mind of a high degree of freedom, this mental freedom is not the highest degree because of the mind being bound by fetters of the most subtle and latent craving.

Unlike Tranquil Meditation, Insight Meditation is concerned with the cultivation of the most unique wisdom, leading to the absolute eradication of all types of craving from one's life. This is like the entire destruction of the roots of a tree so that it can no longer survive. In this way, the mind will be completely free from any craving, no matter how subtle and latent it is, and this will lead to the attainment of the highest level of mental freedom.

CHAPTER 12

MENTAL FACTORS
OF INSIGHT MEDITATION

As previously mentioned, Insight Meditation practice is concerned with the cultivation of Insight Wisdom (Vipassanā Paññā), which directly and thoroughly realizes the ultimate reality of life at the present moment. Attaining this high level wisdom requires the harmonious support of various wholesome mental factors of enlightenment. Out of these mental factors, there are five mental powers which play very important roles in enhancing the effectiveness of Insight Meditation.

The understanding of these five mental powers will enable meditators, especially beginners, to achieve a certain progress in practicing Insight Meditation.

These five major mental powers are:
1. **Confidence Power (Saddhābala)**
2. **Effort Power (Viriyabala)**
3. **Mindfulness Power (Satibala)**
4. **Concentration Power (Samādhibala)**
5. **Wisdom Power (Paññābala)**

1. Confidence Power (Saddhābala)

The mind of some people is dominated by craving (Lobha) to the extent of becoming mentally attached to sensually pleasurable objects. As a result, it becomes subjective and biased as consciously and unconsciously dictated by its own craving. If one is exceptionally fond of something or someone, to him this thing is always good or that person is always right. **For example,** if a man loves his wife, he sometimes sides with her in arguments with other people, even when he knows she is wrong. But when he argues with his wife, he insists that he is always right, thereby revealing his own attachment to his wife and his stronger attachment to his own opinions.

When a government official of some rank such as a judge or police officer, is dictated by his own craving for material wealth, he may be likely to resort to malpractice or malfeasance. The judge may intentionally misjudge a case in favor of a wrongdoer in return for material gain. The police officer may refrain from arresting a smuggler in exchange for a bribe, while accusing the innocent of wrongdoing as a result of his failed extortion attempt.

In practicing Insight Meditation, it is imperative that the mind be free from the inducement of craving, which brings about a certain kind of prejudice. Without this freedom from the influence of craving, the mind will not be able to realize the ultimate reality of life as it really is. This is due to the fact that the craving misdirects the mind so as to prevent it from realizing the ultimate reality, **In order to effectively overcome the adverse effects of craving, one must rely on the power of Confidence (Saddhābala) in practicing Insight Meditation with integrity, leading to the realization of ultimate reality in life.** If this power of Confidence is lacking, the mind will become less firm, and will become susceptible to the influence of craving, which in turn gives rise to the prejudice.

Confidence Power (Saddhābala), which serves as a power base of Insight Meditation, refers to a firm belief in the right meditation practice to the extent of becoming unshaken by the craving as well as being able to rid the craving of its prejudicial influence. This meditation confidence will be further explained in the following section **b.**

Confidence (Saddhā) generally means a wholesome belief in accordance with reality. It is neither a blind faith nor a wrong view, both of which are unwholesome. This wholesome belief has the characteristics of purity and clarity, and by its wholesome influence the egotism subsides and leaves the mind clear and transparent, like a pool of purified water. In this way, the behavior becomes wholesomely refined, benefiting oneself and others. Although this confidence is wholesome and useful, it does not necessarily mean that it is always a mental power of Insight Meditation.

*In fact, there are two types of confidence (Saddhā);
(a) ordinary confidence and (b) meditation confidence.*

a. Ordinary confidence

This refers to confidence in general, which exists in the wholesome mind. In spite of its usefulness, this type of wholesome confidence is not strong and can be easily influenced by craving. Thus, it cannot serve as a power base for practicing Insight Meditation.

b. Meditation confidence

This type of confidence, which serves as a power base of Insight Meditation, is so powerful that it can effectively overcome the prejudicial influence of craving. In addition, **such confidence must be accompanied with wisdom.** This means that there must be a firm belief with right understanding with respect to the practice of Insight Meditation, which will increasingly purify the mind, leading eventually to the cessation of all sufferings. This meditation confidence is also called Confidence Power (Saddhā-bala)

In addition, Confidence Power (Saddhābala) paves the way for the meditator to be on the right path in practicing Insight Meditation, leading eventually to the full realization of ultimate reality and the attainment of "Perpetual Happiness" (Nibbāna). In the following analogy, a timid crowd, standing on a river bank looking at the river with its rapid current, hesitates to swim across to the other side for fear of danger, due to its ignorance of the real condition of this river as well as the right way of reaching the other side. Then a man comes along and jumps into the river and reaches the other side safely. After seeing this successful crossing, the crowd dispels its fear and confidently follows suit. If one tries to eradicate his suffering and to attain "Perpetual Hapiness" (Nibbāna) but does not have the confidence to do it, he will not be able to achieve his goals, just like the diffident crowd who wants to reach the other side of the river but hesitates to do so. However, when he is taught how to practice Insight Meditation with the right and firm understanding that this practice will finally lead to the cessation of all sufferings and to the attainment of "Perpetual Happiness" (Nibbāna) and associates himself with a meditator who has gained considerable and valuable benefits from the effective practice of Insight Meditation, he will gain confidence significantly with respect to Insight Meditation practice. This confidence in turn gives rise to the right effort for practicing Insight Meditation so as to be able to thoroughly realize the ultimate reality which has not yet been attained. This is like the timid crowd following the example of that man in crossing the river after gaining the necessary confidence.

Therefore, Confidence Power (Saddhābala) is one of the most important mental factors in practicing Insight Meditation.

2. Effort Power (Viriyabala)

*Effort Power (Viriyabala) with respect to prac-
ticing Insight Meditation implies an earnest, sustained
attempt with sufficient strength to overpower laziness.*
In the effective practice of Insight Meditation, the
mind must be accompanied with this mental power,
which can only enhance the mindfulness in realizing
the ultimate reality of Nāma (mind and mental constituents) or Rūpa (matter) as it arises, at the present
moment. This is like rubbing two sticks against each
other. If enough effort is exerted, a fire will be ignited.
But, if the rubbing is not hard and long enough, there
will be no fire. Similarly, Insight Wisdom, like the fire,
cannot be attained through Insight Meditation practice
without the exertion of adequate effort.

**Normally, the mind tends to experience conven-
tional reality as its object, which always lacks the
characteristics of ultimate reality. For example,** when
a young man says "I love you" to his girlfriend,
the sound of these words, in the sense of ultimate
reality, is merely the vibration made in the air, but
in the sense of conventional reality, these words carry
a desirable meaning. Upon hearing what the young
man says, the girl automatically accepts the conventional reality, which is the meaning of "I love you",
instead of the ultimate reality.

Even at a time when the mind has ultimate
reality as its object, our ignorant mental constituent
(Moha Cetasika) will cloud the mind with respect

to the true characteristics of ultimate reality. As a result, what is known then contradicts the true reality. **For instance,** upon seeing a visible object such as the light from a fluorescent or neon lamp, which is ultimate reality, one assumes that the light glows all the time, even though it actually arises and falls away rapidly and successively up to about 48 times a second. This truly reflects the impermanent characteristic (Anicca) of neon light. But one's ignorance gives rise to the wrong view that the neon light is on all the time, which means permanency, and this is contrary to the true characteristic of ultimate reality.

For the above reasons, in order to fully realize the ultimate reality through the effective practice of Insight Meditation, one must exert enough effort to be constantly mindful of Nāma and Rūpa at the present moment.

People who begin practicing Insight Meditation through the Direct Awareness of the ultimate reality of Nāma (mind and mental constituents) and Rūpa (matter) for a certain period of time, generally tend to become discouraged or bored so much so that they want to give up the practice. This is the result of their craving for sensually pleasurable objects being unfulfilled or hindered by the meditation practice. As a general rule, we are constantly driven by our own craving to do many things that we want to do, such as listening to favorite songs, tasting delicious food, seeing pleasant sights and bodily contacting pleasurable objects. As a result, during the practice of Insight Meditation, craving can easily arise such as wanting to eat ice cream, wanting to watch a favorite T.V. program or wanting to do other things which are desirable. When this craving is denied or not satisfied, a negative reaction or Dosa will follow. This can be in the form of discouragement, boredom, dissatisfaction or anger.

To live one's life without going against the current of craving will bring about suffering. It is just like a boat going down stream and perishing in the sea. But when one is practicing Insight Meditation in order to do away eventually with all sufferings, it is just like a boat moving upstream against the downward current of craving and finally reaching the shore of "Perpetual Happiness" (Nibbāna).

Therefore, if one's effort in effectively practicing Insight Meditation is not strong enough, craving will step in and induce the meditator to act or behave according to its command just like the boat drifting down the stream. Under this condition, one will become lazy or disheartened causing one to give up the meditation practice. For this reason, being effective in practicing Insight Meditation definitely requires that the right effort be powerful enough to overcome this laziness, and such effort is called Viriyabala. This is just like exerting enough effort to row successfully against the current.

This effort, if sufficiently exerted, plays the vital roles of supporting and strengthening the mind and other mental constituents which arise at the same time, with respect to the practice of Insight Meditation. This is like sturdy pillars supporting the roof of a house as well as preventing it from collapsing. Another illustration follows: in an encounter between a large army and a small one, the latter retreats and its king, upon learning about this, calls upon every possible ally and reinforces his small army. His army then defeats the larger one. So also, effort will not allow the coexistence of strengh and associated mind and other mental constituents to fall back and to recede, but will strengthen and reinforce them.

Therefore, Effort Power (Viriyabala) is one of the most important mental factors of practicing Insight Meditation.

3. Mindfulness Power (Satibala)

Mindfulness Power implies consciousness with respect to lifting the mind above the level of unwholesomeness which brings about harmful effects. This consciousness also sets the mind free from the state of unawareness and confusion.

Mindfulness Power (Satibala), which serves as a power base of Insight Meditation practice, pertains to the mindfulness of the ultimate reality of Nāma and Rūpa at the present moment. At the same time, it is powerful enough to overcome the unawareness and the forgetfulness which give rise to reckless and careless actions.

Ordinarily, when the mind experiences a desirable object through the eyes, the ears, the nose, the tongue, the body or the mind door, and that person lacks mindfulness, he will be pleased or satisfied and becomes mentally attached (craving) to that object. On the other hand, if that object is undesirable, he will be displeased or dissatisfied (Dosa). At the same time, when the mind becomes pleased or displeased, the ignorance (Moha) which clouds the mind from becoming aware of the true reality of the object also arises. Therefore, under this condition, the ultimate reality of life cannot be realized. This holds true even in the case of an indifferent feeling, which is neither pleased nor displeased and which stems from the root of ignorance (Moha).

In our daily activities, the unwholesome mind in the form of craving (Lobha), anger (Dosa) or ignorance (Moha), arises as long as there is no mindfulness. But if one performs wholesome deeds such as assisting those in need, observing precepts, and making a donation for a good cause, while refraining from doing something unwholesome in such forms as committing adultery, harming or lying to others, the mindfulness will arise in his mind which is wholesome.

However, this is just an ordinary mindfulness, and it is different from the mindfulness which is required in practicing Insight Meditation, on the following basis:

a. Ordinary mindfulness does not arise from the constant Direct Awareness of ultimate reality in nature at the present moment. But the Mindfulness Power (Satibala) of Insight Meditation does.

b. With ordinary mindfulness, it may not necessarily be accompanied with wisdom. Even if there is the accompaniment of wisdom, this ordinary mindfulness is not able to enhance the wisdom to fully realize the ultimate reality, simply because it is not the result of awareness as mentioned above. But the Mindfulness Power (Satibala) of Insight Meditation must always be accompanied with wisdom, and enhances the wisdom to fully realize the ultimate reality.

c. Even at the time of its arising, ordinary mindfulness could be easily influenced by the defilements (Kilesa) of mind such as craving, anger or ignorance, so as to become unaware or forgetful, and in this way cannot be used to effectively develop the mind. But the Mindfulness Power (Satibala) of Insight Meditation, if sufficiently developed, will become purified so as to be significantly free from the influence of unwholesomeness such as craving, anger or ignorance. It can also overcome this unawareness or forgetfulness in addition to uplifting the mind to the level above the disturbance of the defilements of mind.

Therefore, it can be seen that Direct Awareness with respect to practicing Insight Meditation is able to cultivate the mindfulness to the highest level. Such mindfulness cannot be attained through any means other than Insight Meditation practice.

The mindfulness of beginners who practice Insight Meditation in order to cultivate the full realization of ultimate reality, will not normally be strong enough to deter the occurrence of unawareness or forgetfulness with respect to directly experiencing Nāma or Rūpa at the present moment. The meditators should not become discouraged or dissatisfied. Instead, they should take this negative effect as a usual occurrence and continue to make further effort to directly experience the ultimate reality of Nāma or Rūpa after becoming aware of it. As one intensifies his effort in practicing Direct Awareness, his mindfulness will be further strengthened so as to become Satibala which will be able to overwhelm the unawareness or forgetfulness. At this stage, the mindfulness will be more and more accustomed to directly experiencing Nāma or Rūpa at the present moment of its arising and falling away.

It should be noted that when mindfulness as a mental factor of Insight Meditation is developed to the extent of becoming a power base (Satibala) of Insight Meditation, the coexistent wisdom will be accustomed to discerning Nāma or Rūpa, leading to its full realization at the present moment. On the other hand, if the mindfulness is not strong enough to become a power base of Insight Meditation, the coexistent wisdom cannot fully realize Nāma or Rūpa. This is simply because with weak mindfulness, unawareness or forgetfulness can easily arise, and this means that the mind will be adversely affected by its defilements (Kilesa) to the extent of being unable to fully realize the ultimate reality of Nāma or Rūpa at the present moment.

Therefore, Mindfulness Power (Satibala) is one of the most important mental factors of practicing Insight Meditation.

4. Concentration Power (Samādhibala)

Concentration Power (Samādhibala) with respect to practicing Insight Meditation refers to the right focusing of the mind upon the Insight Meditation object with adequate strength to overpower mental scattering or wandering. *Concentration is a type of mental constituent called Ekaggatā which gathers together the mind and other mental constituents arising along with it as well as holding them together in order to prevent them from being either distracted or scattered.*

The nature of concentration (Ekaggatā) can be compared to the dome of a gabled house, which binds all the other building material to itself, or to the presence of an army general during a troop inspection, which causes the soldiers to be orderly and to stand at attention. In other words, concentration (Ekaggatā) causes the mind to fix upon one object, just like a steady lamp-flame in a windless place. It is like a firmly fixed pillar that cannot be shaken by the wind.

It should be noted that in practicing Insight Meditation, the mental constituents which arise along with the Concentration Power (Samādhibala) also include the other four mental powers, namely: Confidence Power (Saddhābala), Effort Power (Viriyabala), Mindfulness Power (Satibala), and Wisdom Power (Paññābala). Thus, the Concentration Power (Samādhibala) will cause these four mental powers of Insight Meditation practice to remain calm without scattering or wandering, and will particularly support the Wisdom Power (Paññābala) in the latter's full realization of the ultimate reality as it really is. Without the concentration, there will be no focusing of the mind on the object of Insight Meditation and in this way, it is not possible to thoroughly realize the ultimate reality. Even when there is a certain degree of concentration but not to the extent of Concentration Power (Samādhibala), the mindfulness will become weakened, thereby adversely affecting the full realization of ultimate reality. This is because such concentration is susceptible to mental wandering.

It should be kept in mind that in practicing Insight Meditation, the Concentration Power (Samādhibala) is not concerned with the focusing of the mind on one Insight Meditation object for a long period of time but is just a momentary concentration (Khaṇika-samādhi). Even on this momentary basis, the Concentration Power (Samādhibala) will be strong enough to overcome mental scattering or wandering. For further details, please refer to the previous explanation on "Different level of concentration" in Chapter 10, "How does Insight Meditation differ from Tranquil Meditation".

Therefore, Concentration Power (Samādhibala) is one of the most important mental factors in practicing Insight Meditation.

5. Wisdom Power (Paññābala)

Wisdom Power (Paññābala) with respect to practicing Insight Meditation refers to the thorough realization of ultimate reality as it really is at the present moment, with adequate strength to overpower ignorance (Moha).

Generally, wisdom means realization or right understanding of reality as it really is. This is called the right view (Sammādiṭṭhi). Such wisdom is far above the level of other types of knowing which can be illustrated by the following classifications of knowing:

a. Knowing by Saññā (noting mentally)
b. Knowing by mind (Citta) and
c. Knowing by wisdom (Paññā)

The above three levels of knowing are similar to the following examples: When a child looks at a coin, he merely knows that the object is round, and is ignorant of its monetary purpose. But an adult will know also that the coin has monetary value and can serve as a medium of exchange. When this coin is presented to an expert who deals with money, this expert will also know whether the coin is a fake or a real one, and of what the coin is made. The way the coin is known by the child reflects knowing by noting mentally (Saññā), as he only takes note of the shape of the coin. Knowing by the mind (Citta) is like the case of the adult. But knowing by wisdom (Paññā) is like the knowing of the expert. It can therefore be seen that knowing by wisdom is the most thorough of them all.

This wisdom, which is a type of mental constituent, arises and falls away together with the mind. But it is not necessary that the arising of the mind must always be accompanied with wisdom. In fact, it is rather difficult for this wisdom to arise unless one receives proper mental training in such forms as seeking advice from those who have gained considerable experience in life, reading certain books on how to cope with life's problems, or meditation practice. On the other hand, the arising of the mind must always be accompanied with the Saññā (noting mentally) mental constituent (Cetasika). This is simply because the mind has the nature of knowing the object (Ārammaṇa) and this means that the mind must depend upon the Saññā mental constituent to take note mentally of that object. In other words, the Saññā mental constituent enhances the knowing by the mind, which is the second level of knowing. **For example,** at the time of hearing a sound of the music, hearing is the knowing by mind, but if there is no Saññā, which arises together with the hearing mind to take note of the audible object, the hearing (mind) cannot arise to know the sound. This can be compared to the case where if there is no writing of the letter "A" on a blackboard, the knowing of that object "A" cannot take place. Similarly, if there is no Saññā mental constituent to take note mentally of the audible object of the mind, the hearing mind cannot arise.

It should be again emphasized that when wisdom, a type of mental constituent, arises to understand rightly the reality as it really is, it must always be supported by the Saññā mental constituent and the mind. **For instance,** in the case of Insight Wisdom developed through Insight Meditation practice to fully realize the ultimate reality of life such as mental suffering or physical pain at the present moment, its cultivation must require the support of the Saññā mental constituent and the mind, which arise at the same time. This support is in the form of mentally noting down (Saññā) and the knowing (mind) of the ultimate reality of mental suffering or physical pain (object). These Saññā and the mind cannot fully realize the ultimate reality of this object themselves. However, both of them are helpful in strengthening the Insight Wisdom (Vipassanā Paññā), which thoroughly realizes the ultimate reality of the object of the mind. *This can be compared to a three-legged stool. In order that one of its legs can remain steadfast without falling down, it must have the firm support of the other two legs. The lack of support on the part of either leg could easily cause the stool to fall.*

Similarly, the full realization of the ultimate reality, which is Insight Wisdom, can take place only with the support of both the Saññā mental constituent and the mind. On the other hand, with the lack of support of Saññā and/or the mind, the thorough realization of ultimate reality will never be achieved. In spite of their important roles in strengthening the Insight Wisdom (Vipassanā Paññā), Saññā and the mind themselves can never have sufficient strength to overpower such unwholesomeness as ignorance (Moha). But Insight Wisdom (Vipassanā Paññā) can serve as a power base to help overcome the ignorance (Moha) that obscures ultimate reality. This wisdom is like a light that spreads far and wide and dispels the darkness of the mind, the inability to see things in their true nature and proper perspective. Just as when a neon lamp is turned on, the darkness vanishes and the light manifests itself, so also wisdom has as its nature the shedding of light.

From the above, it can be seen that the first two levels of knowing, namely, knowing by Saññā (noting mentally) and knowing by mind (Citta) cannot effectively cope with the problems in life. Take the case of excessive drinking; if the person involved merely knows by Saññā and by mind that this action is harmful to both his physical and mental health, he will not be able to completely stop this undersirable habit through intellectualization. Only when he knows by wisdom (Paññā) will he be able to voluntarily,

automatically, and immediately put a complete stop
to this unwholesome and harmful behavior without
any feeling of regret, discomfort, uneasiness or
suffering. In fact, he will experience a feeling of
wholesome happiness and contentment.

The mind of most persons is ordinarily obscured
by "darkness" which is the ignorance of life (Moha).
When this mind arises, it usually is accompanied
with a mental constituent of ignorance, which conceals
the ultimate reality of life. But as one cultivates one's
mind through listening to lectures pertaining to the
reality of life or reading books on similar subjects
with right understanding, one's wisdom will arise.
But the light of this wisdom (Sutamayapaññā) is still
dim and therefore will not enable him to thoroughly
realize the ultimate reality of life. Even when the
wisdom is gained through conventional scientific
methodology, the light of such wisdom is brighter in
terms of better understanding of the ultimate reality.
But this second level of wisdom, which is based upon
the use of conventional or symbolized reality as a
medium in discovering a certain truth in nature,
cannot fully and directly realize the ultimate reality.

It is, in fact, the development of wisdom through
Direct Awareness of ultimate reality at the present
moment that will lead to the thorough realization of its
true nature. The light of this third level of wisdom, called
Insight Wisdom (Vipassanā Paññā), is the brightest
and will eventually lead to the complete elimination of

ignorance of mind. For further details, please refer to Chapter 9, "What is Insight Meditation".

The thorough and direct realization of ultimate reality as it really is on the part of Insight Wisdom (Vipassanā Paññā) refers to the full and right understanding of: what is wholesome, what is unwholesome; what is moral and what is immoral; what is useful and what is harmful to life; what are the basic causes of suffering, and what is the path leading to the cessation of suffering and to the attainment of "Perpetual Happiness" (Nibbāna). This is like a doctor who knows for sure which drugs are suitable and which drugs are unsuitable for prescribing to a patient.

In summary, Insight Wisdom (Vipassanā Paññā) thoroughly and directly realizes the ultimate reality (in nature) at the present moment of its arising and falling away in the most precise manner, just like an expert archer who skillfully hits the bull's-eye. This wisdom dispels ignorance in life just like a light doing away with darkness. In fact, Insight Wisdom (Vipassanā Paññā) plays a leading role among all the mental factors of Insight Meditation, and this is the reason why this type of meditation is named after the word Insight (Vipassanā).

Therefore, Wisdom Power (Paññābala) is one of the most important mental factors in practicing Insight Meditation.

The Optimum Balance

The Optimum Balance carries the meaning of the optimum harmony and balance of these five most important mental factors of practicing Insight Meditation

As mentioned previously, the five major mental powers consisting of: Confidence Power (Saddhā-bala), Effort Power (Viriyabala), Mindfulness Power (Satibala), Concentration Power (Samādhibala) and Wisdom Power (Paññābala), are the most important mental factors in practicing Insight Meditation and in bringing about the thorough realization of ultimate reality. Nevertheless, such a realization cannot take place if these five mental powers are not properly optimized. This means that *the excessiveness of some mental powers will hinder this realization of ultimate reality as described below:*

a. If the meditator is overconfident, he tends to believe anything very easily without attempting to find out the real reasons. Even though his belief is based upon reality, this excessive confidence will cause his wisdom to slacken. Under this condition, the wisdom will not be up to the level required in thoroughly realizing ultimate reality.

b. If too much emphasis is placed on wisdom, the meditator often turns to his old way of thinking or to ordinary wisdom which is based on conventional reality. Sometimes, he tends to refer to his theoretical knowledge of Insight Meditation so as to lose track of ultimate reality at the present moment. This can be compared to a visitor to a museum who tries to see a painting from a booklet instead of looking at it directly. By so doing, it will not pave the way to the cultivation of Insight Wisdom (Vipassanā Paññā), simply because there is no Direct Awareness of the ultimate reality of Nāma and Rūpa at the present moment.

c. In exerting too much effort, the meditator will become tense and use up a lot of energy unnecessarily. As a result, he or she can become tired and easily fatigued. Some meditators even experience headaches or bodily pain because of such excessiveness. In other words, the exertion of too much effort will bring about physical pain or discomfort and tiredness so as to discourage oneself from further practice.

d. If there is too much concentration in practicing Insight Meditation, the meditator will fix his or her mind, for a certain period of time, on a particular meditation object which has already fallen away. This means that the meditation object is no longer in existence at the present moment. In this way, the meditator will be prevented from reaching the ultimate reality at the present moment. This is similar to a ripple. The first wave arises and falls away; so does the second wave or the third wave and so on. If the meditator applies excessive concentration on one meditation object for a period of time, it is just like focusing the mind on the first wave, which has already fallen away, while ignoring the subsequent waves at the present moment of their respective arising and falling away. Apart from this, the excessive concentration can bring about a mental image which is a conventional reality and not an ultimate reality at the present moment. In fact, many people who practice Insight Meditation with too much concentration, sometimes can see the arising and falling away of Nāma and Rūpa which are not real and are merely their mental images. This is because they are created by the power of such concentration. These images are useful in our understanding of reality in life, but since they are conventional reality, they can never give rise to Insight Wisdom (Vipassanā Paññā) which thoroughly realizes the ultimate reality of Nāma and Rūpa at the present moment.

Therefore, people who practice Insight Meditation must be careful not to have too much concentration and must be able to distinguish which meditation object is ultimate reality and which is conventional reality. To be able to do so, one must have mindfulness in becoming directly aware of the ultimate reality of Nāma and Rūpa at the present moment as well as wisdom in thoroughly realizing this ultimate reality. Whenever the mind fixes on a particular meditation object for a period of time to the extent of bringing about a certain degree of tranquility and happiness, this clearly indicates that the concentration is excessive.

e. As for the Mindfulness Power (Satibala), it is most advisable for the mindfulness to arise frequently and to intensify its power in becoming directly aware of Body, Feeling, Mind or Dhamma, in accordance with the principles of Direct Awareness (Satipaṭṭhāna). In other words, with mindfulness power (Satibala), Direct Awareness of Nāma-Rūpa can be achieved by a meditator who practices Insight (Vipassanā) Meditation directly without going through the practice of Tranquil Meditation first.

There are two important principles regarding the Direct Awareness (Satipaṭṭhāna) in Insight Meditation. Firstly, there must be Direct Awareness of Nāma-Rūpa without being pleased (Abhijjhā) or displeased (Domanassa) so that the mindfulness will be pure and free from the influence of the defilements (Kilesa) of mind. **Secondly,** the increase in the level of Direct Awareness during the meditation practice will prevent the meditator from being mentally attached to conventional reality as being permanent, self, and so forth. Such attachment is contrary to the true characteristics of the ultimate reality and is detrimental to the practice of Direct Awareness.

The attempt to intensify Mindfulness Power (Satibala) which is one of the five mental powers, is to enhance the effectiveness of these two principles as mentioned above as well as the progress of Insight Meditation practice and to coordinate with the other four mental powers in bringing about the optimum balance.

Thus, in the practice of Insight Meditation, it is advisable for Direct Awareness (Satipaṭṭhāna) to occur frequently and to become intensified so as to lead to the optimum balance of these five mental powers.

CHAPTER 13
MENTAL OBSTACLES TO INSIGHT MEDITATION (NĪVARANA)

In practicing Insight Meditation, meditators are usually mentally obstructed by certain hindrances which prevent them from being successful in the complete and thorough realization of ultimate reality leading to the cessation of suffering in life. If meditators are not well aware of these mental obstacles, they will easily become victims so that their chance to eradicate the causes of suffering will be seriously impaired. Thus, it is imperative for the meditators to realize the nature of these mental obstacles in order to be able to overcome them.

There are six types of mental obstacles (Nīvarana)

1. **Craving for Sensually Pleasurable Objects (Kāmachandanīvarana)**
2. **Dissatisfaction or Anger (Byāpādanīvarana)**
3. **Sleepiness (Thīna-middhanīvarana)**
4. **Mental Wandering and Worrying (Uddhacca-kukkuccanīvarana)**
5. **Scepticism (Vicikicchānīvarana)**
6. **Ignorance (Avijjānīvarana)**

1. Craving for Sensually Pleasurable Objects (Kāmachandanīvarana)

As a general rule, people like to look for sensually pleasurable objects, such as good looks, sweet voices, pleasant odors, delicious tastes, comfort through bodily contact or delightful events as mentally perceived, and become mentally attached to them.

Meditators with a weak awareness of ultimate reality in nature are usually faced with the mental obstacle of craving for sensually pleasurable objects to the extent that their practice of Insight Meditation is ruined. **For example,** during meditation practice, in becoming aware of an unpleasant feeling as it arises at the present moment, the meditator's craving (mental obstacle) may cause him to think that there is no fun in being mindful of this feeling and that it would be better for him to enjoy himself watching a popular T.V. series or listening to favorite music. If the meditator is not well aware of this mental obstacle, he will try to fulfill his desire. By so doing, his mindfulness of ultimate reality will be seriously impaired. Even though he may not experience any more unpleasant feelings for the moment as the result of the fulfillment of his craving, this does not mean that he has really overcome his problem. Actually, in spite of the falling away of his unpleasant feeling for the time being, its causes still remain and could easily bring about further adverse effects in the future, whenever the opportunity allows. Apart from this, the craving itself, which is unwholesome, will further bring about unpleasant feelings in the end even though the meditator may experience happy feelings initially. This means that fulfilling his craving instead of being mindful of the ultimate reality of an unpleasant feeling can only aggravate his adverse condition.

Why does the craving for sensually pleasurable objects obstruct the progress of the Insight Meditation practice ? Generally, the beginner has habitually and regularly satisfied his craving for sensually pleasurable objects in his daily life, but when he is practicing Insight Meditation, he is cultivating mindfulness and wisdom which are wholesome, in place of his craving which is unwholesome. When this craving cannot arise the way it used to, its power will automatically strive for the further arising of the craving, and this has the adverse effect of obstructing the Insight Meditation practice. Some meditators lose out to their craving to the extent of creating in their mind wrong views, such as, "Why should I practice Insight Meditation any further ? Is it not better for me to act according to my craving which requires practically no effort ? There is no point to keep on practicing. To attain happy feelings through craving is much easier and a better way out. Let's quit now". *If the meditators fail to understand this tricky situation, it is likely that they will give up the practice.* This is a great pity for they will miss out on a golden opportunity in life by letting the chance slip through their fingers of opening the wholesome door which leads to a high level of wisdom in overcoming suffering in life.

When this mental obstacle arises, unskilled meditators, more often than not, cope with it improperly by trying to suppress the craving. Improperly attempting to subdue the craving by suppression is ineffective because it is adding an additional craving for suppression to the craving for a sensually pleasurable object, thereby increasing the mental obstacles instead of allowing them to fall away. When this obstacle continues to arise, which is contrary to our unrealistic expectations, it will bring about restlessness and dissatisfaction which in turn defeat the Insight Meditation practice. Instead, the proper and effective way of dealing with this obstacle is for the meditators to become aware that this craving is a natural object of ultimate reality. As this object arises and falls away according to its causes, and is also a type of object of Insight Meditation, why then should the meditator try to get rid of this object upon which his Insight Meditation practice depends? Therefore, the meditator should become directly aware of this craving, giving rise to its realization and leading eventually to the eradication of suffering in life. The meditator must be careful to become directly aware of the craving itself and not the object of the craving. **For example,** when a meditator is listening to his favorite music and becomes mentally attached to this enjoyment, he must become directly aware only of the enjoyment, i.e. the craving itself, and should disregard completely the favorite music, i.e. the object of his craving.

In being directly aware of this mental obstacle, the meditator will find that the power of the craving will automatically be decreased without resorting to any suppression. After having overcome this obstacle, the meditator should continue his Insight Meditation practice through directly experiencing the object of Insight Meditation which manifests itself at that particular moment.

2. Dissatisfaction or anger (Byāpādanīvarana)

Ordinarily, the mind wanders from one thing to another. **For example,** the mind may switch from recalling an interesting conversation during a party held some time ago, to remembering the taste of delicious food as well as the sound of favorite music. When the mind wanders in such a manner, the arising of unawareness or forgetfulness is inevitable. Beginners, in the course of their Insight Meditation practice, become forgetful or unaware of the meditation object such as hearing a sound at the present moment, because of their wandering minds. No matter how hard they try to be mindful of the meditation object, their forgetfulness or unawareness still persists. As a result, they can easily become frustrated, dissatisfied or angry. If this dissatisfaction or anger is allowed to intensify, their ability to practice Insight Meditation effectively could become a remote possibility.

The way to deal effectively with this mental obstacle is to become well aware of the causes which bring about dissatisfaction or anger. At the time of mental wandering, the mind is forgetful or becomes unaware of the meditation object. When the meditator takes notice of his forgetfulness or unawareness and wants to get rid of it in an emotional and unreasonable manner, and fails to fulfill his desire, he will become dissatisfied or angry. But if the meditator understands that his dissatisfaction or anger comes from his emotional wanting or craving, which is unwholesome, the intensity of his dissatisfaction or anger will subside. The meditator should then continue his practice of Insight Meditation through being aware of the meditation object, which is ultimate reality in nature. However, when the power of dissatisfaction still persists, so as to make it difficult to become aware of the meditation object such as hearing, the meditator should not be frustrated or displeased. The meditator should keep in mind that this dissatisfaction or anger is a natural object of ultimate reality which is also a type of Insight Meditation object. Therefore, the meditator should become directly aware of this mental obstacle, giving rise to the realization of it as an obstacle and leading eventually to the eradication of suffering in life.

There is another caution for overanxious meditators who unrealistically expect effective results too soon. They tend to overexert themselves in cultivating mindfulness with respect to becoming directly aware of the meditation object, which is ultimate reality. As a result, such practice could lead to physical pain or discomfort such as tiredness, dizziness, or headaches, which in turn give rise to mental dissatisfaction or anger. Such a mental obstacle is detrimental to Insight Meditation practice. *Therefore, one should not overdo one's intention and effort; instead, one should be aware of the meditation object in a normal manner. This does not mean that one should remain inactive or inert; one should be moderate, and this means following the Middle Path.*

Sometimes during the meditation practice, a meditator becomes dissatisfied by recalling or thinking of something offensive in the past or future. For example, thinking of someone who had insulted us or might harm us would bring about anger or dissatisfaction, thereby obstructing the Insight Meditation practice. When this happens, one must not emotionally and unreasonably try to suppress this mental obstacle. This is simply because the desire to get rid of this mental obstacle through unreasonable suppression is actually a type of craving. But when anger or dissatisfaction does not fall away according to one's wish, this will have the effect of further intensifying dissatisfaction or anger. Therefore, the meditator must be directly aware of the anger or dissatisfaction itself. One important thing that the meditator must avoid is trying to become aware of anything giving rise to this adverse feeling; that is, the person or event that brought about the dissatisfaction or anger. **For example,** when the meditator recalls the time he was insulted by his neighbor and becomes angry, he should be directly aware of anger but not the neighbor. To do so initially is a correct way of practicing Insight Meditation. When anger or dissatisfaction fades out, the meditator should then turn to another meditation object.

3. Sleepiness (Thīna-middhanīvarana)

During meditation practice, some meditators often feel sleepy which is detrimental to the effective practice of Insight Meditation.

This mental obstacle gives rise to a dull, unresponsive or inactive state of mind, which is unwholesome.

Those who experience sleepiness while practicing Insight Meditation should be aware that this mental obstacle is harmful to the progress of Insight Meditation practice. Such awareness can lessen the intensity of drowsiness. How soon and to what extent this obstacle can be overcome depends upon how early one becomes aware of its arising.

At the moment when the mind begins to be inactive through drowsiness, the meditator, through timely awareness, will be able to realize the arising of a mental obstacle to Insight Meditation practice, and thereby cause it to die out immediately. This can be like a situation in which one is about to become a victim of a pickpocket; if one becomes aware of the situation in time, the pickpocket will likely become scared and run away.

When sleepiness sets in and the meditator does not realize it in time, the intensity of this mental obstacle will be strengthened so as to hinder the meditation practice. To deal with this problem, one has to be aware of it. If sleepiness significantly subsides, one should continue practicing Insight Meditation. However, if sleepiness is still present so as to affect the meditation practice adversely, one should take corrective action in the following manner:

Strengthen the mind through deep breathing with the realization that Insight meditation practice generates substantial benefits, such as being the only path leading to the cessation of all suffering in life.

In spite of the above, if sleepiness still persists, then the meditator should try to alert the mind through rubbing the face, arms, legs and body.

At this stage, if one still does not succeed in ridding himself of sleepiness, one should change his posture or try one or more of the following: get up and walk, wash the face, look at the sky or leave the room for a brighter spot. If meditation is practiced at nighttime, it should be treated as if it were daytime. The above method will bringten up the mind so as to free it from dullness or drowsiness.

Should sleepiness persist, even after having taken the above action, keep the mind awake by walking to and fro.

If a lack of adequate rest is the cause of sleepiness, a good rest should be taken before practicing

Insight Meditation. However, the meditator should be aware that this resting is not meant to fulfill laziness, which is a type of craving, but to refesh the body and the mind in order to be in a better position to further practice Insight Meditation.

4. Mental Wandering and Worrying (Uddhacca-kukkuccanīvaraṇa)

Ordinarily, people frequently seek happiness through sensual enjoyment of pleasurable objects in various ways, such as: wanting to see lovely sights, wanting to hear sweet words or sounds, wanting to smell pleasant odors, wanting to taste delicious food and wanting to have bodily contact with pleasurable objects. All these wants will bring about craving or mental attachment to sensually desirable objects. This in turn will further enhance the desire to constantly seek sensually pleasurable objects. The nature of this mental attachment or craving (Lobha) is to search always for new, pleasant objects which are desirable. This means that craving likes to change constantly from one pleasurable object to another. If the same pleasurable object is being enjoyed over and over again, the desire for this object will be significantly reduced, giving rise to a feeling of boredom. **For example,** if one has a craving for a delicious food such as beefsteak, he will enjoy eating it very much. But if he has to eat the same kind of food repeatedly, it will become less and less desirable. This could easily lead to a feeling of tediousness and distaste. On the other hand, if there is a variety of delicious food to choose from, he will experience a feeling of enjoyment instead. It is this craving which causes the mind to scatter or wander.

It should be noted that each type of delicious food which suits one's taste and craving, consists not only of single flavor, but a variety of flavors. **For example,** a delicious pizza has more than one flavor, such as salty, sour or spicy. In addition, it has a nice odor. This means that craving (Lobha) brings about mental attachment to various flavors of a particular dish rather than just one single flavor. Thus, the more craving arises, the more the mind will wander.

Another example of craving bringing about mental wandering pertains to listening to a musical program. Would one like to listen to a song in monotone? Of course not. The song with a variety of harmonous tones and rhythm is more desirable in accordance with the nature of one's craving. This shows that while listening to a song, one is directed by his own craving and becomes mentally attached to the various tones. If instead of just listening to the music, one also has a chance to watch the performance on stage or on T.V., this will suit his craving much more as he will be able to see the colorful lighting which keeps on changing, the singers, the attractive costumes and the beautiful scenery. This also serves to show that craving brings about mental wandering under the influence of various objects.

From the above, it can be seen that people ceaselessly seek happiness accompanied with craving (Lobha), and this craving in turn gives rise to the wandering of the mind. *The intensity of the mental wandering varies correspondingly with the power of the craving.*

As one begins practicing Insight Meditation in order to cultivate mindfulness, one very often experiences mental wandering, which is caused by his own craving, as previously explained. At the moment of mental wandering, one is neglecting the practice of Insight Meditation. When it dawns upon him that he is not being mindful of ultimate reality as it really is, he blames himself for his mental wandering, which has adversely affected his Insight Meditation practice. As a result, he becomes disturbed or uneasy, thereby worsening the situation.

Mental wandering implies an unsettled or distracted state of mind. It is comparable to the disturbed state of a heap of ashes when hit with a stone, whereas worrying implies a disturbed state of mind giving rise to anxiety, distress or uneasiness.

During Insight Meditation practice, this mental obstacle, which is unwholesome, arises because the mindfulness as well as the effort is not strong enough. As this mental wandering keeps on arising, one may even go to the extent of unreasonably blaming oneself for failing to become directly aware of the ultimate reality. This is turn will make one lose self-respect and self-confidence.

When this obstacle arises, the meditator should become fully aware of its arising and take care not to become mentally attached to the event bringing about this adverse mental condition. One should not blame or look down upon oneself so as to become discouraged in continuing Insight Meditation practice. It should be realized that to thus put the blame on oneself will have an unwholesome effect on one's life. On the contrary, the meditator should continue to strengthen his/her effort in cultivating Direct Awareness. Even during meditation, when one's mind switches to thinking of other objects, one should not feel sorry or uneasy, because this mental obstacle is not unusual, especially for the beginner whose mindfulness power is not yet effectively developed.

In trying to cope with this mental obstacle, the meditator may resort to one of the following methods:

a. The meditator becomes directly aware of the initial stage of arising of the mental wandering and worrying. By being able to do so, this mental obstacle will either fall away immediately or will be weakened or fade away. The meditator should continue his Insight Meditation practice. **For example,** while one of the meditators at the Omm Noi Insight Meditation Center, Petchkasem Highway Km.24, Samutsakorn, Thailand, was aware of his bodily posture in the form of the sitting position at the present moment, he was interrupted by the arising of this mental obstacle. But he was able to become directly aware of the initial arising of this obstacle, and as a result, it faded away quickly. He then resumed his practice again, becoming directly aware of his sitting position.

b. During meditation practice, if the mental wandering is so intensified that the meditator can no longer become effectively aware of his/her meditation object such as his/her sitting position, he/she should turn his/her mindfulness towards the mental wandering itself, which is the ultimate reality, while completely disregarding his/her practice of awareness of the sitting position for the time being. Under such an adverse condition, if the meditator tries not to change his/her meditation object from his/her original sitting position to that of the mental wandering, he/she may be discouraged or frustrated to the extent of giving up the practice. Such an occurrence is quite common for some meditators who practice Insight Meditation at the Omm Noi Insight Meditation Center.

This can be illustrated in the following actual case. One of our meditators at the Omm Noi Insight Meditation Center, who had been adversely affected by his own mental wandering to the extent that it ruined his practice, came to the meditation instructor for briefing and consultation. *Here is the gist of the conversation between the meditator and the instructor:*

Meditator: "I can no longer continue practicing Insight Meditation. My mind keeps wandering, making it impossible for me to become aware of the meditation object. No matter how hard I tried to get rid of the mental wandering, I failed, and I feel very discouraged and uneasy. Perhaps my understanding and wholesome accumulations are shallow, rendering the practice of Insight Meditation noneffective".

Instructor: "Is this mental wandering an ultimate reality which arises in nature?"

Meditator: "Yes, it is".

Instructor: "If this is so, why don't you try to become aware of this mental wandering? This mental wandering at the time of its arising can serve as a very good lesson for practicing Insight Meditation. Why don't you make use of it? Be mindful of that mental wandering directly. But do not suppress it, simply because the suppression itself is a kind of mental defilement (Kilesa). The more you try to inhibit the mental wandering, the worse it will become, if the outcome does not turn out according to your expectation. Therefore, you should become directly aware of the ultimate reality without forcing it to fall away. Do you understand ?"

Meditator: "Yes, I do".

Instructor: "It should always be kept in mind that any mental obstacles, when arising, could bring about wisdom leading to thoroughly and completely realizing the ultimate reality of life. They must not be compelled to fall away simply because one does not like them. This can be compared to the case of watching a show. The meditator must act as a spectator watching the show instead of becoming an actor himself. As spectators, have we ever tried to order the actors to perform the way we desire? Of course not. When the time comes for the villain to act his role, we, as spectators, merely watch him act. It is not for us to chase him off the stage just because we do not like his role. Similarly, when a mental obstacle such as mental wandering arises during meditation, we should not try to get rid of it through suppression, but instead we must try only to become aware of it. Is it clear?"

Meditator: "Yes, definitely, and thank you very much for your help. I shall try my best to follow your valuable advice".

Although mental wandering and worrying, as mentioned above, are themselves the objects of Insight Meditation, some meditators unreasonably expect to become fully aware of these ultimate realities much too soon. It is just like trying to reap what has been sown on the same day. Under the condition of over-expectation, which is also a type of subtle craving if things do not turn out as desired, this mental obstacle would become further intensified. Therefore, Direct Awareness of ultimate reality should be free from subtle craving in the form of unrealistic expectations. Otherwise, the Direct Awareness will not be purified to the extent of the complete and thorough realization of ultimate reality leading eventually to the cessation of suffering in life.

In short, if this mental obstacle is arising to obstruct one's meditation practice, he should be directly aware of it. If by so doing, this obstacle fades away, the meditator should resume his Direct Awareness of the previous meditation object. On the other hand, if this obstacle becomes so intensified that the meditator can no longer practice Direct Awareness of the meditation object which is being used, he should make use of this obstacle as his meditation object instead, but make sure that his awareness of the ultimate reality is pure and not directed by craving.

5. Scepticism (Vicikicchānīvarana)

For some meditators, this mental obstacle may cause them to become irrationally uncertain to the extent that their minds are not effectively aware of the meditation object.

This obstacle refers to irrational uncertainty accompanied with indecision and unreasonable doubt pertaining to the real benefit of meditation. They are not sure that Insight Meditation gives rise to the attainment of a high level of Insight Wisdom leading eventually to the eradication of all suffering in life. To them, it is also doubtful whether or not the meditation practice is a right path in life. They may even feel that they have been misled when their meditation practice fails to produce any desirable result over a certain period of time.

As a matter of fact, reasonable doubtfulness does not come under the category of a mental obstacle. It lends itself to meditation practice and leads to the knowledge of its causes which in turn could relieve this doubt. **For example,** during meditation, one may be doubtful and want to know the reason why sometimes he can be succesfully mindful of the meditation object at the present moment, and why at other times he cannot. With this kind of rational doubt, one will try to seek the right answer, and know that perhaps overexpectation with respect to the progress of the meditation practice is one of the causes. In this way, this doubt is helpful to the practice of Insight Meditation through the identification of its causes.

When irrational uncertainty, which is a mental obstacle, is arising, the meditator should be mindful of its presence. The sooner he is able to do so, the better. If by doing so, this obstacle fades away, the meditator should resume his meditation practice as before. On the other hand, if this obstacle still persists to the extent of obstructing the meditation practice, the meditator should not try to suppress it but instead should make use of this obstacle as his meditation object for the time being, until it fades away.

When this obstacle is powerful enough to hinder further the meditation practice despite the mindfulness of the meditator, *thorough understanding and consideration with respect to one or more of the following are required to cope effectively with this problem:*

a. **The uncertainty, indecision and unreasonable doubt are unfounded and often exaggerated without the support of any facts.** Usually, this obstacle takes place even before any real attempt is made to practice Insight Meditation. It is just like the case in which, before delicious food is tasted, one has already formed a preconceived notion that the food is not tasty. This is, in a way, denying oneself the chance of a new and useful experience. Such an attitude is unsound, and is something that one should try to avoid. One should not assume unreasonable doubts, but instead should continue to practice meditation in order to prove its real effectiveness beyond all doubts.

b. **At the Omm Noi Insight Meditation Center,** some meditators have effectively coped with this mental obstacle by utilizing their scepticism as an object of their Insight Meditation. As a result, they became aware of and realize the ultimate reality of their scepticism leading to significant relief of their suffering in life. Thus, the stronger this mental obstacle becomes, the more distinctly it can serve as an object of Insight Meditation. For this reason, instead of being a mental obstacle to the practice of Insight Meditation, it should be usefully turned into an object of Insight Meditation. In this way, scepticism will no longer become a mental obstacle to the practice of Insight Meditation.

6. Ignorance (Avijjānivarana)

Ignorance (Avijjā) is the unwholesome nature which obstructs the wholesome nature with respect to covering up the true reality. It has the characteristic of lacking in the realization of the Four Noble Truths (Ariyasacca) and its function is to obscure the real condition of the object, thereby bringing about the state of total blindness to the ultimate reality, the inability to realize the object (Nāma-Rūpa) of Direct Awareness (Satipaṭṭhāna) as well as the impediment of the Noble Path leading to the attainment of the cessation of all suffering (Dukkha-nirodha) or "Perpetual Happiness" (Nibbāna).

The lack of knowledge and understanding of the principles and techinques of practicing Insight Meditation is a mental obstacle to its practice, because Insight (Vipassanā) Meditation, by its name, is aimed at attaining Insight Wisdom which can thoroughly realize the common characteristics of Nāma-Rūpa which are ultimate reality, as being impermanent (Anicca), unable to retain its original existence (Dukkha) and non-self or dependent upon causes (Anattā). If there is no such realization nor understanding, it is not possible to practice Insight Meditation properly. This is unlike the case of Tranquil Meditation. Even though ignorance (Avijjā) still persists, the meditator can nevertheless be successful in practicing Tranquil Meditation.

Why is it so? This is because the aims of Tranquil Meditation and Insight Meditation are not the same. Tranquil Meditation has the purpose of achieving tranquility and subtle happiness and at the most, Tranquil Meditation can only subdue the defilements (Kilesa) of mind. Generally, the principles of practicing Tranquil Meditation are concerned with the firm concentration on conventional reality so as to give rise to tranquility. It is not for the purpose of realizing the ultimate reality. Therefore, ignorance (Avijjā) is not a mental obstacle of Tranquil Meditation.

As for Insight Meditation, its practice is aimed at thoroughly realizing the ultimate reality. But there is still ignorance, which lacks knowledge and understanding of ultimate reality as well as of the principles and methods of Insight Meditation practice leading to thorough realization of the ultimate reality. Thus, ignorance is a mental obstacle of Insight Meditation.

If the meditator who applies mindfulness accompanied with wisdom in becoming directly aware of Nāma-Rūpa which are ultimate reality, does not know the techniques of Direct Awareness, when facing a conventional meditation object he/she will not be able to realize whether it is conventional reality or ultimate reality. For this reason, it is very necessary for the meditator practicing Insight Meditation to gain knowledge and understanding of principles and techniques of Insight Meditation practice first. In addition, the object of Insight Meditation must be Nāma-Rūpa which are ultimate reality. Otherwise, ignorance (Avijjā) will hinder the practice so that the meditator will not be able to become directly aware of the Insight Meditation object correctly.

Generally, for those who begin to practice Insight Meditation, the way to overcome ignorance (Avijjā), which is a mental obstacle, is to learn about the principles and methods of Insight Meditation practice from the instructor whose understanding of Insight Meditation is based on the guidelines laid down by the Buddha in the TIPIṬAKA. After gaining the necessary knowledge and understanding well enough, the next step is to set the mind prudently, appropriately, and constructively (Yonisomanasikāra) upon the Direct Awareness of Nāma-Rūpa which are ultimate reality, according to the principles of the Middle Path. This means that the meditator is to refrain from practicing the extreme of sensual indulgence (or extreme hedonism) and the extreme of self-mortification (or extreme asceticism). It is like playing a harp with its strings stretched properly, without being too loose or too tight. As a result, the proper practice of Insight Meditation will give rise to Insight Wisdom or Right View (Sammādiṭṭhi) which will be able to get rid of this mental obstacle of ignorance (Avijjānivarana).

CONCLUSION

Even though the above six mental obstacles can hinder the effectiveness of practicing Insight Meditation, all of them are a type of ultimate reality and can be utilized in the cultivation of Insight Wisdom (Vipassanā Paññā), leading to the eradication of suffering in life. Therefore, the meditator must not emotionally regard them as being something detrimental or try to be in conflict with them. Otherwise, the situation can only become worse for the reason that this negative attitude, being unwholesome, can in no way be used to do away with mental obstacles, which are also unwholesome.

Thus, when any one of these mental obstacles arises, the meditator should try not to resort to the unwholesome practice of forcing or suppressing it to make it disappear. Instead, he/she should make effective use of it by turning it into an object of Insight Meditation. With its awareness and realization, the strength of this mental obstacle will subside, leading to its falling away without any further arising. The use of a mental obstacle as a meditation object is, in fact, a type of Insight Meditation practice.

III. DIRECT AWARENESS-THE BASIC APPROACH TO PRACTICING INSIGHT MEDITATION

INTRODUCTION

The practice of Direct Awareness is something unique and is entirely new except to those who have studied and practiced Buddhist Meditation with right understanding. For those people who have never been exposed to such practice, it is impossible to even think about it. It is just like thinking precisely about someone whom we have never met nor seen, which would be impossible.

In order to know someone fairly well, we usually have to meet him and converse with him quite frequently and regularly, rather than doing so once in a while. The same holds true in the case of trying to be familiar with the right method of practicing Direct Awareness (Satipaṭṭhāna), which must be performed constantly and continually rather than infrequently and intermittently. Only in this way will we be able to really know and get used to it.

Even when we have no chance of meeting a person, this does not necessarily mean that there is no way to learn about this person. We can still learn about him indirectly by asking a friend to describe his looks, habits and other personal traits and to show us his photo and the place where he can be met. This indirect introduction serves as a useful basis for knowing him directly when the opportunity to meet him arises. At the time of meeting him for the first time we will know for certain that he is the one described by his friend. Likewise, when one has had no opportunity of knowing directly about the practice of Direct Awareness which is the fundamental step of Insight Meditation, this does not imply that there is no chance of learning about Direct Awareness at all. In fact, there is still a way of learning and understanding about the practice of Direct Awareness indirectly by asking those who have experience in this regard to explain the nature and scope of awareness, its functions, manifestation and causes as well as the technique for practicing Direct Awareness. This indirect introduction serves as a useful basis for practicing Direct Awareness when the opportunity allows. At the time of practicing Direct Awareness for the first time, one would probably know for sure that this is the right way.

The purpose of Chapters 14 and 15 is to familiarize readers with the fundamentals of practicing Direct Awareness, which is an introductory step of Insight Meditation, with respect to the meaning of Direct Awareness (Satipaṭṭhāna) and the general technique of practicing Direct Awareness for the purpose of enhancing the right understanding and the right practice.

CHAPTER 14

WHAT IS MEANT
BY DIRECT AWARENESS

If we are clear first about the misconceived notion of awareness (Sati) as well as about its general meaning, we will be in a better position to thoroughly and correctly understand the real meaning of Direct Awareness.

Misconceived notion of awareness

Some people have the misconception that awareness (Sati) in the context of The Buddha's Teachings (TIPIṬAKA) carries the meaning of having knowledge of something internally and externally, irrespective of whether the intention is wholesome or unwholesome. **For example,** when a house is being burglarized, the burglar, driven by his craving motive, which is unwholesome, must be conscious and cautious in his movements in order to make sure that nobody is awakened. Having this kind of consciousness which is accompanied with the unwholesome intention of stealing from others is not considered as having awareness (Sati) in the true sense of the Buddha's Teachings. This is a misconception for the reason that awareness (Sati) in the Buddha's Teachings must always be accompanied with wholesome intention. Its true meaning will be explained as follows:

General meaning of awareness (Sati)

Awareness in the context of the Buddha's Teachings is called Sati and is characterized by becoming mindful and conscious of what is wholesome, what is unwholesome, what is useful and what is harmful to one's life. This can be like an effective personnel staff of an organization trying to be mindful in order to determine if an applicant is suitable or unsuitable, trustworthy or untrustworthy, productive or unproductive etc.

When awareness arises in one's mind, one will be conscious of what is or is not beneficial in life and what one should or should not be involved with. Looking at its other aspect, awareness (Sati) is concerned with consciousness with respect to lifting the level of mind above unwholesomeness or putting a stop to the power of unwholesome intention. **For example,** when a meditator becomes aware of his anger, during its arising, he will be reminded of the uselessness and harmfulness of his adverse feeling, along with his attempt to get rid of it. In another instance, when one who has the wholesome intention of helping those in need is urged by his friends to try his luck at gambling, he may simply refuse to go along, and instead gives his money to the poor. In this case, it is his awareness that is responsible for making him mindful and conscious of helping others instead of spending the money unwisely, and this is a wholesome and beneficial thing to do.

The following analogy will be helpful in further clarifying the meaning of awareness: a royal guard of a king must be able to screen visitors to determine which ones deserve to see the king and which ones do not; only the former are allowed to enter the gate. The latter are rejected. Awareness can be compared to this royal guard in the sense that it reminds one to acquire only the things which are useful and helpful in life while discarding the things which are not useful, just as the guard screens out undesirable visitors.

Direct Awareness

The characteristics described under the previous heading pertain to all types of awareness (Sati). But under this heading, only one type of awareness called Direct Awareness (Satipaṭṭhāna), which is the only basis of practicing Insight Meditation, will be covered.

This Direct Awareness tops all the others in term of being the only Right Path (**EKĀYANO MAGGO**) leading to:
- complete purification of the mind
- perfect freedom from physical and mental suffering
- eradication of all suffering
- thorough realization of ultimate reality and
- attainment of "Perpetual Happiness" (Nibbāna).

From the time of awakening to the time of sleeping, our mind through six sense doors ordinarily perceives various objects such as visible objects, audible objects, odorous objects, taste objects, bodily contact objects and mental objects. Along with these perceptions either wholesome or unwholesome mind arises. The wholesome mind will always be accompanied with awareness, while there is no awareness whatsoever in the unwholesome mind. The mind, whether it is wholesome or unwholesome, can manifest itself through only three ways as illustrated below:

Ways	Wholesome act	Unwholesome act
1. Physical	helping a blind man to cross the street	causing bodily harm
2. Verbal	asking others to do a meritorious deed	scolding or cursing
3. Mental	thinking of helping others in need	desire to take revenge

It should be noted that the arising of the mind in these three ways, in general, must be either wholesome, which is always accompanied with awareness, or unwholesome, which is never accompanied with awareness.

To be able to really understand the nature of Direct Awareness, it is advisable for one to proceed on a step-by-step basis by learning about:

1. **the arising of the mind (Javana-citta) without awareness (Sati)**

2. **the arising of the mind accompanied with awareness other than Direct Awareness**

3. **the arising of the mind accompanied with Direct Awareness (Satipaṭṭhāna)**

1. The arising of the mind (Javana-citta) without awareness (Sati)

At the time of committing an unwholesome act, the unwholesome mind arises without the accompaniment of awareness (Sati). This is simply because there are three basic types of unwholesome mind; namely, craving mind (Lobha-citta), angry or dissatisfied mind (Dosa-citta) and ignorant mind (Moha-citta). The arising of these three types of unwholesome mind can be exemplified as follows:

Type of unwhole-some mind	Examples
Craving mind - rough form	: mental attachment with delight in stealing from others

Type of unwhole-some mind	Examples
- subtle form	: enjoyment of eating one's favorite food such as ice cream
Angry or dissatisfied mind - rough form - subtle form	: being hateful and abusive to one's enemy : being dissatisfied with a subordinate's late arrival
Ignorant mind - rough form - subtle form	: being oblivious of things around you without the accompaniment of desire or anger : letting the mind wander aimlessly with indifferent feeling and without any likes or dislikes

It should be kept in mind that by their nature the wholesome mind and the unwholesome mind cannot arise at the same time and cannot coexist. This can be like brightness and darkness, which cannot exist at the same time.

2. The arising of the mind accompanied with awareness (Sati) other than Direct Awareness

As previously stated, any physical, verbal or mental action (Kamma) must be either wholesome or unwholesome. This means that when the action is not unwholesome, it must be wholesome, brought about by the wholesome mind which must always be accompanied with awareness (Sati). This is because the wholesomeness (wholesome mind and wholesome mental constituents) by its nature impedes the power of unwholesomeness (unwholesome mind and unwholesome mental constituents). Such impediment cannot be accomplished without the support of awareness (Sati) for the simple reason that the nature of awareness is to cause the mind to become mindful and conscious with respect to lifting the mind above the level of unwholesomeness.

The followings are some examples of wholesome actions which are accompanied with general awareness (Sati) other than Direct Awareness in our daily lives: doing meritorious deeds in the form of buying food to feed one's children; acquiring presents for one's wife or friend; giving things to those in need; offering alms to the monks; cultivating the mind so as to refrain from stealing or telling lies; listening to a lecture on reality which is useful to one's life; forgiving other's misdeeds; extending loving-kindness; possessing the right view concerning which type of action is unwholesome and harmful and which type is wholesome and beneficial.

When the wholesome mind arises, bringing about wholesome action on the part of an individual who has never studied the Buddha's Teachings (TIPIṬAKA) especially the part dealing with Applications of Mindfulness and Buddhist Meditation, there will always be awareness (Sati) but such awareness is not Direct Awareness. The unique way of developing the Direct Awareness (Satipaṭṭhāna) which is the sole basis of practicing Insight Meditation, can only be discovered through the Supreme and Perfect Wisdom of the Buddha.

It should be noted that general awareness (Sati), which is not the same as Direct Awareness, has the following common features:

a. **Being often conscious of conventional reality rather than ultimate reality**
b. **Being often conscious of persons or things external rather than internal to oneself**
c. **Being often conscious of the past rather than the present**
d. **Being often influenced by the defilements (Kilesa) of mind such as craving or unwholesome wanting and/or ignorance**
e. **Being with or without accompaniment of wisdom**

a. Being often conscious of conventional reality rather than ultimate reality

This relates to the consciousness of such conventional reality as:

- Various events or happenings bringing about wholesomeness in life such as accompanying members of a charitable organization to provide relief to fire victims or taking an accident victim to the hospital.

- Wise sayings such as:

"From craving springs grief, from craving springs fear; for him who is wholly free from craving there is no grief, much less fear". (The Sayings of the Buddha)

- Advice given by those who have wisely gained extensive experience in life.

- Parental teachings concerning what is really meant by true friends.

Such consciousness of conventional reality can never be Direct Awareness for the simple reason that as a general rule, Direct Awareness is concerned with ultimate reality.

b. Being often conscious of persons or things external rather than internal to oneself

It can be seen from the above examples as stated in section **a.** above that all of them are external to oneself. In fact, most of what we are conscious of is external to ourselves rather than internal.

At times, the consciousness of what is going on within oneself can also arise, but this does not necessarily constitute Direct Awareness as illustrated by the **following examples:**

At the time of the arising of anger, through awareness one becomes conscious of the anger being unwholesome and harmful and of its bringing about much suffering or misery in life.

One's deed of helping others in relieving suffering in life brings about wholesome and delightful feelings, and it is through one's awareness that one becomes conscious of it.

Even though the awareness in the above two examples arises within oneself and is based on ultimate reality, it is not Direct Awarness. This is simply because at the time of consciousness, there is no real and deep intention to become fully and constantly aware of ultimate reality in order to attain Insight Wisdom (Vipassanā Paññā).

c. Being often conscious of the past rather than the present

Ordinarily, at the time of the arising of awareness, people tend to become conscious of what has already happened for quite some time rather than what is happening currently. **For example,** they become aware of their past wholesome deeds such as making a contribution to a charitable organization or promoting the welfare of the poor. Such consciousness is quite common among old people who reminisce about their past meritorious deeds.

This does not mean that people in general cannot become aware of what is going on at the present moment; this is sometimes possible. With such awareness they can become conscious of an object at the time of its arising; however, this consciousness in itself is by no means Direct Awareness. This is due to the fact that at the time of the arising of this consciousness, they do not mentally follow the present object constantly and continually at the time of its arising. This means that they become aware of other mental objects as well, such as a past object of conventional reality. Taking the example of becoming conscious of one's anger, as cited in section **b.** above, when one becomes aware of one's anger at the time of its arising, the anger, which is ultimate reality, becomes the present object but later when one thinks of its adverse effects, one's object then becomes the past or the conventional reality.

d. Being often influenced by the defilements (Kilesa) of mind such as craving or unwholesome wanting and/or ignorance

For people in general who have not yet cultivated their Direct Awareness (Satipaṭṭhāna), even though their wholesome deeds are always accompanied with general awareness (Sati) other than Direct Awareness (Satipaṭṭhāna), this awareness is often influenced by their own defilements of mind, such as craving or unwholesome wanting (Lobha), dissatisfaction (Dosa) and/or ignorance (Moha). These influences come in various forms as illustrated below:

Influenced by defilements (Kilesa)	Illustration
(1.) Prior to the arising of general awareness	A craving for recognition leads a man to give a generous donation to a well-known charitable organization which will publicize his meritorious deed. At the time of the donation, he will have the feeling of wholesomeness accompanied with general awareness.
(2.) During the arising of general awareness	While saying a prayer, which is a wholesome deed accompanied with awareness (Sati), a person becomes irritated at some children playing noisily nearby.
(3.) After the arising of general awareness	After having contributed to social welfare activities with a wholesome intention over a period of time, a woman becomes arrogant about her wholesome accomplishments.

In actuality, the influence of the defilements (Kilesa) on general awareness other than Direct Awareness is quite complicated and this means that it can arise at various times: before, during, and after the arising of general awareness.

However, in certain cases, the arising of general awareness other than Direct Awareness can be free from the influence of nonsubtle defilements as stated above. **For example,** a person has a pure, deep and wholesome intention of helping others without any unwholesome expectation in return before, during and after committing the act. *However, being free from such influence in itself is not as pure as Direct Awareness for the reason that general awareness is not accompanied with the real intention of becoming aware of the ultimate reality leading to its thorough realization. At the same time this person does not know that Direct Awareness is the only right path leading to the purification of mind in life and the eradication of all suffering.*

From the above, it can be seen that those who have only general awareness other than Direct Awareness (Satipaṭṭhāna), are at least being blinded by their own defilements of ignorance (Moha) so that their general awareness cannot be really free from the defilements, especially the subtle ones.

e. Being with or without accompaniment of wisdom

The arising of awareness (Sati) other than Direct Awareness may not necessarily be accompanied with wisdom. All one has to do is to have the right confidence and the wholesome memory in bringing about the arising of such awareness. **For example,** a young man had been taught all along by his parents that it is good for him to perform meritorious deeds in the form of helping others in need, such as offering things or services to charity organizations or assisting old people or invalids to cross the street. This teaching had been well-received and deeply impressed upon him. One day, when he came across a blind lady who was trying to cross the street in Bangkok, he automatically became aware of her need for help and rendered his assistance accordingly. Up to this point, his awareness had not been accompanied with wisdom. Later, this young man came to study Buddhist Advanced Science (ABHIDHAMMA) and realized that helping others in need is a wholesome deed and that the wholesome effect of this deed would lead to peacefulness and happiness in life. In this way, the arising of his awareness was accompanied with wisdom. Nevertheless, this awareness, even though it is accompanied with wisdom, is still not Direct Awareness as it does not meet the basic requirements of Direct Awareness as explained in the next section.

3. The arising of the mind accompanied with Direct Awareness (Satipaṭṭhāna)

As briefly mentioned and illustrated in section **2.** above, it can readily be seen that Direct Awareness (Satipaṭṭhāna) distinctively differs from the rest of general awareness (Sati). This word "Direct" when used along with "Awareness" carries special meanings as follows:

Constant and continual consciousness only of ultimate reality at its present moment, being accompanied with wisdom as well as being pure and free from the influence of defilements (Kilesa).

For a complete and correct understanding of Direct Awareness (Satipaṭṭhāna) the above meanings should be further clarified based upon the following:

a. **Being conscious of ultimate reality as it really is**

b. **Being conscious of the present object at the time of its arising**

c. **Being constantly and continually conscious of the object which is ultimate reality**

d. **Being always accompanied with wisdom and**

e. **Being pure and free from the influence of defilements**

a. Being conscious of ultimate reality as it really is

As previously explained in Chapter 9, it can be seen that Insight Meditation is concerned with the cultivation of Insight Wisdom (Vipassanā Paññā), which directly realizes the ultimate reality of life as it really is at its present moment of arising and falling away leading to the eradication of defilements (Kilesa) which are causes of suffering, and to the attainment of "Perpetual Happiness" (Nibbāna). This means that only through Insight Wisdom (Vipassanā Paññā) can the ultimate reality be fully realized. **How then can one attain this Insight Wisdom (Vipassanā Paññā)?** If the mind is not well-trained at becoming skillful in knowing the ultimate reality, the wisdom which accompanies this untrained mind can never thoroughly realize the ultimate reality. **How can the mind be trained so as to skillfully and truly know ultimate reality as it really is?** This can only be achieved through Direct Awareness. **This may be illustrated as follows:**

If a reader does not yet really know the meaning of several key words in an article, he will not be able to really and fully understand the content of this article. In order to be able to know their real meaning through reading, he must first learn and become well-versed in the words through spelling, pronunciation and recognition.

The attainment of Insight Wisdom (Vipassanā Paññā) in thoroughly realizing ultimate reality must depend upon the well-trained mind in truly knowing this reality, just like the full understanding of the content of this article depends upon the knowledge of the meaning of the words. The achievement of such a well-trained mind must in turn depend upon Direct Awareness just as the learning and knowing of the real meaning of the words depends upon the skillful practice of spelling, pronunciation and recognition.

Therefore, Direct Awareness (Satipaṭṭhanā) is the first step leading to the attainment of Insight Wisdom (Vipassanā Paññā).

It should be noted that ultimate reality basically consists only of Nāma (mind and mental constituents) and Rūpa (anything other than Nāma which changes due to cold or heat). The detailed explanation of Nāma and Rūpa has previously been given in Chapter 9.

The practice of Insight Meditation leads to the full realization of ultimate reality; that is, Nāma and Rūpa. Since Direct Awareness is a prerequisite for this practice, one must be mindful of Nāma and Rūpa face-to-face in the following ways:

(1.) Mindfulness of Body
    (Kāyānupassanā Satipaṭṭhāna)
(2.) Mindfulness of Feeling
    (Vedanānupassanā Satipaṭṭhāna)
(3.) Mindfulness of Mind
    (Cittānupassanā Satipaṭṭhāna)
(4.) Mindfulness of Dhamma
    (Dhammānupassanā Satipaṭṭhāna)

BUDDHIST MEDITATION FOR RESULTS
INSIGHT MEDITATION
(VIPASSANĀ-BHĀVANĀ)

THE LIGHT OF WISDOM
DISPELS
THE DARKNESS OF IGNORANCE
IN LIFE

(1.) Mindfulness of Body
(Kāyānupassanā Satipaṭṭhāna)

This refers to the constant application of mindfulness upon one's body in the ultimate sense of reality leading eventually to the eradication of suffering.

Ordinarily, people are mentally attached to the body whether it is their own or another's, thinking that it is something pretty or attractive. Such thinking is far from being thorough and accurate. If one wisely resorts to careful and deep contemplation, one will discover without difficulty that in its ultimate sense of reality the body is nothing but a conglomeration of filth. In fact, the evidence of the body's filthiness is easily discernible. One just looks at oneself in the following conditions: if one does not clean oneself, especially in hot weather for a day or two, the body will become smelly and dirty, or if one does not brush his teeth for a day or two, the teeth will become dirty and the mouth will emit bad breath. That is why such products as soap, deodorant, toothbrushes, toothpaste, shampoo, etc., are regularly consumed in order to help clean the accumulated dirt of our body. Even with the use of these helpful products, the filthiness of the body, by its nature, will arise time and time again.

If one searches with mindfulness and wisdom throughout the body of even a very beautiful girl, one has only to look beneath her skin to clearly discover undesirable sights in the form of blood, flesh, veins, bones, kidneys, intestines and so forth, which exist in every human body. This means that the so-called beauty of a body which is a conventional reality is merely skin-deep and would vanish should there be no skin to cover the body. In fact, even the skin, body hair and head hair themselves cannot escape from naturally becoming filthy due to the fact that they undergo a constant degenerative process. **For example,** the skin is cease-lessly being dried up and turned into a waste product. In short, the whole body is naturally full of filth and there is no prettiness in it whatsoever, especially under microscopic examination.

Despite the fact that the human body (Kāya) is really not what people who lack mindfulness and wisdom of it, think or believe it to be, people continue to hold views contrary to ultimate reality and are mentally attached to the body as being something pretty or attractive. **The more of the wrong view one holds, the more suffering one will experience.** This can easily be seen in the case where one resorts to self-deception in the form of considering that his/her own body or that of someone he/she loves or admires is really attractive, and that this attractiveness is permanent and thereby not subject to change. When something adverse happens to the body such as deformity, disfigurement, dismemberment, wrinkled skin, loss of sense of hearing or sight, or ulcerated wounds, one can become greatly disturbed, depressed or even shocked because this natural manifestation represents the ultimate reality, which is in sharp contrast to one's wrong view and mental attachment. In certain cases, this suffering is so immense and unbearable that one turns to self-injury or commits suicide.

The practice of Direct Awareness (Satipaṭṭhāna) in being constantly mindful of the body is tantamount to placing the mind in harmony with the law of nature as well as giving rise to Insight Wisdom (Vipassanā Paññā) in thoroughly realizing the ultimate reality of Nāma and Rūpa. This Insight Wisdom (Vipassanā Paññā) in turn eradicates the wrong view and mental attachment, which are the causes of suffering in life, and by so doing, greatly enhances high level wholesome happiness and blissfulness in life, leading eventually to the attainment of "Perpetual Happiness" (Nibbāna).

One of the methods of practicing Mindfulness of Body (Kāyānupassanā Satipaṭṭhāna) is to become directly aware of major bodily postures which consist of standing, walking, sitting or lying down.

(2.) Mindfulness of Feeling (Vedanānupassanā Satipaṭṭhanā)

This refers to the constant application of mindfulness upon one's feeling with respect to its being pleasant, unpleasant or indifferent, which is itself an ultimate reality.

Ordinarily, one's thinking must always be accompanied with one of these three basic kinds of feelings (pleasant, unpleasant or indifferent). To say it differently, our deeds (Kamma) whether they manifest themselves physically, verbally or mentally must similarly coexist with one of these three feelings (Vedanā). Therefore, in daily life, we cannot do without these feelings (Vedanā) at any time. Such feelings (Vedanā) could adversely influence one's mind with respect to causing one to have a prejudice or wrong view which contradicts the ultimate reality. When a pleasant feeling occupies one's mind, he or she tends to crave for it and becomes blindly and mentally attached to it. Even though several hours have passed, one with this blind craving may think that only minutes have passed. This can easily be seen in the case of two young lovers who have spent several hours chatting and teasing; they, nevertheless, think that they have spent merely a few minutes together. On the contrary, at the time of experiencing an unpleasant feeling, people often think that the time drags on much more slowly than it really has. **For example,** when a young man has to wait anxiously for his beloved girlfriend who arrives ten minutes late, he may inaccurately consider that the waiting period has been more than an hour. The wrong view or self-deception cited in the above examples, is dictated by one's own craving or mental attachment. This is to say that when there is a pleasant feeling, craving (Lobha) brings about a firm mental attachment to this pleasantness. By its nature, craving is an unwholesome and insatiable yearning for this pleasant feeling and this craving wants more and more of it. Thus, even though a pleasant feeling is being experienced for a long period of time, craving for still more of it brings about self-deception in the form of thinking which is contradictory to reality. **For example,** thinking that only minutes instead of hours have actually passed by. On the other hand, an unpleasant feeling is not what one craves for and at the time of its arising, one strongly wishes it to fall away quickly. As a result, one erroneously thinks that this unpleasantness lasts much longer than it actually does.

Apart from this, craving can also give rise to other wrong views in life toward these feelings. It is very common among people to believe or think wrongly that these feelings can retain their original existence which is contradictory to the basic characteristic of existence, Dukkha (inability to retain its original existence).

In actuality, the pleasant feeling which one experiences arises and falls away all the time according to its causes. This can be seen from the following examples:

- At the time of dancing to one's favorite music, one feels very pleased, but when the music comes to an end, so does this pleasant feeling.

- At the time of tasting delicious food, which is much to one's liking, one's feeling of pleasure arises, but when the food is gone, this pleasurable feeling will come to an abrupt end.

The above happenings reflect roughly the basic characteristic of their inability to retain their original existence (Dukkha). But in its deep and thorough sense, **the Dukkha characteristic goes much further than the above explanation.** As a matter of fact, the pleasant feeling which one experiences for a certain period of time, arises and falls away very quickly to be succeeded by the next rapid arising and falling away, instead of remaining unchanged all the time. Even the level of pleasantness varies throughout that period according to its causes.

Even though the pleasant feeling is unable to retain its original existence (Dukkha) all the time, because of one's craving, one becomes mentally attached to this feeling in the form of holding the wrong view that this pleasant feeling is able to retain its original existence. As a result, when one's pleasant feeling is no longer with him/her as it is supposed to be according to his/her wrong view, he or she will become sad, disappointed or miserable.

Therefore, the Direct Awareness of ultimate reality in the form of feeling (Vedanā) is the right method leading to its thorough realization as it really is and to the eradication of the wrong view, which gives rise to suffering in life. By this practice, it will greatly enhance the high level wholesome happiness and bliss-fulness in life which eventually leads to the attainment of "Perpetual Happiness" (Nibbāna).

(3.) Mindfulness of Mind (Cittānupassanā Satipaṭṭhāna)

This refers to the constant application of mindfulness to one's mind, which is ultimate reality. The mind has the specific characteristic of knowing an object (Ārammaṇa), and its arising cannot take place without the object. But in this type of mindfulness, **the mind itself becomes the object of the Direct Awareness and can be classified into a wholesome or unwholesome mind. For example:**

- A person becomes angry while recalling somebody who has insulted him at a party. This means that the arising of his mind is accompanied with anger (Dosa). In this case, being angry is the unwholesome mind and the insulting person is the object of his mind. But in practicing Direct Awareness, its object is not the insulting person but the angry mind itself.

- When one allows one's thoughts to go from subject to subject aimlessly, there is an unwholesome mental state of wandering. In the practice of Direct Awareness, the wandering mind and not the individual subject should be made the object of Direct Awareness.

- While one is having pleasant thoughts of one's past meritorious activity, such as listening to sermons or helping those in need, one's pleasant thinking is the wholesome mind and his past meritorious deed is its object. But the object of practicing Direct Awareness is the pleasant mind and not the past wholesome activity.

In our daily life, we ordinarily cannot escape from feeling or thinking of various objects according to their causes and in fact, this feeling or thinking is always arising and can either be wholesome or unwholesome. It should be noted that the word "feeling" here represents the mind in knowing the object and that it differs from the feeling (Vedanā) which is a mental constituent used in the previous section under Mindfulness of Feeling-pleasant, unpleasant or indifferent (Vedanānupassanā Sati-paṭṭhāna). **The situation in which one feels hot is different from the situation in which one feels pain.** At the time of touching a cup of hot coffee, one feels hot and an unpleasant feeling in the form of pain is also arising. In this case, "feels hot" is the mind knowing the hot condition as its object which means that "feels" and "knows" are synonymous, whereas the unpleasant feeling (Vedanā) in the form of pain exists in the mind itself and it is not the knowing of the object even though the mind can feel or know this pain as its object.

The ignorance of ultimate reality with respect to the mind at its present moment of continuous arising and falling away, will lead one's life to suffering or misery simply because such ignorance gives rise to the wrong view or to mental attachment in the form of thinking that the mind is permanent. **For instance,** when one becomes angry or irritated, one's angry or dissatisfied mind **(Dosa-citta)** arises, thereby bringing about mental suffering. This adverse mental condition is not what one craves for; to the contrary, it is what one would wish to go away. But when it does not cease to exist according to one's desire, the suffering becomes worse. This, in turn, gives rise to the wrong view that the angry mind permanently exists in one's life. The more intensified the wrong view is, the worse one will suffer. Some may even resort to self-injury because of their frustration or irritation at the mere thought that the angry mind accompanied with suffering will be lasting. In other cases, when their wrong view is so great that they really think this intensified suffering will follow them everywhere just like a shadow, they may feel that the most appropriate way out for them is to try to get rid of it by turning to self-destruction.

People who hold the wrong view that the angry mind is permanent are those who never practice Direct Awareness of the angry mind at its present moment in order to thoroughly realize its basic characteristic of impermanence (Anicca). In fact, by its nature, the angry mind is always changing in the form of arising and falling away very quickly to be succeeded by the next rapid arising and falling away. **This successive and very rapid arising and falling away of the angry mind causes one to believe wrongly that it is permanent and remains unchanged.** This can be compared to the case of a neon light. Because of its successive and rapid arising and falling away, people have the false impression that the neon light is on all the time.

Similarly, all other minds, either wholesome or unwholesome, arise and fall away rapidly, so as to bring about the wrong view of their being permanent, leading to mental suffering in life.

Therefore, Direct Awareness of ultimate reality with respect to the mind (Citta) is the right path leading to its full realization as it really is and to the elimination of the wrong view, which gives rise to suffering in life. In this way, the high level of wholesome happiness and blissfulness in life will be significantly enhanced, thereby leading eventually to the attainment of Perpetual Happiness (Nibbāna).

(4.) Mindfulness of Dhamma (Dhammānupassanā Satipaṭṭhāna)

This refers to the application of mindfulness constantly on Dhamma which is ultimate reality. The Dhamma here pertains to the following categories:

- (a.) Mental Obstacles (Nīvarana)
- (b.) Five Aggregates (Khandha)
- (c.) Sense-Organs and Sense-Objects (Āyatana)
- (d.) Seven Constituents of Enlightenment (Bojjhaṅga)
- (e.) The Four Noble Truths (Ariyasacca)

(a.) Mental Obstacles (Nīvarana)

These Mental Obstacles are ultimate reality which obstructs the arising of the wholesome mind. They are classified into 5 types, namely:

- (a.1) Craving for Sensually Pleasurable Objects (Kāmachandanīvarana)

(a.2) Dissatisfaction or anger
       (Byāpādanīvarana)
(a.3) Sleepiness (Thīna-middhanīvarana)
(a.4) Mental Wandering and Worrying
       (Uddhacca-kukkuccanīvarana)
(a.5) Scepticism (Vicikicchānīvarana)

All of the above mental obstacles are unwholesome but nevertheless can become objects of Direct
Awareness.

It should be noted that there are 6 Mental
Obstacles to Insight Meditation. But when Mental
Obstacles are to be used as the object of Direct
Awareness only 5 Mental Obstacles as mentioned
above are applicable for the reason that they are more
discernible. This is in accordance with the Sayings of
the Buddha in the Satipaṭṭhāna Sutta.

(b.) Five Aggregates (Khandha)

These Five Aggregates are ultimate reality consisting of physical (Rūpa), mental feeling (Vedanā),
perception (Saññā), other mental constituents (Saṅkhāra)
and mind (Viññāṇa), and their continuous and successive arising and falling away are conditioned by
various causes. These Five Aggregates are so-called
simply because each of them must have at least 5
features, namely: the past, the present, the future,
the gross and the subtle. **For example,** when one
is experiencing a painful feeling, (one of the Five
Aggregates-Vedanā) from a headache (Vedanā) for a
certain period of time, this adverse feeling arises and
falls away very quickly to be succeeded by the next
rapid arising and falling away instead of remaining
unchanged. At the time of its arising, this particular

feeling is the present and at the same time it has become the future in the past as well as will become the past in the future. This pain can be gross when compared to a lesser pain and at the same time can be subtle when compared to a greater pain. It should be noted that the same thing holds true of the Direct Awareness of other aggregates. The Direct Awareness of this painful feeling from a headache (Vedanā) pertains to the mindfulness and realization with respect to the Aggregates, which is different from that under the Mindfulness of Feeling. In fact, the Direct Awareness of the painful feeling Aggregate goes much deeper than the Direct Awareness of the painful feeling (Vedanā), as described under the previous heading.

(c.) Sense-Organs and Sense-objects (Āyatana)

There are basically six external sense objects and six internal sense-organs. When there is contact between an external sense-object and its corresponding internal sense-organ, the knowing of mind takes place as illustrated below:

External sense-object	Internal sense-organ	The knowing of mind
Visible object	eye organ	seeing
Audible object	ear organ	hearing
Odorous object	nose organ	smelling
Taste object	tongue organ	tasting
Bodily contact object	body organ	body feeling
Mental object	mind	mental knowing

(d.)   Seven constituents of Enlightenment (Boj-jhaṅga)

There are Seven Constituents of Enlightenment in life, namely:

(d.1) Mindfulness Constituent of Enlightenment (Sati Sambojjhaṅga)

(d.2) Realization Constituent of Enlightenment (Dhammavicaya Sambojjhaṅga)

(d.3) Effort Constituent of Enlightenment (Viriya Sambojjhaṅga)

(d.4) Joy Constituent of Enlightenment (Pīti Sambojjhaṅga)

(d.5) Calm Constituent of Enlightenment (Passaddhi Sambojjhaṅga)

(d.6) Concentration Constituent of Enlightenment (Samādhi Sambojjhaṅga)

(d.7) Equanimity Constituent of Enlightenment (Upekkhā Sambojjhaṅga)

(e.)   The Four Noble Truths (Ariyasacca)

The thorough realization of the Four Noble Truths leads to the eradication of all sufferings in life and these Truths consist of:

(e.1) Suffering

(e.2) Causes of Suffering

(e.3) Cessation of all suffering - "Perpetual Happiness" (Nibbāna) and

(e.4) The Right Path leading to the cessation of all suffering.

It should be noted that the "Dhamma", which is the object of the Application of Mindfulness as described above, could be complicated and difficult for those who have never studied Buddhist Science. As a matter of fact, this Mindfulness of "Dhamma" is more suitable for those who have real understanding and deep knowledge of Buddhist Science or who possess a high level of logical and wise thinking.

Generally speaking, Dhamma such as mental obstacles, the five Aggregates, and sense-organs and sense-objects are the ultimate realities which exist in nature irrespective of any supposition or symbolization of them. In other words, their existence is not dependent on any supposition or symbolization. **For example,** when the heat from the steam of a boiling kettle comes into contact with a normal body-organ, the feeling of something hot arises. All of us will feel exactly the same way, irrespective of whether or not different words or languages have been used to describe such a feeling. Apart from this, in the sense of ultimate reality there is no such thing as "I" or "We" existing in the feeling of something hot even though a Westerner may use conventional words to describe this feeling, such as, "I feel hot".

From the above example, it can be seen that when there is a contact between a sense-object and a sense-organ, a natural phenomenon (Dhamma) arises and falls away according to its causes and there is no "I" or "We" in that natural occurrence. In addition, such a phenomenon is non-self (Anattā) and does not come under the command of anyone. But generally people mistakenly tend to think that there is a self in this occurrence which is under one's command instead of its being in accordance with the causes. **For example,** when sound as an audible object comes into contact with the ear-organ, hearing will take place according to the causes and in this hearing there is no "I" or "We". Nevertheless, people incorrectly think that there is a self in this hearing by describing it as "I hear". Basically, such a wrong view will lead to unexpected suffering in life. **For example,** when two people are quarrelling heatedly, some bystanders may be pleased to listen to the abusive words even though they are unpleasant objects. Why is this so? This is simply because the abusive words are not directed toward them. But when a bystander becomes so amused with the quarrel that he bursts into laughter, and one quarrelling party, upon hearing the laughter, turns to scold the bystander, at that moment he will likely feel irritated. Why is this so? It is simply because he wrongly thinks, "The quarrelling party is scolding me!". This thinking of being "me" brings about irritation on the part of the bystander. If one considers carefully this matter of being "me" in the sense of ultimate reality, one can then ask oneself which part of the body is "me". Is the hair "me"? Is the cheek "me"? Is the arm "me"? etc. Of course not. There is no "me" to be found and "me" is merely a supposed or symbolized word. It is just like writing words in the air; nowhere can it be discovered.

There is no "me" in nature, and in fact, one's mind and body consist of five aggregates which arise and fall away according to various causes. It is the wrong view which creates the concept that "I" or "We" exist in this ultimate reality of the five aggregates.

In summary, those ultimate realities which are the objects of Direct Awareness are classified in terms of Body (Kāya), Feeling (Vedanā), Mind (Citta) and Dhamma in accordance with common misconceptions among the general public as illustrated below.

Object of Direct Awareness	Basic form	Misconception	Reality
Body (Kāya)	Rūpa	Body is beautiful	Body is a conglomeration of filth
Feeling (Vedanā)	Nāma	Ability of feeling to retain its original existence	Inability of feeling to retain its original existence
Mind (Citta)	Nāma	Mind is permanent	Mind is impermanent
Dhamma	Rūpa & Nāma	Self	Non-self

Direct Awareness of these 4 types of objects will bring about the elimination of misconceptions and at the same time the attainment of the most purified and right view of ultimate reality.

Any one of the Four Applications of Mindfulness will lead to the achievement of excellence in life; that is, the eradication of all suffering and the attainment of "Perpetual Happiness" (Nibbāna). It is as if there are four different directions to reach a city and travelling along any one of them will lead to the same destination.

b. Being conscious of the present object at the time of its arising

Those who have previously tasted a grape, when they try to think of its taste, may know to a certain extent what the taste is like. Nevertheless, they are not in a position to know it exactly and thoroughly. However, while eating a grape, if one tries to become directly aware of its taste one will know it precisely and thoroughly. This is because the true characteristic of the taste manifests itself only at the time of its arising and this is the only time when its thorough realization can take place. Similarly, those who have already known Nāma (such as a painful or pleasant feeling) and Rūpa (such as an audible or visible object), when they try to think of them may know them somewhat, but not to the extent of a full and thorough realization of them. This is because such Nāma and Rūpa do not exist any longer in the ultimate sense. On the other hand, if one tries to become directly aware of Nāma and Rūpa at the present moment, one may fully and thoroughly realize them because the true characteristics of Nāma and Rūpa manifest themselves only at the time of their arising and this is the only time when their full and thorough realization can occur.

To emphasize again, if one tries to think of the taste of his favorite fruit such as grapes before actually eating it, the precise knowing and thorough realization of the taste can never happen. This is simply because the true characteristic of the taste has not yet manifested itself. In a similar way, the full and thorough realization of Nāma and Rūpa before their arising can never be achieved.

For the above reason, to fully and thoroughly realize the ultimate reality of Nāma and Rūpa, one must become directly aware of their arising at the present moment, and not in the past or in the future. (Please also refer to the details in the section "What is Insight Meditation?" in Chapter 9).

For the purpose of further clarification and proper understanding, it is necessary to define the word "present" in the context of Buddhist Science based on 4 aspects as follows:

(b.1) **Present life** refers to the living which takes place in the period between birth and death in this life. Life before the present life is past life and life coming after present life is future life.

(b.2) Present time span refers to the existing time period. **For example,** the period of childhood is the present time span for the one who has passed the period of infancy but has not reached the period of adolescence. In this way, the past of this person is the period of infancy, whereas the future is the period of adolescence.

The time span such as morning, afternoon or night can be present as long as each respective period is still in existence. **For example,** while one is eating breakfast at 7.00 a.m., this is considered as his/her present time span for the morning period. Even when he/she starts working at 8.30 a.m., this is still considered to be his/her present time span for the morning period.

(b.3) Present succession refers to Nāma or Rūpa immediately after it has arisen and fallen away. **For example,** immediately after the arising and falling away of Nāma in the form of "hearing", there is Direct Awareness of this "hearing". Such "hearing" is the present object of this Direct Awareness in the sense of present succession.

(b.4) Present moment refers to Nāma or Rūpa at the very time of its arising before completely falling away. According to the Buddha's discovery of ultimate reality, Nāma (mind) arises and falls away about one trillion times in one-fifth of a second while Rūpa arises and falls away at a rate 17 times slower than Nāma. Thus, each momentary arising of Nāma or Rūpa occupies an extremely short period of time.

In the practice of Direct Awareness in becoming conscious of Nāma or Rūpa at the present time of its arising, this present arising of Nāma or Rūpa which is the object of Direct Awareness refers only to the "Present Succession" as described under **(b.3)** above. This means that right after the arising and falling away of Nāma or Rūpa one becomes directly aware of it.

c. Being constantly and continually conscious of the object which is ultimate reality

Ordinarily, our mental condition frequently comes under the influence and the dictation of our unwholesome wanting or craving, so that we have to constantly seek a sensually pleasurable object in order to fulfill our desire. By so doing, an unwholesome happiness will be brought about. At the time of the arising of this unwholesome wanting or craving in constantly seeking its desirable object such as, favorite music or delicious food, we usually are blindly pleased with and mentally attached to this object and do not realize its ultimate reality. This can be seen in one who likes to drink whisky. The more he drinks, the more easily he becomes mentally desirous of and attached to it, to the extent of intoxication, and as long as he remains so, there is no way for him to realize that the real nature of alcoholic drink is harmful.

Apart from this, our unwholesome wanting or craving can also bring about a misconception with respect to its object of desire. This misconception pertains to thinking of its object which is "impermanent"

(Anicca) as "permanent" (Nicca) or which is "non-self" (Anattā) as "self" (Attā). Such misconceived ideas which are contrary to ultimate reality, can give rise to misery in life and can adversely influence our future thoughts. **For example,** a young man, by saving his money over a long period of time, manages to gather enough money to buy a new car. One month later, his beloved car hits a lamp post, suffering a significant dent. The owner is so overwhelmed with sorrow that he can hardly sleep for several nights. This is simply because he had become mentally attached to his object of desire (the car) along with having the wrong view that his car could permanently stay new and beautiful, which is contrary to the Law of Nature. He lacks the awareness and the realization that the original condition of his car is impermanent and is subject to undesirable or unexpected changes according to its causes. Based upon the Law of Nature, nothing is permanent, and everything is subject to constant change and degeneration. The arising of such mental attachment and the wrong view dictated by his own unwholesome wanting or craving, will in turn cause future misconceptions. In the above example, his sorrow may be lessened as time passes, but whenever he thinks of his damaged car he will suffer again as long as he cannot relieve himself of such mental attachment and wrong view.

Therefore, the thinking or feeling of people in general is usually influenced by their own misconceptions and mental attachments. In other words, such mental adversity constantly flows into one's life stream. Even when there is an arising of general awareness which is wholesome, one will not be able to get rid of such misconceptions and mental attachments directly. This is mainly due to the lack of constant and continuous Direct Awareness of ultimate reality. Thus, when people are not really familiar with the true characteristics of ultimate reality, the thorough realization of this reality cannot arise. This is similar to the case of those who, being unfamiliar with the English alphabet, are not able to readily comprehend the content of an article written in English.

Before the thorough realization of ultimate reality can arise, there must be Direct Awareness in becoming conscious of it, constantly and continuously. "Constantly and continuously" means that one must become directly aware of ultimate reality (Rūpa or Nāma) frequently, without any unnecessary interruption or break. **For example,** when one is experiencing physical pain, his/her practice of Direct Awareness requires that he/she becomes conscious of this pain on a constant and continuous basis. So if he/she interrupts this direct consciousness by thinking of something which is not helpful to Direct Awareness and then later comes back to the practice, it means that Direct Awareness is no longer being practiced constantly or continuously.

When Direct Awareness is practiced at a Meditation Center without involvement in other activities,

one can become directly conscious of ultimate reality
as its object more effectively, with respect to regularity
and continuity. Under this condition, Direct Awareness
can arise more frequently and easily. Some meditators
may ask a question such as, "If one has to become
directly conscious of ultimate reality constantly and
continuously, does this mean that he/she is not permitted
to do anything else such as thinking?" The answer to
this can be negative or affirmative depending on
whether or not what one does will be beneficial or
helpful in furthering the practice of Direct Awareness.
For example, at the time of practicing Direct Awareness
in a sitting position on a terrace, the thought may
arise in the mind that the sun's heat, which will soon
intensify, will make this place unsuitable for meditation,
and that a move to another suitable place would be
advisable. It should be noted that the object of such a
thought is conventional reality and not ultimate reality.
But nevertheless, this thought can support the practice
of Direct Awareness and such a thought is permissible.
Even though the arising of this thought causes a short
break in the regularity and continuity of the direct consciousness of ultimate reality, it does not bring about
any adverse effect. As a matter of fact, the arising of
such a thought is necessary with respect to supporting
the regularity and continuity of Direct Awareness which
is about to arise again. On the other hand, if the thought
which arises does not render the necessary support

or is damaging to the practice of Direct Awareness, one must avoid it. **For example,** during the practice of Direct Awarness, instead of becoming directly conscious of ultimate reality, a person may purposely think of theoretical aspects of Buddhist Science or any other subjects through intellectualization based on conventional reality. Such thinking, which can adversely affect the practice of Direct Awareness, is not appropriate and therefore not permitted.

d. Being always accompanied with wisdom

As previously stated. Insight Meditation is concerned with the cultivation of Insight Wisdom for a thorough and direct realization of ultimate reality, and Direct Awareness is the first step of Insight Meditation practice. Therefore, Direct Awareness leads towards the attainment of this high level realization of the ultimate reality. In this way, Direct Awareness must always be accompanied with wisdom, in the absence of which a full realization of ultimate reality cannot take place.

However, the wisdom accompanying Direct Awareness is not wisdom which is concerned with thought or with considering the conventional reality, but is a type of high level wisdom which clearly and thoroughly realizes the ultimate reality: Nāma (Mind) or Rūpa, the present object of Direct Awareness. **For example,** at the time of experiencing mental pain as a result of loss of a loved one, one must refrain from considering or thinking that this mental suffering is a natural phenomena while trying to identify its causes. This consideration or thinking reflects merely an ordinary wisdom. On the other hand, in the case of Direct Awareness, there is a clear and direct consciousness and thorough realization of this mental pain without resorting to any thinking or consideration. This is like the direct knowing of saltiness at the time of tasting salt without having to consider or think about it.

The subject of Mindfulness and its accompaniment with Wisdom has been previously explained in Chapter 12, under "Mindfulness Power" (Satibala).

e. Being pure and free from the influence of defilements (Kilesa)

The defilements of mind such as unwholesome wanting or craving (Lobha), dissatisfaction or anger (Dosa), ignorance (Moha), and wrong view (Micchā-diṭṭhi) have a strong influence on one's mind with respect to distorting reality and preventing the mind from realizing the reality as it really is. It is extremely difficult, if not impossible, for one with just ordinary mindfulness to be really free and pure from the influence of his/her own defilements. Such freedom and purity can only be achieved through effective Direct Awareness. As Direct Awareness is the first step leading to the achievement of the direct and thorough realization of ultimate reality, the mind which is accompanied with Direct Awareness must be true to reality without any bias. This is like an honest and competent judge deciding a case objectively, based on facts, without resorting to favoritism or taking bribes.

It is, therefore, imperative that Direct Awareness* be pure and free from the influence of defilements.

---

* It should be noted that there is another method of meditation practice whereby the meditator who has successfully attained a high level of concentration through Tranquil Meditation (**Jhānas**), or whose intrinsic nature is appropriate for relying upon Tranquil Meditation as a base in practicing Insight Meditation, may start out with the mindfulness of conventional reality in order to lead to Direct Awareness of Nāma-Rūpa which are ultimate reality, at a later stage. However, this book does not emphasize such method of meditation practice (**SAMATHAYĀNIKA**); instead, its emphasis is for those who practice Insight Meditation directly without depending upon Tranquil Meditation (**VIPASSANĀYĀNIKA**), which a large number of people, especially laypersons will be able to put into practice extensively.

CHAPTER 15

GENERAL PROCEDURE OF PRACTICING DIRECT AWARENESS

1. Introduction

The understanding of the real meaning of Direct Awareness as explained in Chapter 14 is a prerequisite for the effective practice of Direct Awareness. Such understanding enables the meditator to know the specific characteristics of Direct Awareness which differ significantly from those of ordinary awareness. **When one possesses this knowledge, it is like having a map which will guide oneself toward the right path in life without going astray.**

This Chapter is aimed at introducing a general method of practicing proper Direct Awareness for those who wish to walk effectively on its right path.

In order to bring about the widest benefits from practicing Direct Awareness among people in general, **this Chapter highlights two basic methods,** one of which enables the meditator to apply certain aspects of Direct Awareness in everyday life. The other method pertains to the full Applications of Mindfulness which must be practiced at an Insight Meditation Center or other proper places. These two methods are as follows:

a. General method of applying Direct Awareness in daily life.

b. General method of practicing Direct Awareness at a proper place for Insight Meditation.

Before giving a detailed explanation of these two methods, it is advisable to touch upon the method of classifying Nāma and Rūpa on the basis of the six sense doors (through eye, ear, nose, tongue, body and mind) and the subject of what should be kept in mind, with respect to practicing Direct Awareness. Knowledge and understanding in these two areas are helpful in the effective cultivation of Direct Awareness.

2. Classification of Nāma and Rūpa through the six sense doors

The causes of suffering in life manifest themselves through the six sense doors only and nowhere else.

Sorrow, anger and frustration in life manifest themselves through the six sense doors only and nowhere else.

Wrong view, misconception and ignorance in life manifest themselves through the six sense doors only and nowhere else.

For these reasons, in order to relieve or eradicate the causes of suffering, sorrow, anger, frustration, wrong view, misconception and ignorance in life, one must attain thorough realization by means of cultivating Direct Awareness of Nāma and Rūpa at the present moment of their arising and falling away through the six sense doors.

In Direct Awareness, Nāma and Rūpa are classified on the basis of the six sense doors as follows:

CLASSIFICATION OF NĀMA AND RŪPA THROUGH THE SIX SENSE DOORS

Sense door	Nāma (Mind)	Rūpa	Natural Manifestation
Eye	Seeing	Visible object	Seeing of the visible object can arise only through the eye sense door
Ear	Hearing	Audible object	Hearing of the audible object can arise only through the ear sense door
Nose	Smelling	Odorous object	Smelling of the odorous object can arise only through the nose sense door
Tongue	Tasting	Taste object	Tasting of the taste object can arise only through the tongue sense door
Body	Bodily feeling	Bodily contact object	Physical feeling of the bodily contact object can arise only through the body sense door

Sense door	Nāma (Mind)	Rūpa	Natural Manifestation
Mind	Wholesome or unwholesome	Physical (e.g. standing, sitting, walking or lying down) and verbal (e.g. giving a sermon or scolding)	Bodily posture and verbal expression can arise only through the mind sense door

From the above table, Nāma and Rūpa pertain to ultimate reality, which exists only in nature, and not to conventional reality based on supposition or symbolization, which does not exist in nature. **For example:**

a. Nāma and Rūpa through the eye sense door

When light (visible object) comes into contact with the eye organ, the "seeing" of this present object arises. "Seeing" is Nāma (mind) while "light" is Rūpa. Both of them are ultimate reality.

The "visible object" refers to a type of Rūpa which can come into contact with the eye organ giving rise to its "seeing" at the organ. According to physics, this "visible object" is nothing but light transmitted through ether at a very high speed. The wave length of light by itself contains no color, but because of its extremely rapid movement in succession, different wavelengths create the impression of different colors. It should be noted that this "visible object", at the time of its arising in the form of the light contains no shape nor form whatever.

By "seeing", it is meant that at the time of the "visible object" coming into contact with the eye organ, the seeing of this "visible object" takes place at this organ. At this particular moment, there is no seeing of living beings, things, or symbols. This is because the "seeing" of living beings, things or symbols is not real in the ultimate sense. In fact, it is merely a mental creation based on the aggregation of wavelengths of light. Such mental images in the form of living beings, things or symbols, do not exist in nature at all. As a matter of fact, their arising is caused by one's mind in gathering the aggregation of "visible objects" to serve as a basis for mental creation. This is similar to an electric fan in motion. The quick rotation of the blades of the electric fan will make us see a circle even though there is no such circle existing in nature. To say, "seeing is believing" does not necessarily hold true. The "seeing" of this circle merely reflects the mental creation based upon the quick movement of the blades, and is not the "seeing" of visible objects in the sense of ultimate reality as explained previously.

Ordinarily, people claim to see such colors as white, yellow, black or red, but all these colors are just conventional reality and do not really exist in nature. In actuality, the "visible object" (light) arises and falls away very rapidly in succession. But contrary to this ultimate reality, people generally feel that the color is static and exists in nature.

From the above examples, it should be noted that in the case of "seeing" as meant by people in general, the object of the "seeing" is most likely a conventional reality, not ultimate reality, and does not exist in nature. Whereas in the case of "seeing" with respect to practicing Direct Awareness, its object is always ultimate reality. Nevertheless, this latter "seeing" by itself, cannot realize the "visible object", and, in fact, its realization must come from Insight Wisdom which does not accompany the "seeing".

"Seeing", as well as the "visible object", has the basic characteristics of impermanence (Anicca), inability to retain its original existence (Dukkha) and being dependent upon its causes, selfless (Anattā).

b. Nāma and Rūpa through the ear sense door

When sound (audible object) comes into contact with the ear organ, the "hearing" of this present object arises. "Hearing" is Nāma (mind) while "sound" is Rūpa. Both of them are ultimate reality.

Sound (audible object) is that which can be heard by hearing mind. In physics, it is vibration made in the air with low or high frequency. They are a type of Rūpa and upon their reaching the ear organ, "hearing" takes place at this organ. However, at the instant of this "hearing", one only hears sound with different frequencies and there is no meaning contained in that sound. When hearing, we are the ones who give meaning to that sound. **For example:** in English, the uttered sound "book", even though it has no meaning at all in the ultimate sense, is denoted to mean a literary composition as printed in a bound set of sheets of paper. But in Thai or Chinese, the uttered sound which carries the same meaning as "book" is "nang suer" or "su" respectively, and all these meanings are only conventional reality and do not really exist in nature. As a matter of fact, the sound is a type of ultimate reality which exists in nature. It arises according to its causes and falls away as these causes cease to exist.

By "hearing", it is meant that at the time of an audible object (sound) coming into contact with the ear organ, the "hearing" of the object takes place at this organ. In this instance, all one can hear is sound at specific frequencies without any meaning whatever. In other words, this sound in its ultimate sense contains no meaning as denoted through supposition or symbolization. There is no "hearing" of male or female sound nor complimentary or discordant sound. When one says that he heard a female or male sound, such hearing is not real in the ultimate sense. It merely reflects the mental knowing based upon the hearing of this sound at the present moment of its arising, and mental denotation of the sound based upon past accumulations. **For example,** if a Westerner says to a Thai who knows English well, "You're a rascal", the Thai may become angry upon hearing this sound. This is because, in his mind, he has already accumulated the negative meaning of these words based on this similar series of sounds, and this accumulation, at the time of hearing such sounds, will lead to a mental knowing of these words and their unfavorable meaning directed towards him. In another example, when a Thai uses abusive Thai words "Ai Na Tua Mia" (meaning "You are a coward") against a foreigner who does not know any Thai language, the uncomprehending foreigner can hear this series of sounds which is ultimate reality. As a result, his anger cannot arise because there is no mental accumulation of word meaning in the past. Although the foreigner hears the ultimate reality (the sound), the foreigner has not yet become thoroughly aware of the sound and the hearing. This is because there is no Direct Awareness in becoming conscious of them.

The hearing, as well as the audible object, has the basic characteristics of impermanence (Anicca), inability to retain its original existence (Dukkha), and being dependent upon its causes (Anattā).

c. Nāma and Rūpa through the nose sense door

When an odorous object comes into contact with the nose organ, "smelling" of this present object arises. "Smelling" is Nāma while the odorous object is Rūpa. Both of them are ultimate reality.

Odor is a type of Rūpa which has the ability of coming into contact with the nose organ, leading to the arising of "smelling" at the nose organ. This odor disperses through the air with the wind. **For example:** fragrance from a rose reaches the nose organ, giving rise to its "smelling".

Smelling is a type of Nāma (mind) which has the ability of knowing the smell of the odorous object at the time of its coming into contact with the nose organ. The "smelling" of the odorous object takes place at this organ. At the very instant of "smelling" the odor, all one can smell is the odor without knowing the meaning associated with it in the ultimate sense. **For example,** when a woman says she can smell perfume, such smelling is not real in the ultimate sense. It merely reflects her mental knowing based upon the "smelling" of this odorous object at the present moment of its arising and the mental supposition or symbolization of the perfume based upon her past accumulations.

Smelling, as well as the odorous object, has the basic characteristics of impermanence (Anicca), inability to retain its original existence (Dukkha), and being dependent upon its causes (Anattā).

d. Nāma and Rūpa through the tongue sense door

When a taste object comes into contact with the tongue organ, the tasting of this present object arises. "Tasting" is Nāma (mind) while the taste object is Rūpa. Both of them are ultimate reality.

A taste object is a type of Rūpa which has the ability of coming into contact with the tongue organ leading to the arising of its tasting at this organ. A taste object (sour, sweet, bitter or salty), is ultimate reality existing in nature according to its causes.

Tasting is a type of Nāma (mind) which has the ability of knowing the taste of an object at the present moment of its coming into contact with the tongue organ. The "tasting" of the taste object takes place at this organ. At the very moment of "tasting" the taste object, such as salt, all one can taste is saltiness without knowing the meaning associated with this object in the ultimate sense. **For example,** when one says that a beverage is sweet, such tasting is not real in the ultimate sense. It merely reflects mental knowing based upon the tasting of this taste object at the present moment of its arising and the mental supposition or symbolization of the beverage based upon past accumulations.

The tasting, as well as the taste object, has the basic characteristics of impermanence (Anicca), inability to retain its original existence (Dukkha), and being dependent upon its causes (Anattā).

e. Nāma and Rūpa through the body sense door

When a bodily contact object comes into contact with the body organ, the bodily feeling of this object arises. Bodily feeling is Nāma (mind) while the bodily contact object is Rūpa. Both of them are ultimate reality.

Bodily contact object is a type of Rūpa which can come into contact with the body organ giving rise to its bodily feeling at this organ. Bodily contact objects consisting basically of the elements of coldness, hotness, softness, hardness, tightness or looseness are ultimate reality existing in nature according to their respective causes.

Bodily feeling is a type of Nāma (mind) which has the ability of knowing the bodily contact object at the present moment of its coming into contact with the body organ. At the very moment of bodily feeling of the object at this organ, all one can bodily feel is any combination of the above six bodily contact objects without knowing the meaning associated with this object in the ultimate sense. **For example,** when one says that he touches a female body or a table, such feeling is not real in the ultimate sense. It merely reflects mental knowing based upon the feeling of this bodily contact at the present moment of its arising and the mental supposition or symbolization of a female body or a table based upon past accumulations.

The bodily feeling, as well as the bodily contact object, has the basic characteristics of impermanence (Anicca), inability to retain its original existence (Dukkha), and being dependent upon its causes or non-self (Anattā).

f. Nāma and Rūpa through the mind sense door

The mind which arises through the mind sense door has the ability of knowing all kinds of objects, much more so than Nāma through the other 5 sense doors. What is known to the mind through the mind sense door can be either conventional reality or ultimate reality. At the same time, the mind can manifest itself through physical or verbal expression. The mind basically consists of two types, namely: wholesome mind and unwholesome mind.

With respect to the classification of Nāma and Rūpa through the mind sense door, Nāma is either wholesome mind or unwholesome mind whereas Rūpa (anything which is not Nāma and changes owing to cold or heat) is of various types including such physical postures as standing, walking, sitting, and lying down.

Nāma through the mind sense door is of two basic types, namely: the wholesome mind and the unwholesome mind. In everyday life, at the time when one awakes, one's mind can be either wholesome or unwholesome as follows:

Type of mind		Illustration
(1.) Wholesome Mind	(1.1) without unwholesome wanting or craving (Lobha), instead, accompanied with Alobha which has the characteristic of non-attachment of	Performing meritorious deeds such as donating money or things to charitable organizations or helping those in need. These deeds reflect self-sacrifice and doing away

Type of mind		Illustration
	the mind to any object, like a drop of water on a lotus leaf.	with selfishness and mental attachment to money or things.
	(1.2) without dissatisfaction or anger (Dosa), instead, accompanied with Adosa which has the characteristic of loving-kindness, tolerance or non-resentment like fire completely put out by water.	Extending loving-kindness with such wholesome intention as "May all living beings refrain from being hostile and destructive. May all be free from suffering and attain happiness and safety in life".
	(1.3) without ignorance (Moha), instead, accompanied with wisdom in life (Paññā).	Through meditation practice one becomes aware of and realizes the ultimate reality in life.
(2.) Unwholesome Mind	(2.1) with unwholesome wanting or craving (Lobha), which has the characteristic of grasping an object like a birdlime.	Mental attachment in the form of desire to taste delicious food or to take away another's belongings without permission.
	(2.2) with dissatisfaction or anger (Dosa),	Hurting others physically or mentally.

Type of mind	Illustration
which has the characteristic of reacting hostilely against undesirable objects. This works against the wholesome mind just like an enemy from within.	
(2.3) with ignorance about life (Moha), which has the characteristic of clouding an object and blinding the mind.	At the time of drowsiness, one's mind becomes dull, unresponsive or inactive so as to prevent him/her from becoming aware of and realizing the ultimate reality in life.

Rūpa through the mind sense door consists of such postures as : standing, sitting, walking and lying down, which are used as objects of Direct Awareness. Movement of these physical postures is caused by the power of the mind.

3. What should be kept in mind with respect to practicing Direct Awareness

What the meditator should keep in mind with respect to practicing Direct Awareness is highlighted under 7 major headings as follows:

3.1 The meditator should realize the real purpose of practicing Direct Awareness, which is to cultivate Insight Wisdom (Vipassanā Paññā) for full and thorough realization of ultimate reality leading to the eradication of all suffering in life and the attainment of "Perpetual Happiness" (Nibbāna).

3.2 The meditator must make sure that the intention of practicing Direct Awareness to achieve the real objectives as stated in 3.1 above, is pure. This means that there must be wisdom in realizing the true objectives of meditation practice together with wholesome intention, which is free from any influence of the defilements (Kilesa) of mind. **For example:** when it is known that one of the objectives of practicing Direct Awareness is to do away with suffering in life, a person's desire (Lobha) will make him/her like it. This is because he/she feels there will be no more suffering and only happiness will prevail in life. With this feeling, he/she proceeds to practice Direct Awareness. In this case, the intention of practicing Direct Awareness becomes impure because of the influence of the unwholesome wanting to eliminate suffering and the mental attachment to this desire. The intention, to be pure, must not be dictated by unwholesome wanting or craving (Lobha), but rather by wholesome wanting (Dhammachanda) to eradicate all suffering in life with the accompaniment of mindfulness. Unwholesome wanting and wholesome wanting can be distinguished through the following analogy: unwholesome wanting is like having a desire to taste delicious food, while wholesome wanting is like needing to take medicine with a bitter taste. The former reflects an unwholesome mental attachment to a delicious taste whereas the latter does not reflect any unwholesome mental attachment to its bitter taste. In fact, the sole purpose of needing to take the bitter medicine is to cure the sickness. Therefore, the intention of practicing Direct Awareness to achieve its real objectives must be free from the influence of the defilements (Kilesa) of mind in such form as craving, just as in the case of tasting the bitter medicine.

3.3 The meditator must really understand the difference between conventional reality and ultimate reality so that there will not be any misconceptions or confusion in regarding the conventional reality as ultimate reality. It should be noted that the object of Direct Awareness must be ultimate reality at the present moment.

3.4 The meditator should have a thorough knowledge and understanding of the objects of Direct Awareness. This means that one must know what is Nāma (mind and mental constituents) and what is Rūpa through the six sense doors, and that both of them are ultimate reality. If the meditator is still not clear about Nāma and Rūpa, which are the objects of Direct Awareness, it is advisable to study about them first so as to gain necessary knowledge and understanding.

3.5 The meditator should also keep in mind that in practicing Direct Awareness, one should be free from any influence of the defilements (Kilesa) of mind in the form of unwholesome wanting/craving or dissatisfaction/anger (Dosa). This is achieved by being well aware of these defilements and their adverse effects upon one's meditation, and upon the cultivation of awareness strong enough to cope effectively with them. This is because the power of these defilements causes the meditator to be prejudiced and at the same time prevents one from becoming aware of and realizing ultimate reality. For example, at the time of becoming directly conscious of an unpleasant feeling (such as boredom) as it arises at the present moment, a meditator might suddenly want to taste a juicy steak, which is his favorite dish. The arising of this unwholesome wanting adversely affects the meditation practice to the extent of instigating its discontinuation while trying to fulfill the desire to taste the steak. Because of this unwholesome wanting, the meditator becomes prejudiced into thinking that one is better off to change the object of Direct Awareness from an unpleasant feeling to a pleasant feeling of tasting one's favorite dish. Even though one tries to continue the practice of Direct Awareness while eating the steak, the meditation practice can no longer be effective. This is because the meditator is no longer free from the influence of unwholesome wanting.

On the other hand, when the meditator becomes strongly conscious of the unwholesome wanting to taste the steak and its adverse effect on the meditation, he will likely not try to fulfill that desire. But if the awareness on the part of the meditator is not strong enough, this unwholesome wanting will persist in arising from time to time. This unfulfilled desire (Lobha), in turn will bring about dissatisfaction (Dosa) during the practice of Direct Awareness. Thus, meditation practice will not be free from the influence of dissatisfaction. This means that the meditator, under the influence of this dissatisfaction, renders the practice ineffective.

3.6 The meditator should realize that the cultivation of Direct Awareness does not take place at the eye base, the ear base, the nose base, the tongue base and the body base. As a matter of fact, Direct Awareness must be cultivated through the mind door at the heart base (Hadayavatthu) only, and cannot be cultivated through the other five sense doors. Nāma and Rūpa through five sense doors (eyes, ears, nose, tongue, and body) can only serve as objects of Direct Awareness.

3.7 It should be noted that most people have a misconception about ultimate reality in that they regard impermanence as permanence. The basic aim of practicing Direct Awareness is to get rid of this misconception, which in turn leads to the attainment of purified and right views and the eradication of all suffering in life. For example, a wife may have the misconception that her beloved husband will always be with her. Later, should her husband pass away unexpectedly, she would suffer greatly simply because she has been misled into thinking that her desirable object (her husband) is permanent even though he is impermanent. If she has the right view, gained through practicing Direct Awareness, her suffering will be much relieved.

4. Basic techniques of practicing Direct Awareness

Before one can start utilizing the general method of applying Direct Awareness in daily life or practicing Direct Awareness at a proper place for Insight Meditation, it is imperative to first thoroughly understand how one can become directly aware of the objects of Direct Awareness in the form of Nāma and Rūpa through the six sense doors. Without such understanding, one cannot practice Direct Awareness properly.

It needs to be emphasized again that Direct Awareness can arise only through the mind door at the heart base and it can never take place at the eye base, the ear base, the nose base, the tongue base or the body base. Nevertheless, Nāma and Rūpa perceived through the six sense doors (eyes, ears, nose, tongue, body and mind) can all serve as objects of Direct Awareness as previously explained in 2.

In practicing Direct Awareness, generally a meditator must become directly aware of either Nāma or Rūpa as its object and not both at the same time. This is because one can only be directly mindful of one object (Nāma or Rūpa) at one time. Whether Nāma or Rūpa should be used as the object of Direct Awareness in each particular case depends mainly upon which object, Nāma or Rūpa, is the cause which gives rise to the meditator's misconception of ultimate reality, or which object, Nāma or Rūpa, leads to a better practice result.

Basic techniques of practicing Direct Awareness in becoming directly aware of Nāma or Rūpa through the six sense doors for the purpose of cultivating Insight Wisdom (Vipassanā Paññā) are as follows:

4.1 Eye sense door

At the time of the visible object (Rūpārammaṇa) coming into contact with the eye organ (Cakkhupasāda-rūpa), the "seeing" (Cakkhu-viññāṇa) of the present object takes place at the organ. **The meditator is required to become directly aware of this "seeing" (Nāma) and at the same time to realize it, at the present moment at the eye base.** This requirement of being directly aware of Nāma (seeing) and not Rūpa (visible object) in this case is because of the common misconception about "seeing" in the form of "I see" instead of "Nāma (mind) sees". At the instant of seeing the visible object, there is no seeing of any form, shape or color. What can actually and directly be seen in the ultimate sense is only the visible object. The other reason for using Nāma (seeing) instead of Rūpa (visible object) as the object of Direct Awareness is that, in spite of the "seeing" of the visible object taking place only at the eye organ in the ultimate sense, people in general are misled into thinking that at the time of "seeing", the visible object is somewhere else, away from the eye organ. **For example,** when the light (visible object) from a neon lamp comes into contact with the eye organ, "seeing" of this light arises at this eye organ. But usually we mistakenly feel that this light which is being seen by "the seeing-mind", is located at the neon lamp and not at the eye organ. Therefore, in practicing Direct Awareness, if a meditator is mindful of the light (Rūpa) from the neon lamp instead of "seeing" (Nāma), he/she has no chance whatsoever of realizing the light (Rūpa) as well as "seeing" (Nāma) at the present moment. Such practice of mindfulness will be ineffective because the visible object (Rūpa) and "seeing" (Nāma) can only arise at the eye organ. **This can be illustrated by the following analogy:** a car travelling from the United Nations Building in New York City has an accident in front of the Empire State Building, but if we look for this accident in front of the United Nations Building, how can we see this accident as it really is? It is impossible.

If the meditator continues to practice Direct Awareness properly and regularly until the mental factors of practicing Insight Meditation (consisting of Confidence Power, Effort Power, Mindfulness

Power, Concentration Power, and Wisdom Power), reach the point of optimum harmony and balance (for detail, please refer to Chapter 12), his/her wisdom will thoroughly and directly realize this "seeing" (Nāma) at the present moment. At the same time, the mind will become enlightened, a unique manifestation never before experienced. With this enlightened mind, the misconception in the form of "I see" will be eliminated and in its place, there will be the right view in the form of "Nāma sees". Apart from this, the meditator can distinctly realize that "Nāma (seeing) is not Rūpa" and the light (visible object), which is Rūpa, is not Nāma (mind)", This wisdom, which can thoroughly and directly realize the "seeing" (Nāma) and the light (Rūpa) at the present moment is of the first level, called **"Nāmarūpa-pariccheda-ñāṇa"**, leading to Insight Wisdom.

With this first level wisdom leading to Insight Wisdom (Vipassanā Paññā), the meditator will be able to do away significantly with life's suffering as well as to attain the Right and Purified View in Life. In this way, the meditator will be one step closer to the attainment of "Perpetual Happiness" (Nibbāna).

4.2 Ear sense door

At the time of a sound (Saddārammaṇa) coming into contact with the ear organ (Sotapasāda-rūpa), the "hearing" (Sota-viññāṇa) of this present object takes place at the organ. **The meditator is required to**

become directly aware of this "hearing" (Nāma) and at the same time to realize it at the present moment at the ear base. This requirement, to be directly aware of Nāma (hearing) and not Rūpa (sound) in this case, is because of the common misconception about this "hearing" in the form of "I hear" instead of "Nāma (mind) hears". At the instant of hearing the sound (audible object), all one can actually and directly hear, in the ultimate sense, is the sound, which is ultimate reality, and there is no meaning whatsoever existing in that sound. The other reason for using Nāma (hearing) instead of Rūpa (sound) as the object of Direct Awareness is similar to the reason explained under the previous heading **4.1.**

When the meditator continues to practice Direct Awareness properly and regularly until the mental factors of practicing Insight Meditation (consisting of Confidence Power, Effort Power, Mindfulness Power, Concentration Power and Wisdom Power), reach the point of optimum harmony and balance, his/her wisdom will thoroughly and directly realize this hearing (Nāma) at the present moment. At the same time, the mind will become enlightened, a unique manifestation never before experienced. With this enlightened mind, the misconception in the form of "I hear" will be eliminated, and in its place there will be the right view in the form of "Nāma (mind) hears". Apart from this, the meditator can distinctly realize that Nāma (hearing) is not Rūpa and the "sound" (audible object) which is Rūpa is not Nāma (mind). This wisdom, which can thoroughly and directly realize the "hearing" (Nāma) and the sound (Rūpa) at the present moment is of the first level, called **"Nāmarūpa-pariccheda-ñāṇa"**, leading to Insight Wisdom.

With this first level wisdom leading to Insight Wisdom (Vipassanā Paññā), the meditator will be able to do away significantly with life's suffering as well as to attain the Right and Purified View in Life. In this way, the meditator will be one step closer to the attainment of "Perpetual Happiness" (Nibbāna).

4.3 Nose sense door

At the time of an odorous object (Gandhārammaṇa) coming into contact with the nose organ (Ghānappasāda-rūpa), the "smelling" (Ghāna-viññāṇa) of this present object takes place at the organ. **The meditator is required to become directly aware of the "odor" (Rūpa) and at the same time to realize it, at the present moment at the nose base.** This requirement of being directly aware of Rūpa (odor) and not Nāma (smelling) in this case is due to the fact that "odor" (Rūpa) as the object of Direct Awareness is more discernible than "smelling" (Nāma) at the nose organ, and at the time of being mindful of this odorous object at the nose base, the meditator will not be misled into thinking that it is somewhere else, away from the nose organ. **For example,** when one smells the odor of a rose, one will know for sure that the odor being smelled is at the nose base and not at the rose flower. Therefore, by being directly aware of odor (Rūpa), the meditator will be in a position to realize the odorous object at the present moment.

When the meditator continues to practice Direct Awareness properly and regularly until the mental factors of practicing Insight Meditation (consisting of Confidence Power, Effort Power, Mindfulness Power, Concentration Power and Wisdom Power), reach the point of optimum harmony and balance, wisdom will thoroughly and directly realize this odor (Rūpa) at the present moment. At the same time, the mind will become enlightened, a unique manifestation never before experienced. With this enlightened mind, the misconception in the form of "I smell" will be eliminated, and in its place there will be the right view in the form of "Nāma (mind) smells". Apart from this, the meditator can distinctly realize that "Nāma (smelling) is not Rūpa" and the odor (odorous object) which is Rūpa is not Nāma (mind)". This wisdom, which can thoroughly and directly realize the smelling (Nāma) and the odor (Rūpa) at the present moment, is of the first level, called **"Nāmarūpa-pariccheda-ñāṇa"**, leading to Insight Wisdom.

With this first level wisdom leading to Insight Wisdom (Vipassanā Paññā), the meditator will be able to do away significantly with life's suffering as well as to attain the Right and Purified View in Life. In this way, the meditator will be one step closer to the attainment of "Perpetual Happiness" (Nibbāna).

4.4 Tongue sense door

At the time of a taste object (Rasārammaṇa) (such as sweet, sour, bitter, or salty) coming into contact with the tongue organ (Jivhāppasadā-rūpa), the "tasting" (Jivhā-viññāṇa) of this present object takes place at the organ. **The meditator is required to become directly aware of the taste object (Rūpa) and at the same time to realize it, at the present moment at the tongue base.** The requirement of being directly aware of Rūpa (taste object) and not Nāma (tasting) in this case is based upon reasons similar to those specified under the previous heading **4.3.**

When the meditator continues to practice Direct Awareness properly and regularly until the mental factors of practicing Insight Meditation (consisting of Confidence Power, Effort Power, Mindfulness Power, Concentration Power and Wisdom Power), reach the point of optimum harmony and balance, wisdom will thoroughly and directly realize this taste object (Rūpa) at the present moment. At the same time, the mind will become enlightened, a unique manifestation never before experienced. With this enlightened mind, the misconception in the form of "I taste" will be eliminated, and in its place there will be the right view in the form of "Nāma (mind) tastes". Apart from this, the meditator can distinctly realize that "Nāma (tasting) is not Rūpa" and "the taste object which is Rūpa is not

Nāma (mind)". This wisdom, which can thoroughly and directly realize the "tasting" (Nāma) and the taste object (Rūpa) at the present moment, is of the first level, called **"Nāmarūpa-pariccheda-ñāṇa"** leading to Insight Wisdom.

With this first level wisdom leading to Insight Wisdom (Vipassanā Paññā), the meditator will be able to do away significantly with life's suffering as well as to attain the Right and Purified View in Life. In this way, the meditator will be one step closer to the attainment of "Perpetual Happiness" (Nibbāna).

4.5 Body sense door

At the time of a bodily contact object (Phoṭ-thabbārammaṇa) coming into contact with the body organ (Kāyappasāda-rūpa), the "bodily feeling" (Kāya-viññaṇa) of this present object takes place at the organ. **The meditator is required to become directly aware of this "bodily feeling" (Nāma) or bodily contact object (Rūpa) and at the same time to realize it, at the present moment at the body base.** It should be noted that this particular technique differs from the others in the sense that either the bodily contact object (Rūpa) or "the bodily feeling" (Nāma) can become the object of Direct Awareness depending on which object is more discernible at the time of practicing Direct Awareness through the body sense door. This requirement of being directly aware of the bodily contact object (Rūpa) or "the bodily feeling" (Nāma) is because of the common misconception arising in such form as "I am hot" instead of "Rūpa" is hot" or "I am painful" instead of "Nāma" is painful". Apart from this, the body sense door is not as subtle as the other five sense doors and this makes it relatively easy to become directly aware of both the bodily contact object (Rūpa) and "the bodily feeling" (Nāma). When an object such as coldness, hotness, hardness or softness (Rūpa) touches the body organ thus giving rise to the "bodily feeling" of this bodily contact object, the meditator should become directly aware of it (Rūpa) due to its being most discernible at this particular time. However, in the case when the bodily contact object touches the body organ bringing about the "bodily feeling" of pleasantness or unpleasantness, the meditator should instead become directly aware of this "bodily feeling" (Nāma) for the simple reason that this "bodily feeling" is most discernible at that time. **For example,** when one is taking a hot shower, the hotness (Rūpa) of the water can be most discernibly felt and therefore can be the object of Direct Awareness at that time. However, if this hotness is increased to the extent of causing bodily pain, the meditator must become directly aware of this pain (Nāma) instead.

When the meditator continues to practice Direct Awareness properly and regularly until the mental factors of practicing Insight Meditation (consisting of Confidence Power, Effort Power, Mindfulness

Power, Concentration Power and Wisdom Power), reach the point of optimum harmony and balance, wisdom will thoroughly and directly realize this bodily contact object (Rūpa) or the "bodily feeling" (Nāma) at the present moment. At the same time, the mind will become enlightened, a unique manifestation never before experienced. With this enlightened mind, the misconception in the form of "I feel" hot/cold, hardness/softness, or physically pleasant/unpleasant" will be eliminated, and in its place there will be the right view in the form of "Nāma feels hot/cold, hardness/softness, or physically pleasant/unpleasant at the body organ. Apart from this, the meditator can distinctly realize that "Nāma (bodily feeling) is not Rūpa" and "bodily-contact object which is Rūpa is not Nāma (mind)". This wisdom, which can thoroughly and directly realize the "bodily feeling" (Nāma) and bodily contact-object (Rūpa) at the present moment, is of the first level, called **"Nāmarūpa-pariccheda-ñāṇa"**, leading to Insight Wisdom.

With this first level wisdom leading to Insight Wisdom (Vipassanā Paññā), the meditator will be able to do away significantly with life's suffering as well as to attain the Right and Purified View in Life. In this way, the meditator will be one step closer to the attainment of "Perpetual Happiness" (Nibbāna).

4.6 Mind sense door

When Nāma (wholesome or unwholesome mind)

arises through the mind sense door in such form as the wholesome mind accompanied with wholesome mental constituents (such as loving-kindness, wisdom and wholesome mental feeling) or the unwholesome mind accompanied with unwholesome mental constituents (such as anger, frustration, worry, fear, mental wandering, drowsiness, craving, ignorance and unwholesome mental feeling), the meditator should become directly aware of this Nāma as its object and at the same time realize it, at the present moment at the heart base.

It should be noted that the arising of all Nāma through the mind sense door takes place only at the heart base and not at the brain. Such mental manifestation is clearly evident in the case where one is very frightened or is in a very happy mood. One can distinctively feel that this state of great fright or extreme happiness occurs only at the heart base and nowhere else.

During the time when Nāma, such as loving-kindness or anger, is arising, people in general have the common misconception that "I extend loving-kindness" instead of "Nāma extends loving-kindness" or "I am angry" instead of "Nāma is angry". When the meditator becomes directly aware of and realizes this Nāma at the present moment, he/she will be in a position to eliminate this wrong view, and in this way, mental suffering in life will be automatically relieved.

Nāma through the mind sense door can also bring about various physical actions such as standing, walking, sitting or lying down. The meditator will find that it is relatively easy to become directly aware of these body postures, which are in gross form and occur at all times during one's life. However, in the practice of Direct Awareness using body posture as its object, the meditator must not try to resort to thinking about or imagining the object. Instead, he/she must become directly aware of and realize only the position of that particular posture in question. When the meditator continues to practice Direct Awareness properly and regularly until the mental factors of practicing Insight Meditation (consisting of Confidence Power, Effort Power, Mindfulness Power, Concentration Power and Wisdom Power), reach the point of optimum harmony and balance, wisdom will thoroughly and directly realize this body posture (Rūpa) at the present moment. At the same time, the mind will become enlightened, and a misconception in the form of "I am standing", "I am sitting", "I am walking" or "I am lying down" will be eliminated, and in its place there will be the right view in the form of "Rūpa is standing", "Rūpa is sitting", "Rūpa is walking" or "Rūpa is lying down". Apart from this, the meditator can distinctly realize that "Rūpa (standing, sitting, walking or lying down) is not Nāma" and "Nāma (mind) which causes the arising of the body posture (Rūpa) is not Rūpa". This wisdom, which can thoroughly and directly realize the body position (Rūpa) and mind (Nāma) bringing about this posture at the present moment, is of the first level, called **"Nāmarūpa-pariccheda-ñāṇa"**, leading to Insight Wisdom.

With this first level wisdom leading to Insight Wisdom (Vipassanā Paññā), the Meditator will be able to do away significantly with life's suffering as well as to attain the Right and Purified View in Life. In this way, the meditator will be one step closer to the attainment of "Perpetual Happiness" (Nibbāna).

The above basic techniques of practicing Direct Awareness can be summarized in this table as follows:

Basic Techniques of Practicing Direct Awareness of Nāma and Rūpa Through The Six Sense Doors

Sense door	Rūpa	Nāma	Practice Requirement	Underlying Reason
Eye	Visible object (Rūpā-rammaṇa) or light	Seeing -mind	Being directly aware of and realizing the seeing (Nāma)	Common misconception relating to the "seeing" in the form of "I see" instead of "Nāma sees" People mistakenly think that at the time of seeing, the visible object is somewhere else, away from the eye organ.

Sense door	Rūpa	Nāma	Practice Requirement	Underlying Reason
Ear	Audible object (Saddā-rammaṇa) or sound	Hearing-mind	Being directly aware of and realizing the hearing (Nāma)	Common misconception relating to the "hearing" in the form of "I hear" instead of "Nāma hears". People mistakenly think that at the time of hearing, the audible object is somewhere else, away from the ear organ.
Nose	Odor (Gandhā-rammaṇa)	Smelling-mind	Being directly aware of and realizing the odor (Rūpa)	Odor (Rūpa) as an object of Direct Awareness is much more discernible than "smelling" (Nāma) at the nose organ. At the time of mindfulness of an odorous object through the nose sense door, the meditator will not be misled into thinking that it is somewhere

Sense door	Rūpa	Nāma	Practice Requirement	Underlying Reason
				else, away from the nose organ.
Tongue	Taste object (Rasāram-maṇa)	Tasting-mind	Being directly aware of and realizing the taste object (Rūpa)	Taste object (Rūpa) as an object of Direct Awareness is much more discernible than "tasting" (Nāma) at the tongue organ. At the time of mindfulness of the taste object through the tongue sense door the meditator will not be misled into thinking that it is somewhere else, away from the tongue organ.
Body	Bodily contact object (e.g., hotness coldness, hardness or softness)	Bodily feeling	Being directly aware of and realizing the bodily contact object (Rūpa) or the bodily feeling (Nāma)	Common misconception in such forms as "I am hot" instead of " Rūpa is hot", or "I am in pain" instead of "Nāma is in pain".

Sense door	Rūpa	Nāma	Practice Requirement	Underlying Reason
Mind	(a) Heart base	(1) Wholesome mind with its wholesome mental constituents* (2) Unwholesome mind with its unwholesome mental constituents**	Being directly aware of and realizing the wholesome or the unwholesome Nāma	Common misconception in such forms as "I extend loving-kindness" instead of "Nāma extends loving-kindness", or "I am angry" instead of "Nāma is angry".
	(b) The positioning of the body postures (standing, walking, sitting or lying down)	The mind which brings about the body postures	Being Directly aware of and realizing the position of the body posture which arises at that particular time	Common misconception in such forms as "I stand" instead of "Rūpa stands," or "I walk" instead of "Rūpa walks".

* such as unselfishness, loving-kindness, wisdom and wholesome mental feeling etc.

** such as anger, frustration, worry, fear, mental wandering, drowsiness, craving, ignorance and unwholesome mental feeling etc.

5. General method of applying Direct Awareness in daily life

a. Introduction

In our daily living, if we become aware of and realize the ultimate reality which has a basic role of bringing about sense perceptions and various human actions, we will be able:

- to prevent certain problems in life from arising.
- to cope effectively with life's problems as they arise.
- to relieve suffering in life.
- to enhance the right technique of wholesome living with respect to family life, work life, human relations, the learning process, etc.

This general method is aimed at improving the effectiveness of the above-mentioned awareness and realization. This method incorporates certain techniques of Direct Awareness through adaptation and simplification so as to allow as many people as possible, from all walks of life, especially those who are not in the position to practice Direct Awareness in a meditation center or any other proper place, to practice it, so that they can bring about the widest possible benefits in their daily life.

b. Sense perception and human actions

In our everyday life, we perceive various objects through our six sense doors, namely; eyes, ears, nose, tongue, body and mind. These objects can be either ultimate reality (e.g. light or sound) or conventional reality (e.g. a table, a language or symbols). The sense door perception in turn can give rise to physical, verbal or mental actions. **For example:** standing, walking, sitting and lying down are physical actions, and speaking is a verbal action, whereas thinking is a mental action. These three actions are the manifestation of ultimate reality with or without the involvenent of conventional reality. **For example,** during conversation (a verbal action), what is said must be basically caused by the mind, and the mind and the uttered sound are ultimate reality while the meaning of the sound is conventional reality. The waving of the hand to call someone to come here, which is a physical action, must be basically caused by the mind, and the mind and the movement of the hand (Rūpa) are ultimate reality, whereas the meaning of "come here" through waving the hand is conventional reality. For instance, when a young man thinks of a good time he has had with his girlfriend, which is mental action, thinking (mind) is ultimate reality while the good time is conventional reality.

c. The application of Direct Awareness in daily life

In our daily living, we must perform certain activities common to all (such as taking a shower, brushing our teeth, answering nature's call) as well as other activities which apply only to certain individuals, (such as a policeman who has a different role and performs activities different from those of a salesman or a truck driver, for instance). However, no matter what the individual's activities are, they are inseparable from the individual's sense perception through the six sense doors and manifest themselves in the form of physical, verbal or mental actions.

The application of Direct Awareness in daily life can be broken down on the basis of these activities, as follows:

> **(1.) General experiences in daily life common to all**
>
> **(2.) Specific experiences in daily life pertaining to each individual**

(1.) General experiences in daily life common to all

With respect to general experiences in daily life common to all, there are 10 points to be considered as illustrated below:

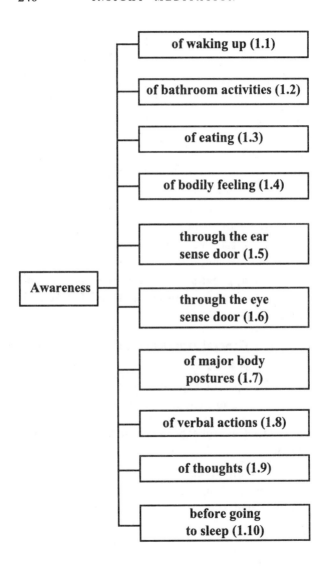

Awareness
- of waking up (1.1)
- of bathroom activities (1.2)
- of eating (1.3)
- of bodily feeling (1.4)
- through the ear sense door (1.5)
- through the eye sense door (1.6)
- of major body postures (1.7)
- of verbal actions (1.8)
- of thoughts (1.9)
- before going to sleep (1.10)

(1.1) Awareness of waking up

One is required to wake up in the morning with regular awareness and realization that sleeping is a means to do away with physical discomfort or pain in the ultimate sense. Since our body cannot retain its original existence, without any rest it becomes weak, fatigued and unbearable. The real reason why one needs rest is to get rid of or to avoid physical discomfort or pain.

However, people often mistakenly feel that a rested body constitutes a type of real happiness. The relief of physical discomfort or pain through resting one's body, and the mental attachment to the happiness resulting from such a relief, can lead to a type of unwholesome wanting to sleep, accompanied by wrong view.

Thus, Direct Awareness and realization will prevent one from being blindly and overly attached to this so-called happiness. In some cases, people are so blindly attached to the happiness from resting or sleeping that they overindulge in this habit. As a result, their habit has become more intensified and at the same time they could become more fatigued than ever.

Apart from this, one is also required to become aware of and realize the subtle unwholesomeness of wanting to continue sleep, which can itself bring about laziness, in order to do away with the adverse effect of oversleeping.

(1.2) Awareness of bathroom activities

(1.2.1) While taking a shower, brushing the teeth or performing other activities in the bathroom, one is required to become aware of and realize that the true purpose of all these activities is only to relieve physical discomfort or pain and to provide measures for avoiding it in the future. One could easily find out the real purpose of these activities by simply asking the question, "what will happen if these bathroom activities are not being performed regularly?" **For example,** without taking a shower for days, one will feel uncomfortable. Physical discomfort or pain becomes more evident in a case where one must delay answering nature's call or when one is famished but cannot immediately satisfy hunger. However, people often overlook the real purpose of these activities and at the same time have a misconception with respect to their being a type of real happiness. This is reflected in such a practice as calling the toilet a "rest room" in accordance with one's desire and misconception, rather than "pain-relieving or pain-avoiding room" in accordance with its real purpose.

(1.2.2) When taking a shower, our body comes into contact with warm or cold water, giving rise to a feeling of warmness or coldness. One is required to become regularly aware of and realize the ultimate reality that warmness or coldness is Rūpa while the feeling of warmness or coldness is

Nāma. However, people often have the misconceived notion that "we are warm or cold" instead of "Rūpa is warm or cold".

This requirement of awareness and realization even for a short period of time will do away with the misconceptions and blind attachments which are the basic causes of suffering in life, and at the same time will make one understand the true nature of this ultimate reality, and this wisdom will bring about happiness in life.

(1.3) Awareness of eating

(1.3.1) Before the meal

One is required to understand that the real purposes of eating a meal are to relieve hunger, prevent hunger pangs from arising, sustain life and provide an opportunity for the improvement and development of one's life.

Whenever a desire (unwholesome wanting or craving) for a delicious food arises, one should become aware of and realize it, instead of trying to suppress it. In letting one's desire for food run its course by indulging one's unwholesome wanting or craving (Lobha), one could lead one's life in the form of "live to eat" and not "eat to live". As a consequence, suffering in life follows. **For example,** some parents spoil their children by allowing them to eat whatever they want even though the food taken lacks nutritive value.

As a result, these children face the problem of malnutrition, which adversely affects their health, giving rise to physical illness.

(1.3.2) During the meal

When one's unwholesome wanting or craving arises for the taste of food, one is required to become aware of and realize this desire. The mere mindfulness of the arising of this desire will lessen its strength and will put it under control. By freely and excessively allowing one's craving for the taste of the food to take its course, one will experience more mental attachment which in turn brings about suffering in life. On the other hand, by controlling this craving (Lobha) through awareness and realization, one will experience a happy feeling without any ill effect. Such control can be compared to containing a fire in a stove instead of letting the fire burn freely and dangerously outside the stove.

When one feels that one has had nearly enough food, one should control the craving through one's awareness and realization in the form of eating moderately instead of excessively. In this way, certain discomforts or suffering will be avoided.

(1.3.3) After the meal

One should examine whether or not one has been lacking in awareness and realization while eating the food, and whether or not one has taken too much food. Some people, during a meal, cannot help themselves in seeking pleasure through eating as much as possible, resulting in indigestion. They sometimes blame themselves for this discomfort by feeling that they should not have been carried away by overeating. If they are aware that their craving was allowed to flow too freely and blindly during the time of tasting the food, they should not worry or feel badly for not having effectively controlled their craving. This is because what has been done cannot be undone. Nevertheless, one should learn from this past mistake by being more aware and careful in the future so as not to repeat the same mistake.

(1.4) Awareness of bodily feeling

(1.4.1) At the time of experiencing a physical pain such as a headache or stomachache, one is required to become aware of and realize this unpleasant feeling in the form of "Nāma is suffering" and not "I am suffering". If one takes this adverse feeling as being "I am suffering", one's physical pain will be worsened, giving rise to mental suffering. On the other hand, one's awareness and wisdom in realizing that Nāma is suffering will prevent one's mental suffering from arising.

(1.4.2) At the time of experiencing a pleasant feeling at the body organ, such as physical pleasantness after taking a shower or after a cool breeze has come into contact with the body, one is required to become aware of and realize this pleasant feeling in the form of "Nāma is pleasant" and not "I am pleasant". If one takes this pleasant feeling as being "I am pleasant", one will become mentally and blindly attached to this pleasantness.

(1.5) Awareness through the ear sense door

In daily life, it is impossible for one to avoid the perception of sound (ultimate reality) or voices (conventional reality) through the ear sense door. At the time, when the audible object comes into contact with the ear organ giving rise to hearing, the sound heard can either be desirable (e.g. sound from a temple or church bell) or undesirable (e.g. the sound from a thunder storm). Further, after hearing it, one may either become blindly attached or react with hostility to it, as the case may be.

When the sounds are generated during a conversation, we ordinarily not only can hear them but also use them as a medium through which their meanings can be formulated. If the sounds are interpreted as being desirable, usually we become blindly attached to them. **For example,** upon hearing flattering words, one will likely become blindly attached to these desirable objects even though they are sometimes accompanied with ill intention. On the other hand, if the sounds are interpreted as being undesirable, we will likely become angry or dissatisfied. **For example,** upon hearing abusive words, one becomes irritated.

(1.5.1) Awareness of an audible object which is desirable

When one's craving or blind attachment (Lobha) arises from hearing the desirable object, one normally is not aware of it. Thus, one should set one's mind to become aware of this unwholesome arising. But there is a point of caution; i.e. one must not try to suppress the craving or blind attachment. This is because such suppression, being a type of defilement (Kilesa), cannot be used to do away with another defilement in the form of craving or blind attachment. In the case when one is being praised by another, one should carefully consider whether or not one really deserves such praise. Even if one is wholesomely praiseworthy, one should not be blindly attached to it, but instead, should try at least to uphold one's wholesome deeds. On the other hand, one should also determine whether or not the person who praises has any sincerity and good intention. If the answer is affirmative, one should extend one's wholesome appreciation. If not, through awareness, one should guard oneself against unwholesomeness so as not to fall into its trap.

(1.5.2) Awareness of an audible object which is undesirable

Upon hearing something which is undesirable, one can easily become dissatisfied or angry (Dosa). With the arising of this unwholesome manifestation, the listener, in all probability, comes under its influence due to lack of awareness. Thus, one should set one's mind to become aware of this unwholesome arising and with the arising of more and more awareness, its unwholesome strength will be lessened leading eventually to its being overcome. In a case where one is being chided by another, one should carefully consider whether or not one really deserves it. If the answer is positive, one should try to improve oneself, keeping in mind that this chiding can serve as a useful guide for self-development. On the other hand, one should also determine whether or not the person who chides has any ill intention. If there is a good intention, one should show thanks and appreciation. If there is bad intention, one should feel sorry for the person's accumulations of unwholesome deeds and, at the same time, extend one's loving-kindness to that person for the sake of one's own self-development.

(1.6) Awareness through the eye sense door

In daily life, it is impossible for one to avoid the perception of visible objects (ultimate reality), colors or shapes (conventional reality). At a time when a visible object comes into contact with the eye organ giving rise to seeing, it can be either desirable (e.g. visible object: light as reflected from a beautiful girl or scenery) or undesirable (e.g. visible object: light as reflected from a horrible sight). Where the visible object is desirable, it is easy to become blindly attached to it, whereas in the case where the visible object is undesirable, one can easily become dissatisfied or displeased.

(1.6.1) Awareness of a visible object which is desirable

When craving or blind attachment (Lobha) arises from seeing a desirable object, one normally is not aware of it. Thus, one should set one's mind to become aware of this unwholesome arising. One must exercise caution not to try to suppress the craving or blind attachment. This is because such suppression, being a type of defilement (Kilesa), can in no way be used to do away with another defilement in the form of craving or blind attachment. Apart from this, one is required to realize that in the sense of ultimate reality, all one can actually see are the visible objects or the light and nothing else. All sights other than light are mental creations which do not really exist in nature, and they are all only conventional reality. With such realization, one is able to get one's craving or blind attachment under control, just as one contains a fire in a stove.

(1.6.2) Awareness of a visible object which is undesirable

Upon seeing something undesirable in such form as a rude gesture, one can easily become dissatisfied or angry (Dosa). With the arising of this unwholesome manifestation, one, in all probability, comes under its influence due to lack of awareness. Thus, one should set one's mind to become aware of this unwholesome arising and also to realize that, in the ultimate sense, all one can actually see are the visible objects or the light and nothing else. All sights other than light are mental creations which do not really exist in nature, and are all only conventional reality. With the arising of each awareness and realization, the strength of this unwholesome manifestation will be lessened leading eventually to its being overcome.

(1.7) Awareness of major body postures

(1.7.1) **In whatever major body posture one** is in, such as standing, walking, sitting or lying down, one is required to set one's mind, as the opportunity allows, to become aware of the body posture as being "Rūpa is standing, walking, sitting or lying down" instead of "I am standing, walking, sitting or lying down". Such awareness will at least enhance one's knowledge of reality as it really is in order to do away with misconceptions and blind attachments which are the basic causes of suffering in life.

(1.7.2) **In changing from on body posture to another** (e.g. from standing to sitting), one often automatically and unconsciously does so according to one's desire for change, which is a type of unwholesome wanting (Lobha). Actually, one must change one's body posture irrespective of whether or not one wants to do so. This is due to the fact that any body posture cannot retain its original existence as a result of physical pain or suffering. What would happen if one remained standing without any movement like a statue for several "hours"? This would become unbearable as the physical pain intensified, and one would be forced to change to another posture. If one always remains in the same body posture without any movement, one will certainly die. In a case where one remains in one posture for too long a period without changing due to lack of awareness, this condition can adversely affect one's health or even shorten one's life. This is evident where employees such as typists, accountants or business executives perform certain jobs which require them to stay in one major posture (sitting) for a long period of time, and they lack the awareness of the necessity of changing this posture.

Therefore, one is required to become aware of and realize the fact that change from one major posture to another is really for the purpose of relieving physical pain and that the major posture should be changed frequently in order to avoid the adverse effects of remaining in one posture for a long time.

In a situation where people are being impelled by an unwholesome wanting (Lobha) to change to another posture, such direction is for the purpose of blindly fulfilling their desire to feel comfortable or happy. When physical pain arises in a major posture (e.g. standing), people, because of their craving

(Lobha), wish the pain to disappear and thus have to resort to changing to a new posture under the influence of their craving. After the change, physical pain disappears and this gives rise to the misconception and blind attachment that the new posture is happy or comfortable. Under this condition, one mistakenly believes that the change from one posture to another is a way to bring about happiness or comfort instead of relieving physical pain.

When one allows one's craving to flow freely with respect to changing one's posture, this reflects a lack of awareness and realization on one's part of reality as it exists, thereby giving rise to suffering in life. This is especially true when one becomes sick or aches all over; no matter what posture one is in, physical pain persists. When this happens, one desires to have this painful feeling disappear by changing to a new posture as done previously. But contrary to one's expectation, the pain still arises and this in turn brings about frustration and mental suffering. The more one changes one's posture according to one's unwholesome wanting, the more one suffers. Therefore, one should try to allow one's awareness, instead of unwholesome wanting, to direct as much as possible the change from one posture to another with the realization that its real purpose is to relieve physical pain. In this way, one will be in a position to do away with the above misconceptions and blind attachments. while cultivating wisdom leading to a more happy and wholesome life.

(1.8) Awareness of verbal actions

Our verbal actions are basically caused by our mind. Without the mind, the verbal actions can never manifest themselves. When we intend to speak, our mind will direct the necessary movements of the vocal chords giving rise to verbal expression.

The mind which brings about verbal actions is normally classified into two main types; namely, the unwholesome mind and the wholesome mind. The verbal expressions caused by the unwholesome mind are in such forms as lying, slandering, harsh speech, and vain talk; those caused by the wholesome mind are in such forms as words of consolation or helpful advice in coping with life's problems.

The right technique of speaking, with respect to enriching one's life, must be based on the wholesome mind with the following five factors:

1) Spoken words are truthful and not deceitful

2) Spoken words are polite and not rude

3) Spoken words are useful and not wasteful

4) Spoken words are lovingly kind and not hostile

5) Spoken words are suitable and not improper

(1.8.1) Before speaking

Before one speaks, one is required to become aware of and realize the usefulness of the verbal expressions. This means that if it is useful, one should speak out; if not, one should avoid it.

(1.8.2) During speaking

At the time of speaking, one is required to become aware of and realize that one's verbal expressions are being caused by the wholesome or the unwholesome mind. People normally accumulate, through verbal actions, wholesomeness as well as unwholesomeness. Those who have regularly cultivated wholesomeness before speaking, will have speech automatically accompanied with awareness. In this way, they will know that their speech, while being given, is caused by the wholesome mind. While speaking, should there be an arising of the unwholesome mind, they will become aware of it and will be able to deter or minimize its adverse effect.

Those who have regularly accumulated verbal actions through the unwholesome mind will automatically be under the influence of their unwholesome intention every time they speak. At the initial stage of cultivating awareness, it is difficult for them to speak with awareness. This is normal for the untrained person. They should not be discouraged or blame themselves. Instead, they should realize that they have not sufficiently practiced awareness before speaking, and at the same time they should try to be regularly aware of the unwholesome mind which basically brings about the spoken words without suppressing this mind. With the arising of each awareness, the strength of the unwholesome manifestation will be lessened, leading eventually to its phasing out, just as when a thief goes away upon being seen by a policeman.

When one who is being blamed for something becomes irritated and speaks out harshly and unwholesomely, he will be able to get rid of this adverse verbal action by becoming aware of and realizing that every time he speaks with an unwholesome mind, he will accumulate the unwholesome power of this verbal action which in turn can cause more unwholesome verbal actions. If such an unwholesome accumulation is allowed to arise more and more, the unwholesome verbal actions will manifest themselves automatically. Once the understanding of the above causal relationship is reached, the unwholesome power of verbal actions can be overcome, just as light dispels darkness. However, if this unwholesome power through past accumulations is very strong, it can only be lessened, and its arising will occur again. In this case, if one is lacking in the awareness and realization of this unwholesome mind, the adverse power of verbal actions will be intensified. On the other hand, if one becomes closely and regularly aware of and realizes its arising, its unwholesome power can eventually be minimized or deterred.

(1.8.3) After speaking

One is required to review to see whether
or not one has awareness and realization while speaking, and whether or not one has followed the above-
mentioned five factors for the right technique of
speaking. If the answers are affirmative, one should
not only try to maintain, but also further develop,
wholesome verbal actions. If the answers are negative,
one should learn from the past deeds by being more
aware and careful for the purpose of self-improvement.

(1.9) Awareness of thoughts

People in general, when they do not occupy themselves with respect to physical or verbal actions, often
think of various things, persons or events. These
thoughts basically consist of two major types; unwholesome thoughts and wholesome thoughts.

(1.9.1) Awareness of unwholesome thoughts

**(a) When one thinks of a desirable ob-
ject, such as a tasty food or a popular song, one is
required to become aware of and realize that this
thought is unwholesome and accompanied with
unwholesome wanting (Lobha). No attempt should
be made to suppress this thought. With such awareness and realization, one will be able to prevent the
arising of frustration, disappointment or dissatisfaction when things do not turn out the way one had**

desired, such as the food not being as tasty as one had expected. On the other hand, if one lacks the awareness and realization of this thought, adverse feeling will follow.

(b) When one shows craving (Lobha) by thinking of oneself or one's loved ones as being superior to others, one is required to be aware of and realize that this thought is unwholesome, being accompanied with unwholesome wanting and conceit. With such awareness and realization, one will be able not only to prevent the arising of the adverse thought but also to lead one's life harmoniously, creatively and successfully.

(c) As previously stated, all things which one is experiencing daily in the ultimate sense of reality, have these basic characteristics: impermanence (Anicca), inability to retain their original existence (Dukkha) and non-self or being dependent upon their causes (Anattā). But one usually thinks that this ultimate reality which consists of Nāma and Rūpa is permanent (Nicca); is able to retain its original existence (Sukha) and has a "self", such as I, he, you and one's table (Attā). Such thinking, which is based on conventional reality, can be used in daily life, but if one blindly holds on to this idea, which is contrary to the ultimate reality with respect to the basic characteristics of existence, this means that already one has the wrong view or mental attachment in life (Micchādiṭṭhi). If this wrong view is allowed to accumulate more and more, suffering in life easily follows. Therefore, one is required to become aware of and realize this misconceived thinking, accompanied with wrong view, and this requirement prevents the arising of an intensified, blind attachment which can bring about suffering in life.

(d) **When one thinks of an undesirable object** such as someone who has caused one trouble, one often becomes dissatisfied or angry (Dosa). In this case, one is required to become aware of and realize this unwholesome thought, which is accompanied with dissatisfaction or anger (Dosa). But one should be careful not to set one's mind upon the undesirable object. Otherwise, dissatisfaction or anger will continue to arise. This is because the troublesome person who is the undesirable object of the thought, is the cause in stimulating the arising of the adverse and unwholesome thinking which is its effect. In short, one should become aware only of the thought which is accompanied with dissatisfaction, and not the undersirable object of the thought. In this way, one will be able to eliminate the cause of the adverse thinking as well as to relieve or do away with the dissatisfaction or anger.

(1.9.2) Awareness of wholesome thoughts

Awareness of wholesome thoughts will enrich one's life with wholesomeness and creativity, leading to the attainment of a happy and successful life.

How is one to know that one's wholesome thoughts are arising? This knowing can come about by just noting the major characteristics of the wholesome thoughts, which include the following:

- non-attachment or non-adhesion of mind to an object (Alobha)

- loving-kindness (Adosa or Mettā)

- understanding of the reality which is beneficial to one's life (Amoha)

At the time of one's wholesome thinking, one is required to become aware of and realize that this thought is wholesome.

In daily living, wholesome thoughts can manifest themselves in various ways such as:

(a) When one thinks of giving away one's material possessions for the purpose of helping others in need, this thought is wholesome and one should become aware of it.

(b) When one thinks of improving oneself by abstaining from verbal or body actions which are harmful or troublesome to others, such as refraining from telling lies or stealing, this thought is wholesome and one should become aware of it.

(c) When one thinks of cultivating mental development through Tranquil Meditation or Insight Meditation, this thought is wholesome and one should become aware of it.

(d) When one thinks of being modest and respectful to those who deserve it, this thought is wholesome and one should become aware of it.

(e) When one thinks of working for the good of the community, this thought is wholesome and one should become aware of it.

(f) When one thinks of extending one's own merits to others, this thought is wholesome and one should become aware of it.

(g) When one thinks of rejoicing in others' meritorious deeds, this thought is wholesome and one should become aware of it.

(h) When one thinks of disseminating the useful truth of life (Dhamma) for the purpose of relieving suffering and attaining a high level of happiness, this thought is wholesome and one should become aware of it.

(i) When one thinks of listening to or attending the teaching of the useful truth of life (Dhamma), this thought is wholesome and one should become aware of it.

(j) When one thinks of purifying one's view in life from misconceptions, this thought is wholesome and one should become aware of it.

In becoming aware of and realizing the thoughts which are wholesome, one's power of wholesomeness will be strengthened, leading to the attainment of a high level of subtle happiness in life.

(1.10) Cultivating awareness before going to sleep

After having been put to work all day long, one's body becomes tired and weak. Under this condition, one needs rest. Thus, at the time of going to bed, one is required to become aware of and realize that sleeping is a means of relieving physical discomfort or suffering. With awareness and realization, one will be in the position of preventing the arising of one's unwholesome wanting (Lobha) to sleep excessively and yet soundly. If this unwholesome wanting is allowed to run its course without its being satisfied, one will end up with restlessness, frustration or many other sleeping problems. **For example,** some people are wide awake most of the night simply because they want to sleep very badly without realizing that their unwholesome wanting to sleep is the condition which keeps them awake. If they are aware of the adverse effect of this wanting as well as the real purpose of sleeping, they will be able to overcome such unwholesome wanting and in this way, they will fall asleep easily and sleep soundly.

(2.) Specific experiences in daily life pertaining to each individual

In everyday life, some people have certain unwholesome experiences which bring about misery in life with no relief in sight, like someone who cannot swim and is on the verge of drowning. The application of Direct Awareness in dealing with problems is like a life preserver preventing one from drowning and enabling that person to reach the shore safely.

These unwholesome experiences are of various types. But only the ones which happen most often are covered here, along with corrective measures through the application of Direct Awareness to overcome them.

The diagram below illustrates seven specific experiences in daily life pertaining to each individual as follows:

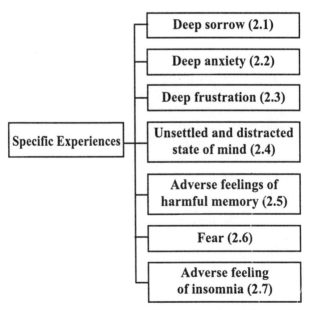

The details of these 7 specific experiences will be highlighted as follows:

(2.1) Experiencing deep sorrow due to the separation from a loved one or loss of status or property to which one is greatly attached

Due to this unwholesome experience, people can hardly eat or sleep. Under this adverse condition, one should realize that such separation from the loved one is a common occurrence in accordance with the Law of Cause and Effect. In fact, one's grief is caused by one's mental attachment to the thought that the loved one will remain with him/her always.

Apart from this, one should further realize that, no matter how sorrowful one is, the loved one who has passed away will never return to him/her and that sorrow is not helpful at all, but instead, can adversely affect one's health.

The most effective way of coping with this grief is to become aware of and realize this adverse mental state directly in the form of "Nāma is sorrowful" and not "I am sorrowful". One should not concern oneself with this mental object of separation because this object stimulates the arising of the sorrow. One should also keep in mind that this sorrow is an ultimate reality and the realization of it could eventually lead to the attainment of "Perpetual Happiness" (Nibbāna). As one frequently and regularly becomes aware of this adverse mental condition, its unwholesome strength will be lessened and phased out in the end without any suppression or wanting it to disappear.

(2.2) Experiencing deep anxiety and worry due to the unreasonable expectation that one's loved one or the things which one possesses with great attachment, will meet with adverse consequences

Under this adverse condition, one should realize that all occurrences must be dependent on their causes in accordance with the Law of Cause and Effect and such overanxiety and overworry, based on unreasonable expectations, run contrary to this Law. **For example,** when a dear daughter travels by car to a remote town, her parents may become very anxious and worried about her safety, unreasonably expecting that she might have an accident even though the chance of it happening is quite slim.

Thus, one should realize that one's own thoughts are unreasonable and do not touch reality, and that one's overanxiety and overworry are caused by one's own craving in the form of excessive mental attachment to the desired object.

The most effective way of coping with this overanxiety and overworry is to become aware of and realize the adverse mental state directly in the form of "Nāma is very anxious and very worried" instead of "I am very anxious and very worried". **One should not concern oneself with the mental object of the unreasonable expectation because this object stimulates the arising of overanxiety and overworry.** One should also keep in mind that these adverse feelings are ultimate reality and that realization of them could eventually lead to the attainment of "Perpetual Happiness" (Nibbāna). As one frequently and regularly becomes aware of these adverse conditions, their unwholesome strength will be lessened and phased out in the end without any suppression or wanting them to disappear. In this way, one will enhance one's wisdom in effectively coping with these problems on the basis of reason and reality.

(2.3) Experiencing deep frustration and irritation due to one's desire being seriously obstructed by others

Some people, when they are being obstructed, especially by persons whom they dislike, so as to prevent them from fulfilling their desire, will become very frustrated and irritated just as if a fire were burning within themselves. Under this adverse condition, one should realize that the frustration and irritation are basically caused by oneself, by means of reacting with hostility and being blindly attached to the undesirable object in the form of that person who causes the obstruction. If one is able to cultivate one's wisdom effectively, one will be in a position to deter or prevent the arising of the unwholesome mind (frustration and irritation) by replacing the adverse feelings with wisdom, just as the light dispels the darkness.

The most effective way of coping with these frustrations and irritations is to become aware of and realize the adverse mental state directly in the form of "Nāma is very frustrated and very irritated" instead of

"I am very frustrated and very irritated". One should not concern oneself with the mental object causing the serious obstruction because this object stimulates the arising of deep frustration and irritation. One should also keep in mind that these adverse feelings are ultimate reality, and their realization could eventually lead to the attainment of "Perpetual Happiness" (Nibbāna). As one frequently and regularly becomes aware of these adverse mental conditions, their unwholesome strength will be lessened and phased out in the end without any suppression or wanting them to disappear.

(2.4) Experiencing an unsettled and distracted state of mind due to one's conflicting desires

In everyday life, people ordinarily let their own unwholesome wanting or craving (Lobha) run its course in the form of desiring various objects (things or persons). If they lack awareness and wisdom in directing this defilement (Kilesa) of mind, their unwholesome wanting or greediness will be boundless. This is like a plastic bag with an open bottom; no matter how hard one tries to fill it, it can never be completely filled. Some people have the desire to acquire more than one thing and when they fulfill their desire for one thing and miss out on another, they still have the urge to fulfill their unsatisfied desire. Under this condition, their desires are in conflict with each other in the sense that one desire is being fulfilled to the exclusion of the other desire, and these conflicting desires give rise to an unsettled and distracted state of mind. **For example,** many Thai students want to go overseas for further studies but when they arrive at their destinations, those who are lacking in awareness become homesick because they are not accustomed to the new environment and miss various desirable objects which can only be obtained in Thailand, such as certain types of Thai food. They then want to return home so as to fulfill their desire for these objects which are not available overseas, but are not in a position to do so. This gives rise to an unsettled and distracted state of mind.

Another example of this adverse state of mind can be seen in the purchase of a T.V. set. Dick wants to buy brand X of a T.V. set because of its design, but at the instigation of his friend, ends up buying brand Y. After the purchase, he may regret it and want to go back to brand X, but is not able to do so. This conflicting condition gives rise to an unsettled and distracted state of mind due to one's lack of awareness.

The most effective way of coping with this mental unsettlement and distraction is to become aware of and realize the adverse mental state directly, in the form of "Nāma is unsettled and distracted" and not "I am unsettled and distracted". One should keep in mind that these adverse feelings are ultimate reality and the realization of them could eventually lead to the attainment of "Perpetual Happiness" (Nibbāna). One should also realize that an unsettled and distracted state of mind basically comes from letting unwholesome wanting or craving freely run its course , especially in desiring something which cannot be attained, and from lack of awareness and wisdom, which prevents one from understanding that certain desires are in conflict with each other and cannot be satisfied at the same time. Apart from this, even the objects which fulfill one's desires, by nature, arise and fall away all the time in accordance with their causes. One should be aware of these disires so as not to let their arising be in conflict with each other to the extent of bringing about mental unsettlement and distraction in life. As one frequently and regularly becomes aware of these adverse mental conditions, their unwholesome strength will be lessened and phased out in the end without any suppression or wanting them to disappear.

(2.5) Experiencing adverse feelings of harmful memory

Some people have a harmful memory and are unable to erase their mental fixation on horrible or frightening sights. Under this condition, one should not direct one's mind to the object of harmful memory, but instead, one should become directly aware of the adverse feeling of the harmful memory. In this way, the adverse feeling will be automatically relieved. This is because **if one tries to direct one's mind towards the object which is the cause of the harmful memory, it will further intensify the arising of the adverse feeling through increasing the harmful memory,** but if one is directly aware of the adverse feeling which is the effect, one will be in the position of doing away with the adverse feeling (effect) which in turn makes the cause (object) lose its strength and eventually phase out. This awareness of the adverse feeling is like a policeman watching over (awareness) a thief (adverse feeling) so that the latter will eventually go away. Without having been watched, the thief would have become more daring. Another analogy: when the owner of a house is fast asleep (lacking awareness), a burglar (adverse feeling) can have a free hand in stealing the household belongings, but if the owner is awake and watchful (having awareness), the burglar usually leaves.

The most effective way to cope with this adverse feeling of harmful memory is to become aware of and realize the adverse mental state directly, in the form of "Nāma feels agitated" instead of "I feel agitated". One should also keep in mind that this agitated feeling is an ultimate reality, and the realization of this ultimate reality could eventually lead to the attainment of "Perpetual Happiness" (Nibbāna). As one frequently and regularly becomes aware of this adverse mental condition, its unwholesome strength will be lessened and phased out in the end without any suppression or wanting it to disappear.

(2.6) Experiencing fear

Some people are so obsessed by their own fear that they lead a very miserable life, full of suffering. One should realize that everything, in the ultimate sense, consists basically of Rūpa and/or Nāma, arising and falling away all the time. A person's fear is basically caused by his/her own mental creation without the realization of the ultimate reality. This can be illustrated by the following situation: when a little ant walks past us, we hardly feel anything. But if it is magnified by means of a microscope and becomes a frightful sight, we could easily become afraid. Our fear of something or someone usually stems from our thoughts, which have been blinded, distorted and exaggerated by our own ignorance (Moha) of ultimate reality. Actually, any frightening sights, in the ultimate sense, are nothing more than aggregations of light so that what we supposedly see is only a conventional reality based upon a mental illusion, and lacks awareness and wisdom. This is evident in the case of people watching a movie and reacting to it emotionally. It is especially true when children are watching a fictitious horror movie and become very frightened due to their ignorance (Moha). In the ultimate sense, they can never have any reaction. This is simply because what one sees is nothing but the mental illusion caused by a rapid movement of each picture frame at 18 frames per second; an aggregation of the transmitted light and the ignorant mind.

From the above illustration, it can be seen that with the awareness and realization of what basically causes the fear, one's fear will be lessened or eliminated. One is also required to become aware of this adverse mental state directly in the form of "Nāma is afraid" instead of "I am afraid" and realize that it is impermanent, arising and falling away all the time. One should also keep in mind that this adverse feeling is an ultimate reality, and that the realization of it could eventually lead to the attainment of "Perpetual Happiness" (Nibbāna).

(2.7) Experiencing the adverse feeling of insomnia due to one's mental wandering or being excessively influenced by one's own craving

Some people's lives have been seriously affected by insomnia. The more earnestly one wants to sleep, the stronger one's insomnia can become. This is because when one falls under the excessive influence of one's unwholesome wanting to sleep, such wanting is likely to prevent sleep. As a result, one will become frustrated and irritated and this in turn further enhances the insomnia. **For example,** a government official in Bangkok went to see a doctor for an annual physical checkup and was advised by the doctor to have at least seven hours of sleep a day. Otherwise, he was told, he would end up with a heart illness. That night, he wanted very badly to sleep, in order to comply with the doctor's advice, but it turned out that he had trouble falling asleep and then kept waking up during the night. Later, he received advice from a lecturer of Buddhist Science at our Buddhist Science Center that he should decrease his excessive desire to sleep in order to be able to sleep better. As a result of putting this advice into practice, he automatically solved his problem of insomnia. For this reason, one should become aware of an excessive desire to sleep, so as to cope effectively with insomnia.

In some cases, people are mentally attached to the happy feeling resulting from sleeping, so that they want to excessively maintain this pleasantness. When, after sleeping throughout the night, they do not feel as happy as they had expected, they become dissatisfied. Because of this unfulfilled excessive wanting, they have the misconception that sleep is the way to attain a happy feeling in accordance with their desire. But, when they do not experience the same happy feeling from sleeping as they did before, they delude themselves into thinking that they did not sleep at all, or hardly slept, even though they really slept throughout the night. This is called pseudo-insomnia. The effective way of coping with this problem of pseudo-insomnia is to become directly aware of this excessive wanting to maintain a happy feeling from sleeping, especially at the time of its arising.

At the time of going to bed, some people's minds wander a lot, changing from one object to the other. **In this case,** one should be aware of the mental wandering directly, and not the objects of the mental wandering, and at the same time, one should realize that "Nāma is wandering" instead of "I am wandering".

d. CONCLUSION

With respect to the general method of applying Direct Awareness in daily life as described above under sections **(1.)** and **(2.)**, one is required to practice regularly, as much as the opportunity allows. If this method is properly implemented, one will certainly reap very substantial benefits in life. In addition to being able to effectively overcome the above problems in daily life, one will be able to enhance one's level of awareness and wisdom, which could eventually lead to the eradication of all sufferings in life and to the attainment of "Perpetual Happiness" (Nibbāna).

6. General method of practicing Direct Awareness at a proper place for Insight Meditation

The general method of practicing Direct Awareness at a proper place for Insight Meditation is the first introductory step in the practice of Insight Meditation. Since the method requires a great deal of explanation, it is felt that covering this subject under a new chapter will be more advisable in facilitating reading as well as understanding. Therefore, the detailed descriptions are highlighted under IV. PROCEDURES AND APPLICATIONS, Chapters 16-21.

IV. PROCEDURES AND APPLICATIONS

CHAPTER 16

INSIGHT MEDITATION– OVERCOMING DISSATISFACTION OR ANGER (DOSA)

1. Introduction

When Dosa, such as anger, fear, annoyance or frustration arises, unpleasantness is experienced. In the natural (but unwholesome) desire to be rid of this adverse feeling, one often wishes that it would simply disappear. But the more one tries to reject and run away from it, the worse the situation becomes, because the real and underlying causes of Dosa still continue to produce their effects. When one does not get what is wanted, he becomes even more agitated.

Some people unwisely and improperly try to overcome the mental suffering caused by Dosa, by drinking alcohol or taking drugs. Instead of the condition being relieved, suffering is likely to increase. Some may even resort to committing suicide.

In attempting to solve the problem, some seek advice from those who have gained considerable experience in life, or read certain books which deal with how to cope with life's problems. Even though these methods can be helpful at times, they do not touch the core of the problem directly and deeply. As a result, they are not as effective as they should be.

The problem can be more effectively confronted and dealt with through the use of Insight Meditation. Insight Meditation is concerned with Direct Awareness of problems as they really are at the present moment. This meditation not only can overcome mental problems on a lasting and comprehensive basis, but can also eventually prevent the arising of other kinds of problems as well.

2. What is to be specifically gained from this Insight Meditation

Apart from attaining the general benefits explained previously in Chapter 11, the effective practice of Insight Meditation will bring about the following:

a. The elimination of unwholesomeness of mind, such as wrong views (Diṭṭhi) and unwholesome wanting, which aggravate Dosa.

b. The ability to cope with Dosa with wisdom, subtlety and calmness, without intensifying its adverse effect.

c. The development of wisdom for full and direct realization of Dosa at the present moment, resulting in the relief of suffering in the future.

d. The ability to enrich the mind with wisdom, subtle happiness, blissfulness and tranquility, which will automatically and naturally prevent Dosa from arising.

e. The acquisition of the right technique of living through the direct and full awareness of Dosa as a means to eventually attaining "Perpetual Happiness" (NIBBĀNA).

3. Nature of Dosa

The theoretical understanding of the real nature of Dosa is the first useful step in the practice of Insight Meditation, and will helpfully lead to its full realization. If the meditator does not really know what Dosa is, how can the full realization of its nature be achieved? It is not possible. By comparison, if one does not know a written foreign language, how can he read and understand a book written in that language? It is really impossible.

Dosa is one of the three basic unwholesome defilements (Kilesa) inherent in the minds of living beings. It reacts with hostility against undesirable objects and works against our wholesome mind, just like an enemy from within.

Dosa manifests itself through:

a) Body: such as physical attack or injury.

b) Verbal Expression: such as scolding or cursing.

c) Mind: such as worrying or agitation.

Adverse Effects of Dosa (Anger, fear, annoyance or frustration)

As a burning match can cause hundreds of houses to burn down completely, "The fire of Dosa" can likewise ruin one's life and property.

If Dosa occurs regularly, its intensity will be increased to the extent that the mind will be burnt up by the fire of Dosa and will eventually explode like a volcanic eruption.

A person who is susceptible to Dosa can be compared to a mind with a chronic ulcerated wound. Whenever one becomes displeased with something or somebody, it will be just as if one's wound were being disturbed, and one will respond most strongly.

In short, Dosa adversely affects both physical and mental health. It shortens one's life and increases one's suffering, thereby making it extremely difficult to live happily and successfully.

The subject of Dosa, which is essential to the practice of Insight Meditation, is clarified under the following headings:

a. General characteristics of Dosa

b. Specific characteristics of Dosa

c. Causes of Dosa

d. Relationship between Dosa and mental suffering

e. Manifestation of Dosa

a. General characteristics of Dosa: Anicca, Dukkha and Anattā

Dosa arises as a result of its causes only and nothing else. When these causes are forceful enough, Dosa will occur automatically; this happening is inevitable. The above can be compared to an electric generator which will produce electricity upon reaching a certain level of performance. As the power of the generator is reduced, the lights will dim; as the causes of Dosa lessen, their effects will correspondingly fall away.

This is also evident in the case where a stone is thrown upward in the air. The throwing is the cause, and the ascent of the stone up into the air is its effect. The throwing produces the force to uplift the stone, but as this force completely diminishes, the ascent of the stone ceases. The same is true in the case of Dosa. Suffering (the effect), caused by Dosa, will fall away as the force produced by its causes ceases to exist. This phenomenon can be clearly seen in the case of thunder. When the sound of thunder is heard, one may become frightened, resulting in Dosa and mental suffering. As the sound stops, so does the fear (Dosa). In this case, the thunderous noise is the cause which gives rise to Dosa and mental suffering as its effect.

For this reason, it can be concluded that Dosa results from the powers of its causes, and that this effect will fall away as the force produced by these causes loses its strength. This manifestation reflects the three basic characteristics of Dosa; namely, Anicca (impermanence), Dukkha (inability to retain its original existence) and Anattā (non-self or being dependent upon its causes which means that no effect can come into existence without cause. Its arising is dependent only upon multiple causes).

(1.) Anicca characteristic

Dosa is impermanent (Anicca), due to its arising and falling away rapidly and successively. If one just remembers past experiences of Dosa, such as frustration, dissatisfaction, anger, etc. he will be reminded that Dosa is transitory.

Nevertheless, this awareness of its characteristic of impermanence is not keen enough because one becomes aware of the falling away only after the Dosa is no longer in existence. In actuality, when Dosa arises, it falls away rapidly to be succeeded by its next arising and so on. **The extreme rapidity of its successive arising and falling away misleads people into thinking that Dosa remains all the time.** This can be compared to the case of a neon light. Usually, we notice the falling away of a neon light only after it goes out, but this observation is not in accordance with its true reality. Why not? Simply because when the neon light is glowing, it does not mean that the light always remains stable. In reality, the neon light arises and falls away rapidly and successively up to about 48 times a second, but since each succession is extremely rapid (Santati), it creates the false impression that the neon light is on all the time.

When Dosa arises, it falls away rapidly, reflecting its transitoriness. Without the effective practice of Insight Meditation, one wrongly thinks that one's Dosa has not fallen away during the time it is being experienced.

With the right understanding of the impermanent characteristic of Dosa, one's mind will harmonize with Dosa's nature. The mind will be prevented from being in conflict with the characteristic of impermanence, resulting in the relief or elimination of mental suffering as well as physical pain which is caused by Dosa.

(2.) Dukkha characteristic

Dosa is characterized by its inability to retain its original existence. Whenever it arises, it must directly fall away. Due to its impermanent characteristic, Dosa cannot remain as it is. And so, anything which is impermanent (Anicca) is Dukkha. When experiencing Dosa, people often feel that Dosa lasts longer than it actually does. This results in an unpleasant feeling. But if one is well aware of the true Dukkha characteristic, one will be much relieved. Actually, Dosa falls away in accordance with its causes, but the rapid and successive arising and falling away tend to obscure its true characteristic.

(3.) Anattā characteristic

Whenever there is Dosa, it is characterized by arising and falling away according to its causes. It arises because of the causes and falls away as these causes no longer exist. Dosa cannot and will not be forced to fall away as long as its causes still remain.

Whatever names are given to describe Dosa, in actuality it does not contain any symbolization. This conventional reality can be compared to the sweetness of sugar; no matter what this inherent taste is called or how it is symbolized, the naming of it does not exist in the sugar. Even the supposed word "sweetness" can never be found in the sugar itself. The sweetness is itself inherent in the sugar by nature without any symbolization or imagination.

Thus, when there is Dosa, its real nature does not depend upon description or symbolization of it. **For example,** when we say "I am angry", there is no such thing as "I" existing in the feeling of Dosa.

b. Specific characteristics of Dosa

Dosa is specifically characterized by an unwholesome nature, which in turn reacts with hostility towards an undesirable object. The details of its nature have been highlighted previously in this chapter, under the heading "Nature of Dosa".

c. Causes of Dosa

There are five major causes of Dosa:

(1.) Habitually getting angry (Dosa Chasayata)

(2.) Lack of thorough and wise thinking (Akampirapa-katita)

(3.) Lack of knowledge of the right technique of living (Uppasutta).

(4.) Experiencing any undesirable object (Anittā rammaṇa smayoko)

(5.) **Experiencing an object which creates Dosa in these ten specific ways (Arkatvat smayoko):**

(5.1) **We are angry with another person, thinking that he did** something unpleasant or harmful **to us,** such as having insulted us.

(5.2) We are angry with another person, thinking that he **is now doing** something unpleasant or harmful **to us,** such as stealing our property.

(5.3) We are angry with another person, thinking that he **will in the future do** something unpleasant or harmful **to us,** such as winning our beloved's heart.

(5.4) We are angry with another person, thinking that he **did** something unpleasant or harmful **to our loved one,** such as having injured our son.

(5.5) We are angry with another person, thinking that he **is now doing** something unpleasant or harmful **to our loved one,** such as scolding our child.

(5.6) We are angry with another person, thinking that he **will do** something unpleasant or harmful **to our loved one,** such as openly disclosing the personal secrets of a close relative.

(5.7) We are angry with another person, thinking that he **has done** something beneficial to or has created a good relationship with **someone we dislike,** such as having lent money to him.

(5.8) We are angry with another person, thinking that he **is doing** something beneficial to or creating good relationship with **someone we dislike,** such as financing someone we dislike who is on the verge of bankruptcy.

(5.9) We are angry with another person, thinking that he **will do** something beneficial to or will create a good relationship with **someone we dislike,** such as giving praise to him.

(5.10) We feel angry for no good reason at all. **For example,** if we happen to stumble over the root of a tree, we may direct our anger against the root by kicking at it, resulting in more pain.

d. Relationship between Dosa and Mental Suffering

Mental suffering is a type of Vedanā Cetasika (literally a "feeling" mental constituent) which manifests itself in the mind (Citta) accompanied with Dosa. Dosa is a kind of mental constituent arising within the mind accompanied with mental suffering. Therefore, mental suffering and Dosa coexist in the same mind. Both of them arise and fall away concurrently and have a common, undesirable object of mind. They also share the same "base". Mental suffering gives rise to Dosa, and Dosa gives rise to mental suffering at the same time. Each is the cause and effect of the other. They mutually support each other like a three-legged stool. If one of its legs is missing, the stool will collapse. Similarly, mental suffering cannot arise without the support of the power of Dosa, or vice versa.

Although mental suffering and Dosa arise together, sometimes the intensity of one is more dominant than the other. For example, when one is in mourning, this deep sorrow is mental suffering existing in the mind accompanied with Dosa. Even though Dosa arises simultaneously, it is nevertheless dominated by the more powerful mental suffering. Sometimes, Dosa is more powerful than the suffering, such as when one becomes angry after being hit or verbally abused.

e. Manifestation of Dosa

Dosa is classified into two types as follows:

(1.) "Persuasive" Dosa

This Dosa occurs as a result of persuasion which manifests itself physically, verbally and mentally. **For instance,** Mr. A. easily becomes angry with Mr. C. after having been persuaded by Mr. B. to dislike Mr. C. Sometimes, persuasion is used with hostile gestures or other bodily actions. Apart from this, mental persuasion can come from one's own mind. For instance, Mrs. D. recalls an unfavorable incident, which in turn makes her furious. In short, persuasion can come from oneself, through other persons or through environmental factors.

(2.) "Non-persuasive" Dosa

This Dosa occurs not as a result of any persuasion, but is conditioned to arise in one's mind automatically and habitually. Some people are full of anger and hatred, which are extremely difficult to control. When the mind with such Dosa comes into contact with an undesirable object, one may tremble with anger, use abusive language or erupt in violence.

4. Meditation Practice

a. What should be kept in mind

(1.) The meditator should realize that the purpose of practice is to become fully aware of the nature of Dosa. Thus, one should not try to get rid of it merely because one desires to. This desire, in itself, is one kind of defilement (Kilesa) of mind adversely affecting the effectiveness of Insight Meditation.

Craving or desire for the elimination of Dosa without the realization of its true nature i.e., its arising and falling away, is not in harmony with nature's Law of Cause and Effect. Wanting to recover from mental suffering caused by Dosa and failing to do so further aggravates suffering and agitation.

(2.) In the practice of Direct Awareness of Dosa, one is required to be objective and not subjective in order to be mindful of Dosa as it really is. Furthermore, the practice does not involve any thinking, symbolizing or imagining, for the simple reason that the meditator is, in fact, directly experiencing the suffering caused by Dosa.

One must not concern oneself with craving for knowledge of the reality of Dosa in the development of Direct Awareness, because this craving is unwholesome and will adversely affect wisdom which is wholesome and which is essential for effective results.

b. What will the practice lead to

Those who have developed the skill of Direct Awareness of Dosa are able to be aware of it even prior to its arising. As a result, Dosa cannot arise, and is replaced instead by wisdom developed through Insight Meditation.

c. How to develop the skill of Direct Awareness

(1.) Stage I - Mindfulness of the occurrence of Dosa

The development of this skill begins with the awareness of Dosa at the time of its arising, the details of which are highlighted in the previous section. It is important to note that Direct Awareness concerns itself only with Dosa, without considering the event that led to its arising. If one tries to be attentive to the event, such as separation from a loved one, loss of property, or verbal abuse, one can only make Dosa worse because these events are in themselves undesirable objects.

Beginners tend to be neglectful or careless in the practice of Direct Awareness of Dosa. This lack of mindfulness is a common occurrence, because of inexperience and lack of skill; therefore, one should not get discouraged nor blame oneself.

To be effective, one should practice Direct Awareness in a natural manner without overexertion or underexertion of effort. This can be compared to tuning a violin, in which the right tones can be attained only with the proper adjustment of the strings. If the strings are too loose or too tight, the violin will be out of tune. Likewise, in Insight Meditation, one should not exert one's efforts too strongly or too weakly. If one mentally focuses on the object of meditation too strongly, one will get tired easily and sometimes even feel uncomfortable or dizzy. On the other hand, if the focus is too weak, awareness will be lost, thereby losing the effectiveness of the meditation practice. **The "Middle Way"** practice of Direct Awareness is therefore recommended.

The Direct Awareness of Dosa involves the close and immediate mental follow-up of its occurrence as it really is at the present moment. One must not be mindful of Dosa which occurred in the past or which will arise in the future.

In everyday life, it may not be possible or appropriate to practice Direct Awareness of the reality of life at all times. For instance, when a high level of concentration is required, such as driving a car along a road with sharp curves, this practice is not advisable.

As mindfulness develops through the constant practice of Direct Awareness, one will become more alert and skillful in becoming aware of Dosa.

As a result, one will realize a brightening of the mind and a contentment in life never before experienced. Prior to the devlopment of awareness, Dosa is allowed to run its course, thereby incurring much suffering. With awareness of Dosa, one is able to cope with it wisely and subtly. This is the wonder of Insight Meditation practice, and one begins to taste the unique value of Insight Meditation.

(2.) Stage II - Mindfulness of the phasing out of Dosa

As one continues to practice Direct Awareness of Dosa effectively at the moment of its occurrence as described in Stage I, the degree of Dosa will not only automatically lose its strength but can also be directly realized without resorting to the use of symbols or imagination. It is just like the tasting of sugar, in which one directly experiences its sweetness without any description or imagination.

As one persistently and closely follows the decreasing strength of Dosa through effective Direct Awareness, one will creatively realize that the suffering caused by Dosa will eventually phase out. As a result, the meditator will achieve a high level of confidence as never before experienced because of the realization that the occurrence of Dosa is not lasting. The occurrence and phasing out of Dosa correspondingly depend upon its causes, consistent with the Law of Cause and Effect.

Even through mere analysis, one can realize that Dosa will eventually phase out. But if one practices this Direct Awareness as well, one will be most certain that the suffering caused by Dosa will surely and finally cease to exist.

When one thus achieves such effectiveness in Direct Awareness of Dosa, one will be better equipped to prudently, calmly and confidently cope with suffering, since more confidence and a higher level of wisdom in life are attained. If the suffering caused by Dosa continues to arise, one will not turn to self-injury, as do people who lack awareness and wisdom, nor will one direct ill feelings toward others. Despite the suffering, one will not become depressed or gloomy simply because wisdom will have been strengthened through the effective practice of Direct Awareness as previously mentioned. For this reason, even at the time of confrontation with Dosa, wisdom will guide one in effectively following through, just as a rudder is used to successfully steer a boat through rough seas.

(3.) Stage III - Mindfulness of the cycle of Dosa

After having successfully practiced Direct Awareness of Dosa as it arises and as it phases out, the meditator will begin to be fully and directly aware of the natural process concerning this sequence.

As one gains more and more experience, one will develop wisdom to the extent of directly realizing Dosa just prior to its occurence. This wisdom replaces Dosa by eliminating the causes which give rise to its occurrence.

5. CONCLUSION

The wisdom gained from Insight Meditation practice is very useful in everyday life. Without this practice, one usually ends up with Dosa when faced with anything undesirable, such as verbal abuse, separation from loved ones, or not getting what has been wished for. Those who have effectively practiced this Insight Meditation will be able to prevent the occurrence of Dosa. Even if this stage is not reached, one can at least lessen Dosa's severity and cause it to diminish and phase out in the end.

Consequently, those who practice Insight Meditation will gain real and special benefits in life. This will ultimately lead to "Perpetual Happiness" (Nibbāna), in which all sufferings will be absolutely and permanently eliminated.

CHAPTER 17
INSIGHT MEDITATION-
COPING WITH MENTAL SUFFERING

1. Introduction

The practice of Insight Meditation in coping with mental suffering follows procedures similar to those described under the previous Chapter 16, "Insight Meditation-Overcoming Dissatisfaction or Anger (Dosa)". This is because both Dosa and mental suffering are ultimate reality and coexist in the same mind. In addition, they arise and fall away and at the same time have a common, undesirable object of mind.

The basic difference between mental suffering and Dosa lies in their respective specific characteristics. This is the basis for treating them separately even though the procedures of practicing Direct Awareness are the same for each. Nevertheless, whether mental suffering or Dosa is to become an object of Insight Meditation depends on the intensity of each at that particular time of practice. If mental suffering is more pronounced than Dosa, the former should be used as the object of Insight Meditation. On the other hand, if Dosa is more intensified than mental suffering, Dosa should be used instead.

Because of the similarity of practice procedures, explanations under certain headings will be left out to avoid unnecessary repetition.

2. What is to be specifically gained from this Insight Meditation

The specific benefits are similar to those mentioned in Chapter 16, "Insight Meditation-Overcoming Dissatisfaction or Anger (Dosa)"

3. Nature of mental suffering

Mental suffering is a type of Vedanā (feeling) Cetasika (mental constituent). Vedanā Cetasika is classified into three categories: pleasant feeling (Sukha-vedanā), painful feeling (Dukkha-vedanā) and indifferent feeling (Upekkhā-vedanā). The pleasant feeling is further subdivided into physical and mental pleasant feelings, while the painful feeling is similarly broken down into physical and mental painful feelings. In the case of an indifferent feeling (Upekkhā-vedanā), there is neither a pleasant nor a painful feeling.

The subject of mental suffering, which is essential to the practice of Insight Meditation, is clarified under the following headings:

    a. General characteristics of mental suffering
    b. Specific characteristics of mental suffering

    c. Causes of mental suffering
    d. Manifestation of mental suffering

a. General characteristics of mental suffering: Anicca, Dukkha, Anattā

Please see the detailed explanations under the same section of the previous Chapter 16.

b. Specific characteristics of mental suffering

Mental suffering is specifically characterized by its unwholesome nature, and is a mental constituent that mentally and unpleasantly feels an undesirable object. This is a painful feeling which adversely affects one's mind by causing sorrow or grief. **For example,** when a loved one passes away, one suffers mentally in the form of mental agitation or anguish, based upon the painful feeling of coming into contact with an undesirable object. This mental suffering can further cause mental illness.

An unwholesome nature is a harmful condition which produces painful and undesirable effects. Under this adverse condition, one is very likely to come into contact with unpleasant and undesirable objects.

c. Causes of mental suffering

The causes comprise two major types:

(1.) Personal loss

(a.) Loss of a loved one, such as a parent, wife, husband or other relatives.

(b.) Loss of property, status or position. **For example,** loss of possessions through fire or theft.

(c.) Loss of health.

(d.) The deterioration of personal qualities.

For example: Changing

from	to
being honest	being dishonest
telling the truth	telling a lie
being a non-drinker	being an alchoholic
being constructive	being destructive
having the right view of the reality of life	having the wrong view of the reality of life

(2.) The existence of the mind accompanied with Dosa

When the mind is accompanied with Dosa in such forms as dissatisfaction, anger and frustration, mental suffering will inevitably arise.

d. Manifestation of mental suffering

There are various degrees of mental suffering as follows:

(1.) Sorrow

A sorrowful feeling within one's mind is a type of mental suffering of slight degree. This can be compared to cooking oil being heated in a frying pan.

(2.) Weeping sorrow

Mental suffering which is intensified to the extent of causing one to weep or lament. This can be compared to hot cooking oil which is bubbling.

(3.) Grief-stricken sorrow

Mental suffering which greatly disturbs one's mind to the extent of causing one to behave abnormally. This high degree of mental suffering can create physical pain for others as well as for oneself. **For example,** when mental suffering reaches this critical stage, some people resort to injuring or destroying themselves by knocking their head senselessly against a wall, throwing themselves on the floor, kicking and cursing, or committing suicide. This suffering may even cause one to physically hurt or kill others.

(4.) The most severe sorrow accompanied by acute Dosa

Mental suffering of the highest degree, in which one feels as if the mind has completely withered away. There is no will-power for one to combat this most adverse feeling.

This suffering can manifest itself in such forms as people being stricken dumb, blacking out, becoming psychotic, or committing suicide. This acute suffering is likely to happen to those who unexpectedly face a great loss in life. **For example,** if one experiences an incurable illness, the sudden passing away of his dearest one, or complete destruction of his property by flood or fire, the most severe sorrow accompanied by acute Dosa may result. This can be compared to cooking oil which is smoking and burning away.

It should be noted that even the right understanding of Buddhist Science (BUDDHIST DHAMMA) is helpful in relieving or preventing mental suffering. Furthermore, if one is able to practice Insight Meditation to the extent of being able to control and limit mental suffering, through the Direct Awareness of it, the suffering can be arrested without the use of any mental force of concentration. This comes about due to one's full awareness of the characteristics of mental suffering as they occur each moment. As a result of this full awareness, one will attain a subtle level of pleasure and happiness as never before experienced.

4. Meditation practice

The practice procedures described under the previous Chapter 16, can also be applied here.

5. Conclusion

Please refer to the concluding section of Chapter 16.

CHAPTER 18

INSIGHT MEDITATION–
COPING WITH PHYSICAL PAIN

1. Introduction

To all human beings, physical pain is inescapable; some even suffer miserably throughout their lives due to ill health. As a result of the physical pain, mental suffering follows, thereby aggravating the condition. This is clearly evident among many hospital patients, who often moan and groan and react to pain intensely with much agitation and frustration. This occurs because they lack the right technique to cope adequately with physical pain. But those who have effectively practiced Insight Meditation are able to get rid of the mental suffering which is caused by physical pain; they are able to relieve physical pain and to face their afflictions wisely and tolerantly.

Sometimes people who have never before experienced serious physical injury suddenly meet with an accident, causing unexpected great pain. Some may damage or even lose part of their body and suffer physically and/or mentally throughout the rest of their lives. If they are well prepared to face the physical pain through the practice of Insight Meditation, suffering will be considerably relieved and some may even be able to lead more useful and significant lives. Even those who have just begun to practice Insight Meditation are often able to deal effectively with physical pain as well as develop wisdom despite their suffering.

There are many who have never suffered from serious physical injury during their lifetime. But there is no guarantee that they will continue to be free from such suffering. Therefore, one should be ready, through the practice of Insight Meditation, to meet wisely with any adverse situations that may arise in the future.

Those who have never suffered major physical pain still experience minor physical pain in the course of everyday life, such as headaches, digestive upsets, elimination distress or muscle tension. Although such pain may be tolerable and of comparatively little importance, one should not overlook its significance. If we are not aware of its true nature, the pain can unknowingly give rise to the accumulation of defilements (Kilesa). This calls for the practice of Insight Meditation, which enables one to be aware of the real nature of pain and makes life happier, more peaceful and successful, thereby eventually leading to the attainment of "Perpetual Happiness" (Nibbāna).

2. What is to be specifically gained from this Insight Meditation

In addition to the general benefits described previously in Chapter 11, the effective practice of Insight Meditation will yield the following:

a. The prevention of mental suffering caused by physical pain.

b. Elimination of an unwholesome mind which causes delusion or self-deception to the extent of aggravating one's physical pain.

c. The handling of physical pain with subtle wisdom as it occurs.

d. The attainment of wisdom in Direct Awareness of physical pain at the time of its occurrence, the promotion of better physical health, and the ability to cope effectively with physical pain in the future.

e. The acquisition of the right technique of living by direct and full awareness of physical pain as a means of eventually achieving "Perpetual Happiness" (Nibbāna).

3. Nature of physical pain

There are 3 basic kinds of feelings (Vedanā): pleasant, unpleasant and indifferent. Physical pain is an unpleasant feeling. **The specific characteristic of all Vedanā is that it experiences the objects of the six senses in terms of pleasantness, unpleasantness or indifference:** i.e., visible object, audible object, odorous object, taste object, bodily contact object, and mental contact object. **For example,** when the body comes into contact with the softness of a pillow, a pleasant feeling (Sukha-vedanā) will arise. Such a pleasant feeling is one characteristic of Vedanā. When something excessively hot touches the body, physical pain (Dukkha-vedanā) results. This unpleasantness is another kind of Vedanā. The third kind of Vedanā is an indifferent feeling (Upekkhā-vedanā), which is neither pleasant nor unpleasant. The details of Vedanā have been highlighted in Chapter 17, under "Nature of mental suffering."

Dukkha-vedanā, the unpleasant feeling, pertains not only to physical pain and/or suffering but also to mental suffering.

Although the nature of physical pain is a subject of very great detail, only certain essential points which are fundamental to the practice of Insight Meditation will be covered under the following headings:

    a. General characteristics of physical pain
    b. Specific characteristics of physical pain
    c. Major causes of physical pain
    d. Types of physical pain

a. General characteristics of physical pain

Physical pain arises because of its causes only and nothing else. When these causes are powerful enough, their painful effects are inevitable. This is like an electric generator, which will produce electricity only when it is sufficiently activated to reach a certain level of performance. When the power of these causes fades, the effects will fall away. Being transitory by nature, the effect of these causes is impermanent, leading to its eventual extinction. This phenomenon gives rise to three basic characteristics of physical pain consisting of impermanence (Anicca), inability to retain its original existence (Dukkha) and non-self or being dependent on causes (Anattā).

(1.) Anicca characteristic

Physical pain is impermanent (Anicca), as it arises and falls away rapidly and successively (Santati). If one simply looks into one's past experience of physical pain, such as a headache, stomachache, toothache or muscle tension, one will realize that these physical pains are transitory.

But even with this realization of its characteristic of impermanence, the awareness is not subtle enough. This is because one becomes aware of its falling away only after the physical pain ceases to exist. In reality, when physical pain arises, it falls away rapidly to be succeeded by its next arising, and so on. Its extreme rapidity in successively arising and falling away misleads people into thinking that physical pain is constant. This situation can be compared to the operation of a neon light. Usually, we take notice of the falling away of the neon light only after it goes out; such realization is not subtle at all and contrary to reality. This is simply because when the neon light is still on, it does not mean that the light is constantly glowing. In the actual phenomenon, within one second the neon light arises and falls away rapidly and successively up to about 48 times, but since this succession is very rapid, it gives the false impression that the neon light is on all the time.

When physical pain arises, it falls away rapidly. This means impermanence. But because one does not effectively practice Insight Meditation, he mistakenly thinks that physical pain has not fallen away during the time he is experiencing the pain. This is due to the extremely rapid sequence of arising and falling away.

When real understanding of the impermanent characteristic of physical pain is reached, one's mind will be in harmony with its nature. This will prevent his mind from being in conflict with the characteristic of impermanence, and will result in the relief or elimination of mental suffering which is caused by physical pain.

(2.) Dukkha characteristic

Physical pain is characterized by its inability to retain any of its original existence. Whenever physical pain arises, it must directly fall away. Because of its characteristic of impermanence, the physical pain cannot remain as it is: anything which is impermanent (Anicca) is Dukkha. When people are suffering, they often feel that the pain lasts longer than it does; this causes frustration. But if they are well aware of its true characteristic, i.e., physical pain is not able to retain its existing condition, they will be significantly relieved. In reality, physical pain falls away according to its causes, but the successive and rapid arising and falling away tend to obscure its true characteristic.

(3.) Anattā characteristic

Whenever there is physical pain, it is characterized by arising and falling away in accordance with its causes. It arises because of its causes and as they cease to exist, the pain falls away. The pain cannot be forced to fall away as long as its causes still remain.

No matter how the pain is symbolized, such as by giving it a name like headache, it, in reality, does not contain any symbolization. This can be compared to the saltiness of salt. No matter what this inherent taste is called or how it is symbolised, the naming of it does not exist in the salt. The supposed word "saltiness" does not exist in the salt itself. The saltiness is itself inherent in the salt by nature.

Thus, when there is physical pain, its real nature does not depend upon a description or symbolization. The feeling of this physical pain is called Vedanā. Even though the word "I" is used instead of Vedanā, in the actual phenomenon physical pain does not contain the word "I" at all. **For example,** when we say "I" feel pain, there is no such thing as "I" in the feeling of pain.

b. Specific characteristics of physical pain

Physical pain here refers to pain which can arise all over the body except the hair, the tips of the nails, and dead skin. When one has a pain in his arm, he tends to have a wrong view (Micchādiṭṭhi) by thinking that his arm hurts. **It should be noted that physical pain is not physical, but it is so-called because it has the body as its base. The snow mobile is so-called because it runs on the snow, but the vehicle itself is not snow. The analogy is true for physical pain.**

Physical pain is the feeling (Vedanā) caused by body contact with an undesirable object. **For example,** if a rock hits your head, the painful feeling will have an unfavorable effect on the body, which in turn creates anger, frustration or unpleasantness in those who lack awareness and wisdom. This physical pain can also lead to mental suffering and can cause prolonged physical illness. For these reasons, physical pain is detrimental to our well-being and difficult to tolerate.

c. Major causes of physical pain

Physical pain comes from several causes. A receptive physical body element and an undesirable bodily contact object are two important and obvious causes of physical pain.

(1.) Receptive physical body element (Kāya Pasāda-rūpa) is an extremely subtle object which cannot be seen with the naked eye, even with the help of a microscope. This element can only be perceived through a trained mind. It permeates the body with the exception of the hair, fingernails, toenails, teeth, and dead skin. Its form is similar to thinly and finely-spread cotton of several layers saturated with oil. This receptive element is able to make contact with bodily-contact objects. In the case where physical pain arises, this receptive element has come into contact with an undesirable object.

(2.) Bodily-contact object can be anything which comes into contact with our receptive body element, giving rise to painful (or pleasant) feelings. **For example,** the contact of our body element with burning charcoal causes physical pain. If one's head is hit by an iron rod, i.e. when the receptive physical body element makes contact with an undesirable bodily-contact object, physical pain arises. During the cold season our skin may become dry, resulting in physical discomfort; when excessive gas in the stomach touches our receptive body element, physical pain is also evident.

d. Types of physical pain

Physical pain can be classified into two types according to the degree of the suffering; minor physical pain and major physical pain.

(1.) Minor physical pain

This type of physical pain is not readily observable by others, and its condition can be known only if the sufferer mentions it or is questioned about it. This is simply because the pain is at a low level. This type of pain can occur either regularly or occasionally in daily life. The former includes such minor pains as simple headaches, elimination distress and other pains or discomforts arising from remaining in the position of standing, lying down, sitting or walking for a certain period of time. The latter covers pain such as headaches, digestive upsets, toothaches or rashes.

(2.) Major physical pain

This type of pain can readily be observed by others without resorting to any questioning or verbal acknowledgement, because the pain is obviously more intense.

This pain is evident in severe afflictions, such as knife or gunshot wounds or a severed limb.

4. Meditation Practice

a. What should be kept in mind

(1.) One is required to be well aware that the purpose of Insight Meditation practice is to gain insight into the nature of physical pain as it really is.

(2.) Before practicing, one should understand that physical pain is a type of natural feeling (Vedanā) which arises as the result of multiple causes.

(3.) Whenever there is physical pain, one is generally mistaken in thinking that it is "I" who feel the pain instead of the pain being Vedanā (natural feelings). With this misconception, an attempt is often made to mistakenly direct Vedanā according to one's personal desires without the realization of its true nature; i.e., causes solely bring about the arising and falling away of Vedanā. This point has been highlighted previously in detail in this chapter, under "Nature of physical pain."

(4.) People associate the natural feeling of physical pain with "I", "Je" in French, "Wor" in Chinese, or "Chan" in Thai, In fact, these words never really exist in the natural feeling of pain, but people tend to automatically give a meaning to these words which is not consistent with the real characteristic of this natural feeling (Vedanā). To say "I" feel pain, suggests that this natural feeling (Vedanā) of pain comes under one's personal command without taking into account its origins. In reality, pain arises from causes and falls away as its causes cease to exist. No one can contradict this natural phenomenon because the causes always produce the corresponding effects.

(5.) **The notion that "I" feel pain causes one to suffer more.** An apt analogy is that of a house burning down; if the house belongs to strangers, there is little or no sense of personal loss. On the other hand, if **I** own the house, that means **my** house is destroyed and I will suffer great pain. Therefore, when there is physical pain, one must consider the pain as being a type of natural feeling without becoming "attached" to the pain; that is, not thinking that "I" feel the pain. In other words, one should disassociate oneself from any connection with the pain.

(6.) To be effective in Insight Meditation, the mind should be set free from any unwholesome desire or Dosa. Also, one should keep in mind that the purpose of this Insight Meditation practice is to be mindful of the true nature of physical pain at the time of its occurrence through Direct Awareness. In addition to these, wisdom must be incorporated into mindfulness for increased effectiveness.

(7.) In the beginning, mindfulness is still weak, causing the meditator to be forgetful, both in being closely aware of the physical pain and in realizing it. Because of this, he will not be able to cope with the physical pain effectively. It is automatic to take the position that "I" feel the pain, thereby making the pain unbearable or causing more suffering. In spite of this, one should not get discouraged, but instead one should try again to be mindful of the physical pain as it occurs. Try to disregard what has been improperly practiced as it is a normal experience, especially for beginners. As one continues to be mindful of physical pain through Direct Awareness, one will become more skillful.

b. Coping with minor physical pain

(1.) Because minor physical pain normally occurs many times each day, one should closely and regularly follow it directly at the moment it arises. With such Direct Awareness, the meditator will understand the reality of life directly rather than have knowledge based on supposition, which does not lead to the full realization of the true reality of nature. The development of such direct mindfulness and wisdom will enhance the attainment of full realization. Apart from this, one will not only become fully aware of the basic causes which aggravate physical pain, but also will be fully aware of the accumulation of such causes, which will produce undesirable results in the future.

(2.) Direct Awareness must be purified by freeing it from defilements (Kilesa)

If we are not fully and directly aware of the true nature of physical pain, this pain can cause defilements to arise unknowingly, resulting in further suffering, restlessness, frustration and agitation.

Although minor physical pain occurs many times daily and can be tolerated, it is nevertheless undesirable. This will lead to certain actions to get rid of the pain. **For example,** when physical pain arises because of standing too long, we will change our position by sitting or lying down in order to relieve

or do away with this pain. When one feels hunger
pangs or elimination distress, he takes corrective
action accordingly. Even though every action is taken
to eliminate the pain or discomfort, people generally
overlook this reality and mislead themselves into
thinking that the action is basically taken to create
comfort or pleasure. This thinking is contrary to the
fact that the real purpose of this corrective action is
only to relieve or to get rid of the pain or discomfort.
When physical pain is eliminated, one tends to become
mentally attached to the pleasant condition arising
from the relief of physical pain. This, in turn, leads
to further belief that the new condition in which
physical pain no longer exists, is a state of happiness.
In other words, when physical pain occurs from
standing too long, one will change into another posture, such as sitting. While remaining in the sitting
position, physical pain in the leg will be relieved.
As a result, pleasant mental attachment, which is a
defilement (Kilesa) of mind, follows immediately,
and this automatically creates the feeling that this
sitting position is a happy one. On the contrary, to
change from a standing to a sitting position is only
to remedy physical pain. One not only enjoys the
comfort of changing to a sitting position, but also
firmly misleads oneself into thinking that this posture
brings about real happiness. This misunderstanding
is due to the fact that during the subsequent sitting

position, one is not able to retain the original condition. This position is impermanent, leading to the feeling of pain. People tend to overlook or misunderstand the true reality of life. Their belief and understanding are contrary to its real nature, thereby obstructing the gaining of Insight. Therefore, when this type of physical pain arises, if we are mindful by means of Direct Awareness we will realize that the changing of physical positions is only a means of relieving physical pain.

Another example is evident in the case of itchiness. When there is an itch, one has a desire to scratch the affected part. During the scratching, the itching will not be felt. As the scratching ceases, the itchiness often reappears. The scratching can be further intensified until the skin is damaged. But the scratcher often mistakenly feels that there is real happiness while scratching, even though the scratching is meant to relieve the discomfort rather than to bring about happy feelings. In actuality, the scratching, if excessive, is harmful to the skin, resulting in physical pain. Some people cannot resist the comfort derived from scratching excessively, and often skin disease or infection results. With the right understanding, there will be wise action taken and the unwholesome desire of scratching the affected part, resulting in worsening physical pain, will be prevented. This is because wisdom is developed through Direct Awareness of the minor physical discomfort called itching. Even if

scratching is used to cope with minor physical discomfort, it should be done wisely for the sole purpose of
relieving the discomfort without causing any damage
to the skin. The development of mindfulness will
enable one to wisely face the physical pain called
"itching", without a feeling of discomfort or dissatisfaction at the time of its occurrence. In this way, the
mind becomes more firm, more secure, more prudent
and more at ease as the result of the effective practice
of Insight Meditation.

With other minor physical pain also, the Direct
Awareness of this pain at the present moment can
prevent the occurrence of the unwholesome action of
wrongfully coping with the pain.

(3.) Be careful not to let unwholesome desire influence the Direct Awareness of physical pain

While practicing Direct Awareness, some people
purposely create physical pain, **For example,** they try
to remain in the sitting position or press a heavy
object such as a chair against their leg, until physical
pain arises, in order to be directly aware of the pain.
Such a practice reflects the existence of unwholesome
desire to the extent of adversely affecting Direct
Awareness. The pain, thus arisen, is an invented one
and is not in harmony with true reality. For this
reason, when such Direct Awareness is influenced
by unwholesomeness, one cannot fully realize the
true reality of physical pain.

(4.) Care should be taken during the practice not to be directly aware of the wrong meditation object

When physical pain occurs, even though it is realized that the feeling of pain (Vedanā) is a natural phenomenon arising from its causes, the beginner often mentally acknowledges this realization to himself. With this type of acknowledgement, the mind will become attached to a conventional word instead of closely and directly following up on the physical pain as it really is. This can be compared to tasting the sweetness of sugar; i.e., instead of directly becoming aware of the real sweetness, one mentally cites the word "sweetness". This mentioned word is not true reality but merely the conventional truth. Therefore, one must refrain from using conventional words which will only distort the true picture of reality.

(5.) Direct Awareness of wrong view which leads to the belief "I feel pain"

Sometimes while directly experiencing physical pain, the meditator will realize the wrong view arising in his mind which incorporates the conventional word "I" in the feeling of pain. In other words, it is the mistaken belief that there is "I" who feels pain, which causes mental suffering. When we are really aware of this misconception, we will fully realize, as never before experienced, that physical pain is a natural feeling (Vedanā), without the existence of "I". In reality, there is no such thing as "I" in the feeling of pain.

(6.) **Physical pain arises from various postures,** such as; standing, sitting, lying down, extending the arms and legs, etc. If the posture is maintained for a period of time, physical pain follows, so as to cause a change to a new posture. In this way, minor physical pain fades away. With this experience, one will be convinced that minor physical pain cannot retain its original condition, and that it eventually ceases to exist.

According to a saying of the Buddha, to remain in any posture for too long a period of time will adversely affect one's health or may even shorten one's life.

Even physical pain which is caused by other than the four major postures cannot remain as it is, and must fall away in the end.

(7.) **When there is a right practice of awareness of minor physical pain,** which involves Direct Awareness of the pain as it arises at the present moment, mental suffering can be effectively deterred. Even at the time of the occurrence of physical pain, one will be able to experience subtle and wholesome happiness in terms of achieving tranquility, relief and soothed feelings.

(8.) If the Direct Awareness of the pain at the time of its occurrence is constantly practiced, the true nature of physical pain will become more and more evident until one can fully realize its basic characteristics: impermanence (Anicca), inability to retain its original existence (Dukkha) and non-self or being dependent upon causes (Anattā). Furthermore, one will become aware of the root cause of physical pain, i.e. craving (Taṇhā). This awareness will eventually lead to the attainment of "Perpetual Happiness" (Nibbāna) through the complete eradication of this basic cause.

c. Coping with major physical pain

(1.) Direct mindfulness of major physical pain
One should directly and mindfully become aware of the major physical pain at the time it occurs. This means that one should become directly aware of the pain as it really is whenever it arises. The details of Direct Awareness practice have been covered in previous sections.

(2.) Difficulties in meditation practice
Due to the fact the major physical pain significantly weakens one's body and mind, Direct Awareness is often made more difficult. Thus, one should be well-prepared to cope with pain, as indicated in the next section.

(3.) Preparedness in coping with major physical pain

In preparing oneself to cope with major physical pain more effectively, one must regularly practice Direct Awareness of the true reality of life as it occurs at the present moment, especially in the area concerning minor physical pain. This will serve as a basis for effectively dealing with major physical pain, which could unexpectedly arise in the course of one's life. Apart from this, such preparedness will have a significant effect in relieving the severe mental suffering which will surely follow this pain.

(4.) Increased level of perseverance and inspiration through dealing with major physical pain

Major physical pain could have a strong and lasting effect on one's life, both physically and mentally. This undesirable condition is what most people generally try to avoid to the greatest extent possible.

But those who have practiced effective Direct Awareness will have the courage to directly face their physical suffering with wisdom. This is the first step towards achieving a higher level of perseverance and inspiration, which is essential to further the development of Insight Meditation.

(5.) Prevention of mental suffering and Dosa caused by major physical pain

Sometimes major physical pain arises with such intensity that it causes one to moan in agony. Even with this degree of suffering, an attempt should be made to be directly mindful of the physical pain, and to realize that because the pain really is intolerable, moaning is a normal reaction. One should not be discouraged or feel sorry if the strength of Insight Meditation practice is weak. Instead, one should be glad that even with a low level of mindfulness from Direct Awareness, one is able to deter the uncontrollable restlessness of mind which will bring about mental suffering and Dosa. The full realization of major physical pain as it occurs at the present moment will make the mind stronger and firmer, more tolerant and calm in facing this pain. In this way, mental suffering, which is certain to follow physical pain, can either be prevented or lessened.

In short, one can even experience happy feelings at the time of major physical pain, because one has attained wisdom through Insight Meditation.

(6.) A real case

Based on his actual experience, Mr. Amnuay Ting-On, a student of Buddhist Advanced Science (ABHIDHAMMA) at the Abhidhamma Foundation (Wat Pho), related the following:

"On the morning of January 29, 1978, I felt happy and cheerful while conversing with my fellow workers, and at 8.30 a.m. I started my work as a cutting-machine operator. One hour later, I bent down to pick up some material to feed the cutting machine, and as I looked up I felt faint. At that moment, I used my right hand to get hold of the machine to prevent my falling down. When I came to, I took a look at my hand and realized that four fingers had been cut off. At first, I experienced numbness and didn't feel the pain, but a moment later, terrible pain followed. I began to recall my Buddhist Advanced Science teachers and their teachings, and managed, through Tranquil Meditation practice, to suppress my terrible pain to a certain extent. At the same time, I was mindful of the pain through Direct Awareness.

"My fellow workers and other people who were nearby came to help me, but when they saw my hand, which bled profusely, they were shocked. Some turned their faces away, while others simply walked away. Some people had pity on me, but they just did not know how to help. After their initial shock, my supervisor, the company doctor, and some fellow workers took me to the hospital.

"While in the hospital, my boss, relatives, and friends came to visit me. Each of them expected to see me in a sorrowful and suffering state. But to their surprise and gladness, I did not show any sign of grief or suffering, as they expected. On the contrary, I behaved normally, as if nothing had happened, and this made the visitors much relieved and happy. The fact that I was able to cope effectively with this kind of major physical pain was due to my study of Buddhist Advanced Science (ABHIDHAMMA) and my practice of meditation, especially Insight Meditation. I realized that there is nothing permanent in one's life. If I had not studied and practiced Buddhist Science, I would have suffered great pain and would have felt misery and much grief because I had lost the fingers of my right hand. Thus, to me, "the taste of Buddhist Science" excels all others. Without such study and practice, I would not have realized the excellence of Buddhist Advanced Science (ABHIDHAMMA)."

From this real experience, it can be seen that the practice of Direct Awareness can prevent mental suffering and that, at the same time, physical pain can also be relieved to a great extent. In addition to this, one will be mentally calmer, stronger and firmer.

5. CONCLUSION

As one gains more and more experience in being directly aware of physical pain as it occurs at the present moment, mindfulness will be further strengthened up to a certain subtle level, which can become an important factor in the development of enlightenment in life. As a result, Insight Wisdom, (Vipassanā Paññā) will arise, so that one will fully realize the basic characteristics of existence (Anicca, Dukkha and Anattā) as well as the root causes of physical pain. It should be noted that such realization does not rely on any thinking or imagination. Even

if the basic causes can be correctly known by means
of thinking or investigating, this understanding, nevertheless, is not subtle enough and it is not possible
to completely destroy the roots of these causes. But
through Insight Wisdom (Vipassanā Paññā) one
becomes fully and directly aware of physical pain and
can thoroughly realize the basic cause of physical pain-
Craving (Taṇhā) leading to the complete eradication
of this basic cause and to the ultimate attainment of
"Perpetual Happiness" (Nibbāna).

Of all diseases hunger is the greatest,

Of all sufferings the conditioned states,

Knowing this (the wise realize Nibbāna)

Which is the Highest Happiness

The Sayings of the Buddha

CHAPTER 19
INSIGHT MEDITATION – DIRECT AWARENESS OF PLEASANT FEELING (SUKHA-VEDANĀ)

1. Introduction

During happy times, one becomes intoxicated with pleasure, while during times of sadness or suffering, one becomes disoriented. Such behavior reflects a lack of wisdom. How to practice Insight Meditation in effectively coping with mental suffering as well as physical pain has been covered in the previous Chapters. People often mistakenly believe that the pleasant feelings which bring about intoxication and unawareness are the essence of their lives, without being aware of their unwholesomeness, leading to misery in life. On the other hand, they fail to realize that certain types of pleasant feelings are wholesome, resulting in greater happiness.

Intoxication with unwholesome sensual pleasures could result in anxiety, frustration, insomnia, or suicide. This is because pleasantness is associated with an unwholesome mind, consisting of various defilements (Kilesa) such as craving (Lobha), ignorance (Moha) and mental wandering (Uddhacca). This craving for sensually pleasurable objects is unquenchable. It creates unrealistic hopes that cannot be fulfilled, resulting in disappointment, restlessness, etc. As for the ignorance (Moha) defilement (Kilesa), it blinds one to the right way of life which brings about wholesome happiness. The mental wandering (Uddhacca) defilement causes the mind to become unsettled, distracted or scattered. These defilements coexist with unwholesome feelings, giving rise to mental discomfort or sufferings.

Upon winning a grand prize in a lottery, a person can become so overwhelmed with extreme exaltation that he may suffer a fatal heart attack. Such an unfortunate incident is the result of a lack of awareness and wisdom which prevents him from effectively coping with this unwholesome feeling.

For these reasons, one should cultivate awareness and wisdom by studying and practicing Insight Meditation through Direct Awareness of happy feelings. In this way, one will be able to be on the right path of life leading to wholesome happiness, while being able to avoid life's pitfalls.

Gaining knowledge and real understanding of pleasant feelings (Sukha-vedanā) not only can help to prevent the arising of mental sufferings but also can enhance greater happiness.

If one has the chance of practicing Insight Meditation by directly experiencing pleasant feeling during its occurrence at the present moment, he will become fully aware of its ultimate real nature. This awareness will give rise to greater happiness while accumulating the natural conditions that will eventually lead to the attainment of "Perpetual Happiness" (Nibbāna).

2. What is to be specifically gained from this Insight Meditation

Apart from attaining the general benefits as described previously in Chapter 11, the effective practice of this Insight Meditation will give rise to the following specific benefits:

a. The elimination of intoxication with pleasant feelings and blind attachment to them.

b. The understanding of the difference between the pleasant feeling which brings about pleasantness, and the pleasant feeling which results in greater unpleasantness. This leads respectively to a decrease of harmful and unpleasant feelings and, at the same time, to the increase of wholesome and creative happy feelings in life.

c. The development of wisdom in thoroughly and directly realizing a pleasant feeling at the present moment, resulting in the elimination of suffering.

d. The acquisition of the right techniques of living through the direct and full awareness of pleasant feelings as a means of eventually attaining "Perpetual Happiness" (Nibbāna).

3. Nature of pleasant feeling

The theoretical understanding of the real nature of pleasant feeling is the first important step in the practice of Insight Meditation, leading to its realization. As previously mentioned, a pleasant feeling (Sukha-vedanā) is a type of Vedanā (feeling) Cetasika (mental constituent), which is classified into 3 categories: pleasant feeling (Sukha-vedanā), unpleasant feeling (Dukkha-vedanā) and indifferent feeling (Upekkhā-vedanā). The pleasant feeling is further broken down into physical and mental pleasant feelings.

The subject of pleasant feeling, which is essential to Insight Meditation practice, is clarified under the following headings:

a. General characteristics of pleasant feeling
b. Specific characteristics of pleasant feeling
c. Types of pleasant feeling
d. Causes of pleasant feeling

a. General characteristics of pleasant feeling

Since a pleasant feeling arises in accordance with its causes, it contains the three basic characteristics of existence: Anicca, Dukkha and Anattā.

(1.) Anicca characteristic

Pleasant feeling is impermanent, as it arises and falls away rapidly and successively according to its causes. If one just simply takes note of one's past experience of pleasant feeling, one will realize that pleasant feeling is transitory, like a dream. The thorough realization of the Anicca characteristic of pleasant feeling will prevent one from being intoxicated with and blindly attached to the pleasantness as well as from being worried and frustrated about missing or losing the pleasant feeling.

(2.) Dukkha characteristic

The pleasant feeling is characterized by its inability to retain its original existence. Whenever it arises, it must directly fall away. Because of its impermanent characteristic, the pleasant feeling cannot remain as it is. Thus, anything which is impermanent (Anicca) is Dukkha.

(3.) Anattā characteristic

Whenever there is a pleasant feeling, it is characterized by arising and falling away according to its causes. It arises because of its causes, and falls away as these causes no longer exist. In other words, a pleasant feeling cannot and will not be forced to remain according to one's desire, when the power of its causes is no longer there.

b. Specific characteristics of pleasant feeling

A pleasant feeling is a type of mental constituent that pleasantly feels a desirable object at the body base and the mental base. When this pleasant feeling arises at the body organ, one will experience physical pleasantness. When it arises at the mental base, one will experience mental pleasantness. **For example,** when a cool breeze comes into contact with the body organ, a physical pleasant feeling will arise. When one recalls complimentary words, or practices Tranquil Meditation, a mental pleasant feeling will arise.

c. Types of pleasant feeling

A pleasant feeling is classified into 3 types, according to its common occurrence among people in general as follows:

(1.) Physical pleasant feeling
(2.) Mental pleasant feeling which is unwholesome
(3.) Mental pleasant feeling which is wholesome

(1.) Physical pleasant feeling

This is the pleasantness which arises at the body organ, as a result of its coming into contact with a desirable object such as coolness or softness. The arising of such physical feeling is the effect of past wholesome Kamma (deed), and this physical feeling itself is neither wholesome nor unwholesome, simply because there is no accompaniment of wholesome mental constituents (awareness, right confidence and wisdom) and unwholesome mental constituents (craving, anger and ignorance).

(2.) Mental pleasant feeling which is unwholesome

Mental pleasant feeling which is unwholesome is the pleasantness which is accompanied with unwholesome wanting or craving and eventually gives rise to suffering. It arises through the heart base, as a result of its coming into contact with a desirable object, but there is no accompaniment of awareness. This means that not only there is the arising of a pleasant feeling, but also a blind craving for this pleasantness. With this type of pleasant feeling, one will have a blind and intense craving for it, just like a fish after coming into contact with water. In this way, one will desire this pleasantness more and more, and when one does not attain it the way one wants, one will experience suffering. Therefore, this type of mental pleasant feeling is unwholesome.

(3.) Mental pleasant feeling which is wholesome

Mental pleasant feeling which is wholesome is the pleasantness which is accompanied with awareness and eventually gives rise to happiness. It arises through the heart base as a result of its coming into contact with a desirable object, but there is no accompaniment of mental attachment, just like a drop of water which cannot be absorbed by a lotus leaf. This pleasant feeling comes from such activities as helping others in need, listening to the useful truth of life (Dhamma) and practicing Tranquil Meditation. Therefore, this type of mental pleasant feeling is wholesome.

d. Causes of pleasant feeling

(1.) The arising of a physical pleasant feeling is basically caused by:

(a.) Bodily contact object, and

(b.) The body organ which is being contacted by that object.

For example, a cool breeze which is a bodily contact object, blows against the body, bringing about a physical pleasant feeling.

(2.) The arising of a pleasant mental feeling which is unwholesome, is basically caused by:

(a.) A desirable object through mind sense door, such as sweet words or money, which stimulates the arising of the mind, and

(b.) "Automatically Imprudent Judging" (Ayonisomanasikāra) of that object under the influence of the past accumulations of craving.

For example, upon recalling complimentary words, one's pleasant feeling accompanied with craving, arises immediately. This reflects the influence of the accumulations of craving for that object (complimentary words), in the form of bringing about this "Automatically Imprudent Judging", which in turn causes the arising of this pleasant mental feeling, accompanied with craving.

(3.) The arising of a pleasant mental feeling which is wholesome, is basically caused by:

(a.) A desirable object through the mind sense door which stimulates the arising of mind, and

(b.) "Automatically Prudent Judging" (Yonisomanasikāra) of that object under the influence of the past accumulations of such a wholesome mental constituent as awareness.

For example, upon recalling complimentary words, one's pleasant feeling, accompanied with awareness, arises immediately. This reflects the influence of the past accumulations of awareness of that object (complimentary words), in the form of bringing about this "Automatically Prudent Judging" which in turn causes the arising of this pleasant mental feeling, accompanied with awareness.

4. Meditation practice

a. What should be kept in mind

(1.) The meditator is required to have a full understanding of the real purpose of practicing the Direct Awareness of pleasant feeling. This practice is aimed at achieving the full and thorough realization of the ultimate reality of pleasant feeling in order to do away with misconceptions and the defilements (Kilesa) of mind which endlessly bring about suffering in life.

(2.) Before the practice, one should understand that the pleasant feeling is Nāma in the ultimate sense of reality.

(3.) When a pleasant feeling arises, one should realize that "Nāma is feeling pleasant" and not "I am feeling pleasant".

(4.) Care should be taken not to let the practice come under the adverse influence of defilements (Kilesa) of mind such as craving.

(5.) One should also understand that craving is always for pleasant feelings and that because of misconceptions, there is a blind mental attachment to pleasant feelings as being permanent (Nicca), being able to retain their original existence (Sukha) and being "self" (Attā).

(6.) One should fully understand the three types of pleasant feelings.

b. How to develop the skill of Direct Awareness

(1.) When a pleasant feeling arises, whether in the form of a physical pleasant feeling, a mental pleasant feeling which is unwholesome, or a mental pleasant feeling which is wholesome, one is required to become directly aware of and realize that "Nāma is feeling pleasant", at the present moment. One must not imagine or think about this pleasant feeling but must directly feel this pleasant feeling as it really is, just like actually tasting a grape.

(2.) While experiencing the pleasant feeling, if the meditator does not exercise enough care, his/her defilements such as unwholesome wanting or craving will arise to the extent of adversely influencing the practice of Direct Awareness. These defilements

(Kilesa) of mind cause one to be blindly, firmly and desirably attached to this pleasantness, like a birdlime. Under this condition, one should be aware of this defilement, but should not try to force it to disappear. With awareness, one will not be adversely governed by this unwholesome wanting or craving, and this will lead to the eventual, thorough realization of the pleasant feeling. This is because unwholesome wanting or craving, if left unchecked, will essentially obscure or conceal the ultimate reality of the pleasant feeling.

(3.) At the time of experiencing a physical pleasant feeling, while one is taking a bath or exposing oneself to a cool breeze on a hot day, one should become directly aware of that pleasant feeling at the body organ, at the present moment. In this way, one will be able to prevent the arising of craving, which causes one to be blindly and desirably attached to physical pleasant feeling, and in turn brings about the mental pleasant feeling which is unwholesome.

At the initial stage of practicing Direct Awareness, one's awareness and wisdom are still not strong enough to go against one's craving with complete success. Thus, the craving (a type of mental constituent) which used to enjoy this physical pleasant feeling, mentally instigates the meditator to form such ideas as "Why should I continue the practice any further? Is it not better for me to follow what my craving desires?

There is nothing to be gained by such practice. Gaining pleasantness through craving is a much easier and better way out. Better quit now." The meditator should become aware of this craving and realize that the decrease of pleasant feelings accompanied with craving amounts to doing away with causes of suffering at a certain level, and at the same time cultivates the causes of a real happiness. Therefore, the meditator should not fall prey to this craving or be tricked into it.

(4.) **If one lacks awareness** at the time of tasting a delicious food, listening to a desirable sound, seeing a pleasant sight or smelling a nice fragrance, the mental pleasant feeling, accompanied with unwholesome wanting or craving, will arise. With this arising, the meditator is required to become directly aware of and realize this mental pleasant feeling which is unwholesome.

(5.) **At the time of thinking about persons, events or other desirable objects** through the mind sense door, if a mental pleasant feeling which is unwholesome, arises, one should become aware of it.

(6.) **In a case where one is having a mental pleasant feeling which is wholesome,** one should become directly aware of it and realize that "Nāma is feeling pleasant". One should be aware that the subtle craving which is desirably attached to this wholesome pleasantness, is about to arise. Otherwise, the practice of Direct Awareness will be adversely affected because of the influence of this subtle craving. It should be noted that the craving which is desirably attached to the mental pleasant feeling which is wholesome, is in a subtle form, and that the craving which is desirably attached to the physical pleasant feeling or the mental pleasant feeling which is unwholesome, is in a gross form.

(7.) While practicing the Direct Awareness of pleasant feeling, the meditator should realize that "Nāma is feeling pleasant" at the present moment. **For example,** if the physical pleasant feeling arises at a certain part of the body such as the face, one should clearly feel that "Nāma is feeling pleasant" at that part. In the case where there is a physical pleasant feeling arising all over the body, one should also realize that this pleasant feeling arises at only one specific part of the body organ at a time, and not at all parts of the body organ at the same time. But at the initial stage of Direct Awareness, one usually has the misconception that this physical pleasant feeling arises all over the body at the same time. Therefore, one should do away with this kind of misconception so as to be able to become directly and correctly aware of and realize the physical pleasant feeling at its present moment. This means that one should not become aware of the physical pleasant feeling collectively. Otherwise, the practice is not subtle enough, and obstructs the thorough realization of the physical pleasant feeling as it really is and especially brings about misconceptions in the form of "I am feeling pleasant".

As for the mental pleasant feeling, one should realize that this pleasant feeling arises at the heart base. Without such realization, one usually resorts to thinking instead, and in this way, one will not be able to directly and thoroughly realize this pleasantness as it really is.

(8.) The meditator is also required to practice Direct Awareness of the pleasant feeling regularly and continually whenever this feeling arises. As one properly practices it more and more until the mental factors of practicing Insight Meditation (consisting of Confidence Power, Effort Power, Awareness Power, Concentration Power and Wisdom Power) reach the point of optimum harmony and balance, one will thoroughly and directly realize this mental pleasant feeling as being Nāma, and its basic characteristics of existence: Anicca, Dukkha, and Anattā. This in turn gives rise to the full realization of the root causes of suffering, leading to its cessation.

5. CONCLUSION

Most people, when experiencing a pleasant feeling, become carefree and intoxicated. This is especially true when people allow the unwholesome mind to arise frequently and uncontrollably. **The more the unwholesome mind arises, the more intoxicated and careless in life they become.** Even people who often cultivate the wholesome mind but lack Direct Awareness of this pleasant feeling can become care-free and intoxicated. **For example,** when one practices Tranquil Meditation and attains a pleasant feeling which is wholesome, but has not yet practiced Insight Meditation, one can easily become intoxicated and attached to this pleasantness, thereby eventually giving rise to suffering. This is evident in the case where one attains this pleasant feeling through the practice of Tranquil Meditation and later loses it because of inadequate practice. As a result, one feels disappointed, and this reflects that one's craving is desirably attached to this pleasantness.

Direct Awareness as mentioned previously, cultivates a thorough and full realization of the pleasant feeling. In this way, one will not be blindly and desirably attached even to the pleasant feeling which is wholesome. This means that the craving, which is the cause of suffering, will not be permitted to desirably attach to all kinds of pleasant feelings. Under this condition, even numerous arisings of pleasant feelings will not be followed by unpleasant feelings, because the meditator does not become carefree and intoxicated with the pleasantness. The ultimate aim of practicing Direct Awareness of pleasant feelings is to attain the highest level of happiness, which is not pleasant feeling but "Perpetual Happiness" (Nibbāna), reflecting the complete eradication of all sufferings.

Health is the highest gain
Contentment is the greatest wealth
Trustful are the best relatives
Nibbāna is the greatest happiness
The Sayings of the Buddha

CHAPTER 20
INSIGHT MEDITATION-DIRECT AWARENESS OF MAJOR BODY POSTURES

1. Introduction

In our everyday life, at the time of being awake, we cannot do without the body postures, which keep on changing. Yet, most of us are unaware of their reality. As a matter of fact, we often unconsciously have misconceptions about them and at the same time, have overlooked their potentiality and usefulness in cultivating our wisdom for overcoming problems in life. As a result, mental worry, restlessness or other sufferings could follow.

The Direct Awareness of body postures can be practiced at any time while being awake. Apart from this, all body postures (Rūpa) are in gross form, and this makes it much easier for them to serve as objects of awareness than in the case of Nāma. This in turn facilitates the practice of Direct Awareness.

2. What is to be specifically gained from this Insight Meditation

Apart from attaining the general benefits explained previously in Chapter 11, one will also gain the following, through the effective practice of this Insight Meditation:

a. The elimination of misconceptions concerning the body postures.

b. The ability to abstain from being blindly attached to the body postures.

c. Provision of a way to effectively develop wholesome physical behavior.

d. The realization and overcoming of subtle, unwholesome wanting or craving, which influences the body postures.

e. The attainment of wisdom in realizing the ultimate reality of the body postures as a means to eventually achieve "Perpetual Happiness" (Nibbāna).

3. Nature of the body postures

When one is asked whether or not one can see the body postures, such as standing, walking, sitting or lying down, one will not hesitate to give an affirmative answer. It is obvious that this person is sitting, or that person is standing. Nevertheless, the body posture which is known through the eye sense door is not real in the ultimate sense. In fact, it is merely a mental creation based upon conventional reality. All one can really see is the visible object or light, and not the shapes or colors, as previously mentioned in

Chapter 15. The ultimate reality of the body postures cannot be known through five sense doors: eye, ear, nose, tongue and body. It can only be known through the mind sense door. This is because the arising of all the body postures is basically caused and supported by the mind, with respect to their maintenance and movements. It has been stated previously that Direct Awareness and the realization of the ultimate reality of Nāma and Rūpa can manifest themselves through the mind sense door only.

The subject of body posture, which is essential to the practice of Insight Meditation, is clarified under the following headings:

a. Characteristics of body postures
b. Major causes of body postures
c. Types of body postures

a. Characteristics of body postures

While in deep sleep, which is free from dreaming or talking, the body cannot be held in position or moved by itself at all. This is evident when the hand of one who is sleeping soundly is being raised by someone. As soon as it is released, the hand drops automatically. Actually, it cannot hold any position by itself. This is because the mind which arises during deep sleep (Bhavaṅga Citta) has no power to produce the positioning or the movement of the body. On the other hand, while one is awake, one can hold various physical positions such as standing, sitting, walking and lying down, and has the ability to move about. This reflects the fact that the mind which arises while one is awake has the power to produce the positioning and/or the movement of the body. The exceptions to this are: when the body is very weak or becomes paralyzed, or is not sufficiently developed, as in the case of a very sick person, an invalid, or an infant. Also, when one is experiencing a great mental strain such as that of a murderer who, upon hearing the death verdict from a judge in a courtroom, cannot hold his standing position any longer; or in the case of parents who, upon hearing the news of the unexpected and sudden death of their beloved child, can no longer maintain their present posture.

In short, while awake, one's mind can cause the positioning and/or the movement of one's body, giving rise to various body postures such as standing, sitting, walking and lying down. Due to the fact that the mind arises and falls away all the time according to its causes, the body posture brought about by the mind also arises and falls away all the time. This manifestation reflects the three basic characteristics of existence: impermanence (Anicca), inability to retain its original existence (Dukkha), and non-self or being dependent upon causes (Anattā).

(1.) Anicca characteristic

All the body postures are impermanent (Anicca) because of their arising and falling away rapidly and successively (Santati). **For example,** at the time of standing, the arising of the mind causes the holding of the body in that posture and as the mind falls away, so does this body posture. As the mind arises again, the body posture also arises, but as the mind falls away again, the body also follows suit, and so on. This can be compared to a neon light; every time it receives an electric current from a power generator, its light arises, but as the supply of the electric current falls away, so does the light. As mentioned previously, the neon light arises and falls away rapidly and successively at the rate of about 48 times per second; this rate, in fact, corresponds with the rate of the arising and falling away of the generator.

The only way to fully realize the ultimate reality of the body postures as being impermanent (Anicca) is to practice Insight Meditation.

(2.) Dukkha characteristic

All the body postures are characterized by their inability to retain their original existence (Dukkha). When a body posture arises, it must directly fall away. Due to its characteristic of impermanence as mentioned previously, the body posture cannot remain as it is. Thus, anything which is impermanent (Anicca) is Dukkha. The changing of one body posture to another all the time is a clear indication that any body posture cannot retain its original existence. However, in the ultimate sense, even while one is maintaining the same body posture (sitting) without changing to another posture (standing), the sitting posture arises and falls away all the time, reflecting the Dukkha characteristic.

The only way to fully realize the ultimate reality of the body posture as being Dukkha is to practice Insight Meditation.

(3.) Anattā characteristic

All the body postures are characterized by their being non-self or dependent upon causes. They are a type of Rūpa, the arising of which is basically caused by the power of the mind. When one says that one stands, sits, walks or lies down, these are just the supposed words used in one's daily life. If one is blindly attached to this conventional reality in the form of "I stand or sit", one's misconception of ultimate reality as it really is will certainly arise. This is because, in the ultimate sense, it is "Rūpa stands or sits" and not "I stand or sit".

The only way to fully realize the ultimate reality of the body postures as being Anattā is to practice Insight Meditation.

b. Major causes of body postures

The arising of all body postures is basically caused and supported by the mind which arises while one is awake. In the case of changing from one posture to the other, there must always be an intention to do so first, to be immediately followed by the mind which gives rise to the change. Thus, the mind basically causes and supports the holding and the movement of the body.

When it is stated that the arising of all body postures is basically caused by the mind, it does not mean that the mind is the sole cause. It merely means that the mind is the principal cause. As a matter of fact, there are other causes which are secondary as well, consisting of one's intention, the heat element and Vāyo-dhātu, which is the element giving rise to motion, vibration, oscillation and pressure within one's body, as well as sound physical health.

The emphasis that the mind basically causes the arising of body posture, relates to the practice of Direct Awareness. After one becomes aware of and realizes Nāma and Rūpa with respect to body posture, one will not have any misconceptions concerning the body posture, and at the same time will be enlightened to the reality that the body posture is Rūpa, and that Nāma basically brings about the arising of the posture.

c. Types of body postures

Body postures can be classified into two types: major body postures and minor body postures.

(1.) Major body postures

In the practice of Direct Awareness, there are four major body postures, consisting of standing, walking, sitting and lying down.

(a.) Standing posture - The maintenance of this posture is basically caused and supported by the mind. The posture is characterized by its inability to retain its original existence all of the time, and undergoes constant change due to its being forced by physical discomfort or pain.

(b.) Walking posture - The movement of this posture is basically caused and supported by the mind. The posture is characterized by its inability to retain its original existence all of the time (Dukkha). Since there is constant movement in this posture, to become directly aware of its inability to retain its original condition is easier than with the other postures. Apart from this, the walking posture undergoes constant change at a faster rate than the sitting and the lying down postures, due to its being forced sooner by physical discomfort or pain.

(c.) Sitting posture - The maintenance of this posture is basically caused and supported by the mind. The posture is characterized by its inability to retain its original existence all of the time. Since, in this case, the arising of physical discomfort or pain is slower in coming than in the case of the standing and walking postures, one will be able to maintain the sitting posture longer before one changes to another posture.

(d.) Lying down posture - The maintenance of this posture is basically caused and supported by the mind. The posture is characterized by its inability to retain its original existence all of the time. Since in this case, the arising of physical discomfort or pain is the slowest in coming when compared with the other major body postures, one will be able to maintain this posture the longest before changing to another posture.

(2.) Minor body postures

The minor body postures can be in such forms as stretching out the body or its limbs, looking up or down, or any other physical activities which are not major body postures as described above.

4. Meditation practice

a. What should be kept in mind

(1.) The meditator is required to have a full understanding of the real purposes of practicing Insight Meditation upon the body postures. The real purposes have to do with the thorough realization of the ultimate reality of the body postures, in order to do away with misconceptions, suffering in the cycle of birth, old age, ill health and death, and all the lesser sufferings which occur in daily life. The meditator should have the right understanding of the causes and the effects with respect to the eradication of suffering in life. This means that the ultimate realization of the body postures as they really are, simultaneously accomplishes the elimination of the causes of suffering in life. This is like the disappearance of darkness upon the arising of light.

(2.) The meditator should rightly understand what is Rūpa and what is Nāma with respect to practicing Insight Meditation on the body postures. These body postures are a type of Rūpa, brought about by their corresponding causes, whereas the mind (Nāma) basically causes and supports the maintenance and the movement of the body as described under the previous section 3., "Nature of the body postures". On the other hand, one should not resort to verbal expression or thinking, with respect to the body postures being Rūpa.

(3.) The Meditator should realize that the body postures conceal suffering and that Direct Awareness of them destroys this concealment. When such concealment of suffering is eliminated, one will be able to realize suffering as it really is.

(4.) The meditator is required to become directly aware of and realize the body postures at the present moment. One should not concern oneself with past or future body postures.

(5.) During the meditation practice, one should not only become directly aware of the body posture as it really is, but also at the same time wisely and clearly feel that it is Rūpa.

(6.) One is also required to practice Direct Awareness of the body postures **constantly** and **continually.**

(7.) The body postures to be used as objects of Insight Meditation must be the ones which we assume normally and naturally in daily life. One must not try to create a special or unusual posture, simply because such a creation is dictated by unwholesome wanting or craving (Lobha). This, in turn, causes the practice to become impure, thereby adversely affecting the effectiveness of the meditation. **For example,** this special or unusual posture can be in the form of walking very slowly. Some meditators wrongly think that if they have to walk at their normal pace, they could not practice Direct Awareness upon the normal postures effectively, because the pacing will be too fast for them. As a result, they purposely walk in slow motion in order to be able to realize it better. In this way, such a pretentious and exaggerated posture is governed by one's own unwholesome desire or craving (Lobha).

(8.) One should not try to select a particular posture according to one's desire, by preferring one over the others. Otherwise, Direct Awareness becomes impure under the influence of craving.

(9.) **Before changing one's posture,** one must have good reasons for the change, such as changing out of necessity or changing in order to overcome physical discomfort or suffering. One should not change in order to fulfill one's unwholesome wanting.

b. How to develop the skill of Direct Awareness

After the meditator has a clear and right understanding of Nāma and Rūpa, he/she can proceed with practicing Insight Meditation on the body postures as follows:

(1.) **At the time of standing, walking, sitting or lying down, one should become directly aware of it, and at the same time,** one should wisely and clearly feel that Rūpa is standing, Rūpa is walking, Rūpa is sitting or Rūpa is lying down, and not just feel Rūpa only. It should be noted that the incorporation of the supposed words, "standing", "walking", "sitting" or "lying down" with Rūpa, is to indicate that even though all the body postures are Rūpa, their positioning differs from each other and arises and falls away at a different time. On the other hand, if one just merely uses the word "Rūpa" to describe various body postures, it is easier for one to misunderstand that all the body postures are the same Rūpa without each respective arising and falling away, and this in turn gives a false impression that they are permanent (Nicca).

(2.) **After sitting for a certain period of time,** physical discomfort or pain (Dukkha-vedanā) arises at the sitting Rūpa, and the meditator is required to become directly aware of, and realize that, this sitting Rūpa is "suffering" (Dukkha). A similar requirement is also applied to the other body postures.

(3.) **When there is an arising of physical discomfort or pain in any body posture,** one should not desire this adverse feeling to disappear. This is because such a desire is a defilement (Kilesa) of mind, which prevents one from realizing the reality as it really is. While practicing, the meditator should be directly aware of body posture as if one was the observer of a play, without becoming an actor or directing the play.

(4.) **Every caution should be taken at all times to make sure that the meditation practice is not being influenced by a defilement of mind.** Under the influence of a defilement, Direct Awareness will become prejudicial or impure. According to the Buddha, the meditator must not allow his/her satisfaction or dissatisfaction to govern the meditation practice. **For example,** when the physical discomfort or pain disappears, one becomes satisfied, but when it does not go away as one wishes, one becomes dissatisfied. When some meditators, who have extensive experience in practicing Tranquil Meditation, become subtly attached to a peaceful and blissful feeling, and turn to practicing Insight Meditation upon the body postures, their minds concentrate on the postures too deeply, to the extent of attaining tranquility and happy feelings. As a result, they become satisfied and mentally attached to the desirable effect. This reflects the influence of subtle craving upon the meditation practice, thereby adversely affecting its effectiveness.

(5.) When physical discomfort or pain arises during the meditation practice, one should realize that the change to the other posture is made for the purpose of relieving or curing the pain, and that one has to change due to being compelled by suffering. People in general, when forced by pain, want to change to another posture and make the change in accordance with their desire. The thought that one changes the posture because one wants to, is not correct. In reality, regardless of whether one wants to change the posture or not, one must do it on account of one's being forced by pain.

For this reason, before changing his/her posture, the meditator should carefully consider why the change has to take place, and whether or not the change is beneficial to the meditation practice. **In the case where craving causes one to change one's posture to fulfill one's desire, this change is improper** and not beneficial to the meditation practice and therefore, one must avoid it through awareness. On the other hand, if the physical pain causes one to change one's posture for the purpose of relieving or curing pain, this change is proper and beneficial to the meditation practice and therefore one must pursue it further.

(6.) **Before changing posture,** one should realize that the real reason for the change is to relieve or cure pain. Without such realization, one will be misled into thinking that the new posture, especially just after changing to it, is a type of real happiness. Some beginners are frequently forgetful in realizing this real reason so that after the pain is relieved or cured, due to the change to a new posture, they become blindly and desirably attached to it and consider it to be happiness. Therefore, they should become aware of this mental attachment or unwholesome wanting. In this way, they will not be governed by this desire, and will prevent it from defiling Direct Awareness.

(7.) **As the meditator gains more experience through the constant and continual practice of Direct Awareness of the body postures,** at the time of changing the posture he/she will realize that not only is the old posture suffering (Dukkha), but also is the new one. In this way, this posture can no longer conceal its Dukkha characteristic. Without such regular and continuous practice of Direct Awareness, the meditator cannot have a thorough realization of the body postures, especially the new one. **For example,** while practicing Direct Awareness of the sitting posture, the meditator who does not have the necessary skills, due to lack of regular and continual practice, will realize it as being suffering, only after the arising of physical discomfort or pain. But one will not realize that a new posture, which one has just changed to, is also suffering. In this case, after the initial changing of the body posture from sitting to lying down, one will not realize that lying down is also suffering and at the same time will have a misconception that the new lying down posture is happiness. Therefore, one should constantly and continually practice Direct Awareness of major body postures in order to realize that both old and new postures are suffering.

(8.) When there is an arising of suffering to cause a change of posture, one is required to realize that Rūpa (sitting posture, standing posture, walking posture or lying down posture) is suffering. Without this Direct Awareness, one will be misled into thinking that "I am sitting", "I am standing", "I am walking" or "I am lying down" really exists in nature, and this in turn brings about misconceptions in the form of "I am suffering" and not "Rūpa is suffering". With this requirement, the meditator will be able to walk on the right path, leading to the thorough realization of the body postures as they really are, and at the same time, he/she will not walk on the wrong path, while thinking that it is the right one.

(9.) If there is an arising of mental wandering while practicing Direct Awareness of the body postures, one should merely be aware of this arising, and not try to follow it through. One is then required to become directly aware of the present body posture once again. This can be compared to learning how to ride a bicycle. Due to lack of skill, it is likely that the rider will fall off the bicycle many times. After falling down, the rider should try to get on it again and again, instead of turning to do something else. Thus, the meditator, especially the beginner, must exert enough effort to keep on practicing Direct Awareness of the body posture, despite his/her being obstructed by this mental obstacle.

(10.) Some beginners, after being strongly obstructed by the arising of mental wandering, try unsuccessfully to go back to practicing Direct Awareness of the body posture. In spite of their further effort to continue their practice on the body posture, this mental obstacle continues to prevail. Under this condition, one should be careful about the arising of dissatisfaction and should not blame oneself, otherwise, one can easily get discouraged. One should also realize that this mental wandering is a natural manifestation, based upon its causes. When its strength is predominant, one is required to become directly aware of and realize this mental wandering as being "Nāma is wandering" and not "I am wandering", without forcing it to disappear. Care should also be taken not to become directly aware of persons or events bringing about mental wandering. Otherwise, one will end up with more mental wandering. However, after practicing Direct Awareness of this mental wandering until it loses its strength and eventually phases out, one can then return to the practice of Direct Awareness of the body posture once again.

(11.) The meditator is required to become directly aware of and realize the body posture, at the present moment. This is the most crucial prerequisite. Many meditators assume that their object (body posture) of meditation is at the present moment, but they are wrong. This is because it is not as easy as they think it to be. Actually, the present arising of the body posture (meditation object) manifests itself in an extremely short period of time. It is like trying to catch a fish in the water with one's bare hand. One thinks that it is easy to catch the fish because it stays still. But when one actually grasps the fish, it slips out of one's hand, either going forward or backward. For this reason, to be able to practice Direct Awareness of the body posture at its present moment, one must have a thorough understanding of what the present object or the past or the future object is, and at the same time, one must practice it regularly and continually. Otherwise, one will not be able to realize the ultimate reality of the body posture as it really is.

(12.) While practicing at meal time, the meditator should also consider that the real purpose of eating food is not to fulfill one's desire or unwholesome wanting, but only to relieve hunger pangs as well as to sustain one's life. Otherwise, defilement (Kilesa) of mind (craving) will step in, adversely affecting the effectiveness of the meditation practice. In the case where one takes food in order to relieve hunger, it can serve its real purpose even if it is not tasty. But if one takes food because of one's desire or unwholesome wanting, and the food is tasty according to one's desire, one can become blindly and mentally attached to it. However, if the food is not as tasty as one's desire, one can become dissatisfied or displeased. Therefore, one is required to become aware of and realize the real purpose of eating.

(13.) Similarly, at the time of performing bathroom activities, one should also consider their real purposes of relieving one's discomfort or suffering.

(14.) In the case of putting on a dress, one should also consider that its real purpose is to relieve physical discomfort or suffering with respect to giving warmth to the body or protecting one from insect bites, and not to fulfill one's desire for good looks, status and/or fame, where one's craving lies.

(15.) As for minor body postures, such as stretching out the body and its limbs, looking up or down, turning the head left or right, or turning the body, they will be fully realized only after the effective practice of Direct Awareness of the major body postures can be accomplished.

(16.) As one practices Direct Awareness of body postures regularly and continually, until the mental factors of practicing Insight Meditation (consisting of Confidence Power, Effort Power, Mindfulness

Power, Concentration Power and Wisdom Power), reach the point of optimum harmony and balance, one will thoroughly and directly realize the following:

- the body posture as being Rūpa
- the mind which causes and supports the arising of the body posture as being Nāma
- Nāma which is fully and wisely conscious of that particular Rūpa in such form as the sitting posture, and
- their basic characteristics: Anicca, Dukkha and Anattā.

5. CONCLUSION

The Direct Awareness of the body postures as described above is not concerned with practice based on a certain set of laid-down rules and regulations in accordance with one's blind faith in others. It is concerned with the thorough and right understanding of the real reasons why the practice is carried out in this way. This understanding is the core, leading to the full realization of ultimate reality as it really is. Without this, success in practicing Direct Awareness can never be achieved.

In practicing Direct Awareness of the body postures, one must begin with the understanding of its real objects, and the means by which these objects can be attained. The means consists of the following:

- Right understanding of what is Nāma and what is Rūpa.

- Knowing how to make awareness pure and free from the influence of defilements (Kilesa).

- Understanding the real purposes of changing the body postures.

- Wise consciousness of the present meditation object (body posture) at the time of its arising, regularly and continually.

- Know-how in effectively coping with mental obstacles.

- Maintenance of the meditation practice.

When one acquires such understanding, it is like having a light to show the way of meditation practice, in order to enable the meditator to walk on the right path with full confidence with respect to the relief or eventual eradication of suffering, leading to the attainment of "Perpetual Happiness" (Nibbāna).

> **These wise, frequently meditative**
> **Ever earnestly persevering**
> **Attain the bond-free supreme Nibbāna**
> The Sayings of the Buddha

CHAPTER 21

INSIGHT MEDITATION– DIRECT AWARENESS OF MIND AND FIVE SENSES

1. Introduction

Even though it is relatively difficult to practice Direct Awareness of the mind and five senses, the practice offers substantial benefits in life similar to the previously-mentioned practices of Insight Meditation. The subject of these types of Direct Awareness has been somewhat covered in III., "DIRECT AWARE-NESS-THE BASIC APPROACH TO PRACTICING INSIGHT MEDITATION", and this chapter will take up the areas which have not been previously mentioned.

2. What is to be specifically gained from this Insight Meditation

Apart from the general benefits explained previously in Chapter 11, one will also gain the following through the practice of Insight Meditation:

a. The provision of a means to cope effectively with the arising of unwholesome mind by being free from its harmful influence.

b. The direct understanding of the wholesome mind, resulting in improvement of mental qualities, which enchances greater wholesome happiness in life.

c. The realization of what is ultimate reality and what is conventional reality through the six sense doors, so as to eliminate misconceptions in life.

d. The cultivation of wisdom in directly realizing the ultimate reality of the mind and five senses, leading to the eventual attainment of "Perpetual Happiness" (Nibbāna).

3. Nature of mind and five senses

Mind, which is Nāma, has the specific and unique characteristic of knowing the object (Ārammaṇa) in the forms of knowing the sound, knowing the taste, knowing the smell, knowing the visible object and knowing other ultimate realities as well as knowing conventional reality.

The five senses consist of seeing, hearing, smelling, tasting and bodily feeling, and arise when the external sense-object (e.g. visible object) comes into contact with the respective internal sense-organ (e.g. eye organ).

The mind and the five senses have the basic characteristics of existence: impermanence (Anicca), inability to retain their original existence (Dukkha), and non-self or being dependent upon their causes (Anattā).

4. Meditation practice

a. What should be kept in mind

(1.) The meditator is required to have a full understanding of the real purposes for practicing Insight Meditation with the mind and the five senses. This practice is aimed at gaining the full and thorough realization of the ultimate reality of the mind and the five senses, in order to do away with misconceptions and with the defilements (Kilesa) of mind, which endlessly give rise to sufferings in life.

(2.) The meditator should rightly understand what is Nāma and what is Rūpa through the six sense doors.

(3.) Care should be taken not to let the defilements of mind adversely influence the practice of Direct Awareness.

(4.) One should fully understand the real reasons behind the practice, in becoming directly aware of the arising of Nāma and Rūpa as they really are, through the five sense doors.

b. How to develop the skill of Direct Awareness

(1.) The mind

(a.) When the mind accompanied with un-wholesome wanting or craving (Lobha), arises, the meditator is required to become directly aware of and thoroughly realize it.

(b.) When the mind which is free from unwholesome wanting or craving, arises, the meditator is required to become directly aware of and thoroughly realize it.

(c.) When the mind accompanied with dissatisfaction or anger (Dosa), arises, the meditator is required to become directly aware of and thoroughly realize it.

(d.) When the mind which is free from dissatisfaction or anger, arises, the meditator is required to become directly aware of and thoroughly realize it.

(e.) When the mind accompanied with ignorance (Moha), arises, the meditator is required to become directly aware of and thoroughly realize it.

(f.) When the mind which is free from ignorance, arises, the meditator is required to become directly aware of and thoroughly realize it.

(g.) When the mind accompanied with sleepiness, arises, the meditator is required to become directly aware of and thoroughly realize it.

(h.) When the mind accompanied with mental wandering, arises, the meditator is required to become directly aware of and thoroughly realize it.

(2.) The five senses

The procedures of practicing the Direct Awareness of the five senses have been described under III., "DIRECT AWARENESS-THE BASIC APPROACH TO PRACTICING INSIGHT MEDITATION.

5. CONCLUSION

In the practice of Direct Awareness of the various types of mind, and Nāma and Rūpa through the five sense doors, the meditator should have a clear and deep feeling of the meditation object (Nāma or Rūpa), at its present moment. As one gains more and more experience through proper and continual practice, one will be able to directly and thoroughly realize the ultimate reality of the mind and five senses. This in turn leads to the relief or eventual eradication of suffering and the attainment of "Perpetual Happiness" (Nibbāna).

The flickering, fickle mind
Difficult to guard, difficult to control
The wise straightens,
As a fletcher, an arrow
        The Sayings of the Buddha

V. CONCLUSION

Insight Meditation (Vipassanā-Kamaṭṭhāna) is the unique cultivation of Insight Wisdom (Vipassanā Paññā), which is the highest level of wisdom among all the worldly wisdoms. With this Insight Wisdom, one will be able to directly and fully realize ultimate reality as it really is, without any thinking or imagining or the use of any conventional reality. Insight Meditation brings about a special type of wisdom (Vipassanā Paññā), which is ultimate reality, in thoroughly realizing the three common characteristics of Nāma or Rūpa; Anicca, Dukkha and Anattā.

Direct Awareness (Satipaṭṭhāna) is the first and only prerequisite of Insight Meditation in leading toward **the Noble Eightfold Path.** There are four basic types of Direct Awareness, namely; Direct Awareness of Body, Direct Awareness of Feeling, Direct Awareness of Mind and Direct Awareness of Dhamma.

This book highlights two general methods of practicing Direct Awareness. One is concerned with applying Direct Awareness in daily life, while the other with practicing Direct Awareness at a proper place for Insight Meditation. No matter how busy one is, one should not let the golden opportunity of practicing Direct Awareness slip through one's fingers. Whenever there is an opportunity, one should try to apply, in one's daily living, the practice procedures as described in this book. Such application will result in the attainment of wisdom in place of suffering or mental stress and strain, in the most subtle and prudent manner. This wisdom, gained through Insight Meditation or Direct Awareness, is full of power. Even with the application of certain aspects of Direct Awareness in daily life, one will be able to achieve the "light of wisdom", leading the way to the right path of life in the forms of:

- **absence of wrong view or misconceptions of reality,**
- **absence of blind and intoxicated attachment to reality,**
- **absence of retreat from reality,**
- **attainment of the right view of reality,**
- **realization of reality as it really is,**
- **ability to face reality in the most effective and prudent manner.**

This wisdom will become firmly implanted in one's life without fading away, and its usefulness will not only be applied to this life, but also to the future lives through its accumulations. This is an important step leading eventually toward the cessation of sufferings, the getting out of the cycle of birth and death, and the attainment of "Perpetual Happiness" (Nibbāna).

There are no lights that shine brighter than the "light of wisdom" and the "light of wisdom" gained through Insight Meditation shines the brightest among all the worldly wisdoms.

One gramme of meditation practice is worth more than one ton of its knowledge. This is because only when one puts this knowledge into effective practice, will one really be able to gain the highest level of subtle and wholesome happiness.

In the practice of Insight Meditation for the purpose of crossing the "ocean of suffering", one must thoroughly understand the proper procedures and techniques and practice them with perseverance, Direct Awareness and wisdom until there is a spontaneous arising of all these eight types of power, called **"the Noble Eightfold Path" (Ariyamagga),** consisting of right understanding (Sammādiṭṭhi), right thought (Sammāsaṅkappa), right speech (Sammāvācā), right action (Sammākammanta), right livelihood (Sammā-ājīva), right effort (Sammāvāyāma), right mindfulness (Sammāsati) and right concentration (Sammāsamādhi). **It is only when there is such a spontaneous arising, that the "ship of life" will be able to successfully cross the "ocean of suffering" and reach the "shore of Perpetual Happiness" (Nibbāna). At this ultimate stage, all the sufferings can arise no more and the "Perpetual Happiness" (Nibbāna) remains everlastingly permanent (Nicca).**

May we wish you every success in cultivating high level wisdom through meditation practice with the ultimate aims of eradicating all suffering in life and attaining "Perpetual Happiness" (Nibbāna).

Yours in the Dhamma,
Author and editorial staff.

APPENDIX

1. BIBLIOGRAPHY

1. Buddhaghosa "Attasalini"
   (London, Luzac & Company, Ltd., 1958.)
2. Buddhaghosa "The Path of Purification"
   (Ceylon: M.D. Gunasena & Co., Ltd., 1975.)
3. Byrom, Thomas, "The Dhammapada-the Sayings of the Buddha"
   (New York, Vintage Books, 1976.)
4. Kovitaya, Vanna; U. Sivakul, Vinai, "Buddhist Psychiatry in Thailand"
   (Bangkok, The Wacharin Publishing Co., Ltd., 1978.)
5. Mahaniranonda, Naeb, "Development of Insight"
   (Bangkok: Reproduced in 1979.)
6. Narada, "A Manual of Abhidhamma"
   (Ceylon: Tisara Packaging Industries, 1966.)
7. Phra Khantipalo, "Dhammapada-The Path of Truth"
   (Bangkok, Mahamakut Rajavidyalaya Press, 1977.)
8. "Tipiṭaka, Digha-Nikaya" (in Thai)
   (Bangkok: Mahamakut Rajavidyalaya Press, 1980.)
9. "Tipiṭaka, Majjhima-Nikaya" (in Thai)
   (Bangkok: Mahamakut Rajavidyalaya Press, 1980.)

10. "Tipiṭaka, Satipaṭṭhāna-Vibhaṅga, Abhidhamma-Piṭaka" (in Thai)
    (Bangkok: Mahamakut Rajavidyalaya Press, 1980.)

11. U. Sivakul, Vinai, "Applied Buddhist Science" (in Thai)
    (Bangkok, Sudhisan Printing, Third Edition, 1979.)

12. U. Sivakul, Vinai, "The Differences Between Tranquil Meditation and Insight Meditation" (in Thai)
    (Bangkok: Sudhisan Printing, Second Edition, 1981.)

13. U. Sivakul, Vinai, "Buddhist Psychology" (in Thai)
    (Bangkok: Precha Printing, 1980.)

14. U. Sivakul, Vinai, "Powers: Causes of Life" (in Thai)
    (Bangkok: Prachak Printing, 1980.)

15. Warren, Henry Clarke, "Buddhism in Translation"
    (New York, Atheneum, 1976.)

2. AN INTRODUCTORY OUTLINE OF BUDDHIST ADVANCED SCIENCE (ABHIDHAMMA)

Introduction

Among all the sciences which are beneficial to mankind, the science which concerns itself with the following Noble Truths of life excels all others:

- the realization of the ultimate reality of suffering (Dukkha); i.e., suffering in its deepest sense

- the most effective ways and means of eradicating the causes of suffering

- the right path leading to the cessation of all suffering

- the attainment of "Perpetual Happiness" (Nibbāna)

Only Buddhist Advanced Science (ABHIDHAMMA) deals comprehensively with the above Noble Truths.

Even with a general understanding of Buddhist Advanced Science, one can become wholesomely blissful and lighthearted. In this way, one will be able to develop his/her wisdom so as to cope with problems in life more effectively.

What is Buddhist Advanced Science (ABHIDHAMMA)

1. Buddhist Advanced Science has universal applications, as it deals with the ultimate reality of nature. Buddhist Advanced Science does not belong to any one group of people, nor does it exist in the imagination. As a matter of fact, Buddhist Advanced Science is the true nature of reality discovered by the highest level of wisdom of the Buddha, who disseminated his discoveries among the general public for the purpose of relieving and permanently eradicating their suffering and helping them attain a high level of happiness, leading eventually to "Perpetual Happiness" (Nibbāna).

2. The word "science" denotes a system of thorough and verifiable knowledge based on right understanding according to ultimate reality.

As for the word "Buddhist" in the context of Buddhist Science, it does not really stand for a group of persons who profess Buddhism, but rather, it pertains to the superb and creative wisdom in life arising from the thorough awareness and realization of the true nature of reality as it really is. Such wisdom is the light of life which prevents one from falling into pitfalls in one's daily life. Apart from this, with this wisdom one will be able to live an intelligent, happy, wholesome and calm life as never before experienced, as well as to eventually attain "Perpetual Happiness" (Nibbāna).

3. It can therefore be seen that Buddhist Advanced Science is highly beneficial to all, irrespective of one's religion, creed, culture, color, sex or race. All of us can benefit by studying and practicing Buddhist Advanced Science (ABHIDHAMMA).

In conclusion, Buddhist Advanced Science is a universal system of knowledge of true reality giving rise to superb and creative wisdom. This high level of wisdom can in turn be utilized to help one cope effectively with problems in life, to enable one to attain wholesome happiness, and to foster the attainment of the path towards achieving "Perpetual Happiness" (Nibbāna).

Is Buddhist Advanced Science (ABHIDHAMMA) a scientific approach

1. In the study and practice of Buddhist Advanced Science, there are no requirements for blind faith and unconditional obedience on the part of individuals.

2. In view of the fact that Buddhist Advanced Science contains the true reality of life, it can withstand any verifications with no time limitation. Rational and scientific criticism and objective analysis are therefore encouraged. It is most important to realize that in order to thoroughly understand Buddhist Advanced Science, one must also rely on one's own efforts and wisdom developed through the practice of Tranquil Meditation and Insight Meditation.

What is covered under Buddhist Advanced Science (ABHIDHAMMA)

1. **Various levels of realities and structures of all existence.**

2. **Mind and thoughts of living beings.**
   What is mind? What are types of mind? How does the mind process work? (This is to enhance one's mental ability in order that one can lead a successful and happy life.)

3. **Dreams and their nature:**
   Why some dreams come true while others do not.

4. **Mental constituents.**
   Effective techniques are given for purifying the mind and enabling the mind to become more calm, more productive, and happier.

5. **Buddhist matter and energy with reference to life.**

6. **Nature of behaviors** manifested through the body, verbal expression, and the mind, along with the causes of behaviors that will lead to a sound body, a sound speech and a sound mind.

7. **True nature of life.**
   Law of birth and death of living beings, life after death, planes of existence, psychic power, hypnotism, invisible beings, diagnosis and treatment of certain illnesses by means of psychic power.

8. **Law of causal relation of life.**

9. **The path leading to "Perpetual Happiness" (Nibbāna).**

10. **Tranquil Meditation and Insight Meditation:** their differences, benefits and methods of practice.

What are the benefits to be gained from studying and practicing Buddhist Advanced Science

Benefits to oneself:

1. Enhancing learning power and effective observation and thinking.

2. Improving memory and ability to cope effectively with the unpleasant and painful feelings arising from the recall of undesirable past experiences.

3. Attaining deep physical rest and relaxation and improved physical health.

4. Achieving complete mental rest along with experiencing a high level of happiness.

5. Cultivating awareness and wisdom to deal effectively with problems in daily life as well as overcoming worry, dissatisfaction, anxiety, fear, frustration or irritation.

6. Promoting initiative and creative wisdom.

7. Bettering the personality and the effectiveness of job performance.

8. Encouraging deep, restful and pleasant sleep, free from nightmares.

9. Relieving physical and mental suffering and ridding the mind and body of certain illnesses.

10. Enhancing enlightenment of life.

11. Fostering the attainment of the path towards achieving "Perpetual Happiness" (Nibbāna).

Benefits to family:

1. Promoting happier, more peaceful, more secure and more successful living within the family.

2. Overcoming the problems arising from the generation conflict.

3. Enhancing the state of preparedness to face an undesirable or tragic event, such as separation or loss of a loved one.

4. Providing a technique that will help to have a child be born without disabilities.

5. Enhancing proper methods of bringing up children for a successful and happy life.

6. Enabling members of the family to make themselves useful to each other.

Benefits to Society:

1. Establishing security, peacefulness, and happiness within society.

2. Preventing and remedying social problems, such as crime, drug addiction or drug abuse.

3. Enabling the general public to engage in activities which are useful to them as well as to society, without causing any serious harm or undesirable consequences. **For example,** those who study and practice Buddhist Science will not resort to the use of harmful food additives to make the food look more attractive or taste better.

4. Enhancing the effective utilization of resources without being wasteful or without being inconsiderate of the next generation. For instance, such practices as the irresponsible destruction of the forests or the wasteful consumption of energy will be avoided.

5. Creating a good social environment for the promotion of physical and mental health.

6. Enabling the government officials of each country to really work for the benefits of the society within their own country as well as others' without resorting to corrupt practices or seeking domination over others economically, politically or militarily, thereby increasing the stability and peacefulness of the world.

CONCLUSION

In conclusion, it can be seen that the study and practice of Buddhist Advanced Science

(ABHIDHAMMA) have great value and benefits in daily living for all of us irrespective of our religion, creed, culture, color, sex or race. It is Buddhist Science which provides effective techniques of overcoming suffering at all levels.

Apart from this, Buddhist Science will enhance wisdom in life, enabling us to understand the nature of all types of happiness and their effects. With this realization, we will be able to differentiate between the unwholesome happiness which will bring about suffering, and the wholesome happiness which will give rise to peacefulness and contentment in life. Buddhist Science also points out the right path leading to the attainment of "Perpetual Happiness" (Nibbāna).

For the above reasons, it is relatively easier for one who studies and practices Buddhist Science than for one who does not do so, to wisely attain the high level of happiness which is wholesome and beneficial.

With the study and practice of Buddhist Science, even over a short period of time, one will be able to realize and appreciate its benefits and significance in daily life.

If we do not really understand the true nature of suffering, how will we be able to cope effectively with our suffering?

If we do not really understand the true nature of happiness, how will we be able to effectively attain a high level happiness?